FLAWS IN THE ICE

David Day has been a research fellow at Clare College in Cambridge, a visiting professor at University College Dublin, the University of Aberdeen, and the University of Tokyo, and an ARC senior research fellow at La Trobe University. He is currently an honorary associate at La Trobe University in Melbourne and a visiting fellow at the Australian National University in Canberra. His many books include bestselling histories of World War Two, biographies of Australian prime ministers, and a study of Winston Churchill and Robert Menzies that has been made into a television documentary. His books have won or been shortlisted for several literary prizes, with *Claiming a Continent* winning the nonfiction prize at the Adelaide Festival. *Conquest: How Societies Overwhelm Others* has appeared to acclaim in Australia, Britain, and the United States, and has been translated into several languages. His most recent book is the widely acclaimed *Antarctica: A Biography*.

To the members of the Australasian Antarctic Expedition,
who went in search of a continent and found themselves.

FLAWS IN THE ICE

In Search of Douglas Mawson

DAVID DAY

LYONS PRESS
Guilford, Connecticut
Helena, Montana
An imprint of Rowman & Littlefield

Lyons Press is an imprint of Rowman & Littlefield

Distributed by NATIONAL BOOK NETWORK

Copyright © 2014 by David Day
First published by Scribe Publications, 2013

Maps drawn by Kelly Day
Indexed by Richard McGregor
Typeset in 12/15.25 pt Minion Pro by the publishers

National Library of Australia Cataloguing-in-Publication Data available

British Library Cataloguing-in-Publishing Information available

Library of Congress Cataloging-in-Publication Data available

ISBN 978-1-4930-0750-9 (paperback)

∞™ The paper used in this publication meets the minimum requirements of American National Standard for Information Sciences—Permanence of Paper for Printed Library Materials, ANSI/NISO Z39.48-1992.

This project has been assisted by the Australian government through the Australia Council for the Arts, its arts funding and advisory body.

Australian Government

Contents

This is a map of the Antarctic coastline, as it was imagined to be at the time of Mawson's expedition in 1911.

A map of the Ross Sea coastline, showing the sledge journey of Edgeworth David, Mawson, and Mackay across sea ice and land toward the presumed position of the South Magnetic Pole.

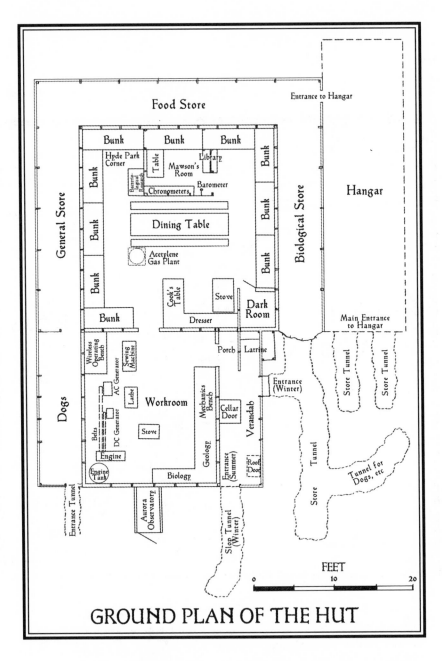

GROUND PLAN OF THE HUT

The cramped expedition quarters are starkly revealed by this plan of the hut and its attached workroom.

A map showing the position of the expedition huts and the surrounding features.

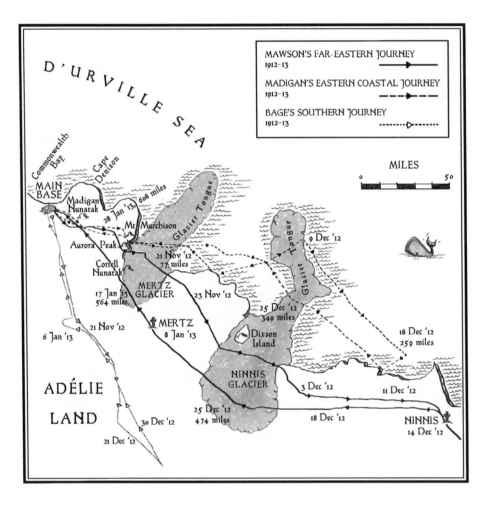

A map of the competing journeys by Mawson, Madigan, and Bage, as they raced to outdo each other.

List of Expedition Members

Main Base

Douglas Mawson	Expedition leader
Lieutenant Robert Bage	Astronomer, assistant magnetician, recorder of tides
Frank Bickerton	Aircraft mechanic
John Close	Marine collector and photographer
Percy Correll	Mechanic
Walter Hannam	Wireless operator (first year)
Alfred Hodgeman	Draftsman
John Hunter	Biologist
Frank Hurley	Photographer
Charles Laseron	Taxidermist and biological collector
Cecil Madigan	Navigator (sledging)
Dr. Archibald McLean	Medical officer and bacteriologist
Dr. Xavier Mertz	Ski expert
H. Dyce Murphy	In charge of stores (originally meant to be leader of third base)
Lieutenant Belgrave Ninnis	Surveyor and in charge of dogs
Frank Stillwell	Geologist
Eric Webb	Magnetician
Dr. Leslie Whetter	Surgeon
Sidney Jeffryes	Wireless operator (second year)

Western Base

Frank Wild	Leader
George Dovers	Surveyor
Charles Harrisson	Biologist
C. Archibald Hoadley	Geologist
S. Evan Jones	Surgeon
Alexander Kennedy	Magnetician
Morton Moyes	Meteorologist and surveyor
Andrew Watson	Geologist

Glossary of Terms

Burberry   Close-weaved garments made by the maker of the same name, which were designed to provide protection against the cold wind.

Drift   Wind-driven surface snow.

Glaxo   Dried milk.

Hoosh   The traditional food of polar explorers, the usual ingredients being pemmican, ground biscuits, and water.

Ice shelf   An ice sheet extending out from the coastline, often with much of it floating and its outside edge comprising a tall cliff.

Nunatak   An outcrop of rock standing above the surrounding ice.

Pack ice   Ice of various shapes and sizes floating in different concentrations on the surface of the ocean and often blocking access to the continent.

Pemmican A mixture of dried beef and fat.

Pithing   Killing penguins by inserting a needle into their brain or spinal cord.

Plasmon   Soluble milk protein added to sledging biscuits.

Sastrugi   Compacted snow formed into ridges or other shapes by the prevailing wind.

Serac   Ice surface with ridges or pinnacles.

Imperial-to-Metric Conversions

Length

1 inch	2.54 centimeters
1 foot	30 centimeters
1 mile	1.6 kilometers

Weight

1 ounce (oz)	30 grams
1 pound (lb)	450 grams
20 pounds	9 kilograms

Temperature

32° Fahrenheit	0° Celsius
0° Fahrenheit	–18° Celsius
–20° Fahrenheit	–29° Celsius

"A flaw in one's character will nowhere become so glaringly apparent as here."

Diary of Frank Bickerton, in Stephen Haddelsey, *Born Adventurer: The Life of Frank Bickerton, Antarctic Pioneer,* Sutton Publishing, Stroud, 2005, p. 61.

Preface

This book was meant to be part travelogue and part history. I was going to travel in the wake of Mawson's 1911 expedition to Antarctica, so that I could visit the hut in which he and other members of the expedition had sheltered for nearly two years, and look out at the windswept vista of ice and snow that had beckoned them into the unknown. However, it was not to be. As explorers have discovered over the centuries, the Antarctic has ways of disrupting carefully laid plans. In my case, a huge glacier the size of Luxembourg had floated westward to become stuck across the entrance to Commonwealth Bay, where Mawson's hut is located. The position of the glacier caused pack ice to build up and become so thick that it was impossible for our ship to force its way through to the continent. Even had the ship been able to penetrate the ice, its access to Commonwealth Bay would have been blocked by the glacier, which was stopping sea ice in the bay from being broken up by wind and wave and swept into the ocean. Two successive voyages ended in the same disappointing result. Although the continent was tantalizingly close, we had to be content with exploring the offshore pack ice.

Crossing the mist-draped Antarctic Convergence had promised much more. Yet the pack ice became a magical experience in itself. In the cold and calm conditions, the Zodiacs wound their way among the jumble of convoluted shapes of blue and white, as Adélie penguins porpoised past and snow petrels wheeled overhead. It made the long days crossing the Southern Ocean worthwhile. Indeed, the life-filled and sometimes storm-tossed Southern Ocean, with its whales and albatrosses and petrels, was just as magical — as was the sight of the first icebergs, far from the continent. Most of Mawson's men had been similarly amazed at their first sight of ice. And they had feelings of relief and awe when the *Aurora* finally came within sight of the continent, with its protective ramparts of snow-covered rock and forbidding cliffs of ice. Despite its small size, the *Aurora* was able to push through the loose pack ice and effect a landing. However, within weeks, Mawson discovered to his horror that he had established his base at the windiest place on earth. By year's end, the expedition was facing disaster. Mawson had led Xavier Mertz and Belgrave Ninnis to their deaths, and six others were marooned with Mawson for another year.

As with many tragic developments, there was no single cause of the events that took the lives of Mertz and Ninnis — Ninnis falling down a crevasse, and Mertz dying on the journey back to the hut. While most historians ascribe the deaths of the two men to bad luck, my reexamination of the existing evidence, and a reading of the new evidence, reveals that their deaths were caused by Mawson's relative inexperience, overweening ambition, and poor decision-making. Until now, there has been little questioning of the official account that Mawson gave to explain the deaths of his companions and his own, seemingly miraculous, survival. This is partly because historians have been hampered by a shortage of evidence. After all, Mawson was the only surviving witness to the events that occurred on the trek, which meant that historians have had to rely largely on his diary and the two-volume book that he compiled about the expedition, which privileged his story and activities above others. Historians also were not helped by Mawson's diary being frustratingly devoid of much description or emotion. Days would pass without any entry at all. The diary was seemingly written for fellow scientists, or perhaps simply as a jog to Mawson's memory, and wasn't published until 1988. Due to the paucity of alternative primary material, historians have been reluctant to question Mawson's account or to dispute his status as Australia's Antarctic hero.

The few accounts that have been published until recently by other members of the expedition have done little to detract from the heroic image that Mawson consciously created for himself. There was an understandable hesitancy on their part to question, at least in public, their leader's competence and character. After all, their own heroic status was due to their association with Mawson. The diaries of Mertz and Ninnis might have painted a different picture, but Ninnis's diaries have not yet surfaced. Although he aspired to be the expedition's Samuel Pepys, the diary that he wrote on the sledging journey with Mawson has disappeared. Mawson had it in his possession at the end of the expedition and promised to send it to Ninnis's family in Britain. However, there is no record of it ever having been received. As for the diary that Ninnis wrote in the hut, it has yet to be published, and remains under wraps at the Scott Polar Research Institute. Mertz's diary of the sledging journey has also disappeared. Although Mawson returned the original diary to Mertz's family, and a transcript of the German original was made, the diary itself has vanished from view.

Despite the problems with the diaries of Mertz and Ninnis, the centenary of Mawson's expedition has caused a great deal of new material to emerge. Much of it has been hidden away for the last century. It includes the diaries of Archibald McLean, Robert Bage, Frank Stillwell, John Hunter, Charles Harrisson, and several others. The most explosive diary of all was kept by Cecil Madigan, the leader of the eastern coastal party and of the rescue party that remained behind to search for Mawson and his two companions. So scathing was Madigan that he apparently instructed that his diary was not to be published until the last of Mawson's children had died. Now that it has been published, and other diaries and letters have appeared, a more complete portrait of Mawson and a more balanced assessment of the expedition have become possible.[1]

During my preparation of this book, many people have been helpful with advice, and with providing access to papers and giving me permission to quote from them. My thanks are particularly due to Julia Madigan, Lady Elizabeth Kennet, Alun Thomas and the estate of the late Sir Douglas Mawson, Gordon McLean, Heather Rossiter, Bernadette Hince, Jenny Hunter, Peter FitzSimons, Ross McMullin, Sherrie-Lee Evans, Anna Lucas, Mark Pharaoh of the South Australian Museum, Naomi Boneham of the Scott Polar Research Institute, the staff of the Mitchell Library, the State Library of South Australia, the State Library of Victoria, the Cambridge University Library, the National Archives of Australia, and the Australian Antarctic Division Library. Some of the ideas in this book were discussed in lectures I gave aboard ship in the Southern Ocean, and I am grateful to the passengers and my fellow expedition staff, particularly Michael and Andrea Marsh, Di Patterson, Don McIntyre, and Margie McIntyre for their contributions. I am also grateful to Caroline Homer and the Tasmanian Historical Research Association for providing me with the opportunity to explore some of the arguments in this book when presenting the 2013 Eldershaw Lecture in Hobart. Thanks are also due to my daughter Kelly for preparing the maps.

I am also grateful to my friends, John Moore and Lesley Garton, and Claude and Irene Wischik, for their input over several long dinners. Henry Rosenbloom of Scribe has been everything a publisher and editor should be. Lastly, my wife, Silvia, has been my constant companion and sounding board during the research and writing.

CHAPTER ONE

To the South Magnetic Pole

Encased in an ice cave on the edge of the polar plateau, Douglas Mawson pondered the tragedy of his situation. With the muffled sound of a blizzard blowing overhead, the exhausted explorer had reached his underground refuge with its welcome store of food, including freshly deposited pineapples and oranges. He was just five miles from his hut, and could be confident that his life was safe. However, his reputation might well turn out to have been ruined. After all, having set out with two companions on a 300-mile trek with dog sledges along the Antarctic coastline in November 1911, the thirty-year-old leader of the Australasian Antarctic Expedition had staggered back alone. One of his companions had fallen to his death down a deep crevasse, while the other had died a slow death from starvation and the bitter cold.[1] Instead of returning in triumph, with their sledges full of scientific curiosities and carefully noted observations, Mawson had barely returned with his life. It was a terrible end to an expedition that had begun full of promise and eager anticipation.

From the late nineteenth century, there had been several proposals for an Australian-financed expedition to the Antarctic. But sufficient money had never been forthcoming from either official or private sources. Australians aspiring to go south had to attach themselves instead to a British expedition, which is what the young Douglas Mawson did when the Antarctic explorer Ernest

Shackleton arrived in Australia in late 1907. Tall, handsome, and ambitious, Mawson was then a recently graduated geologist from Sydney University who had completed a geological survey of the New Hebrides before being hired as a lecturer by the University of Adelaide. Mawson was interested in the ancient glaciation of South Australia, and was keen to see active glaciation at first hand. He also wanted to make a name for himself. When he learned that Professor Edgeworth David, his academic mentor from Sydney University, was going south with Shackleton, Mawson offered to go, too.[2]

The Yorkshire-born Mawson had arrived in Australia as a two-year-old with his parents in 1884. His father was the son of a farmer, but had turned to running a drapery business in a nearby town. Now he was taking his young family to the other side of the world, hoping to turn a small fortune into a larger one. He was destined to be disappointed. Mawson's father was a failure at the various businesses he tried in New South Wales, from raising pigs to canning fruit. Whether it was due to his personal shortcomings, or simply resulted from the vicissitudes of the 1890s depression, he abandoned his businesses and worked as an accountant for a timber merchant in inner Sydney. The family were also forced by their straitened circumstances to take in lodgers at their rented accommodation in the inner suburb of Glebe. It was a humiliating position for young Mawson, who was admitted to the engineering faculty at Sydney University in 1899, and graduated with reasonable results in 1902. He did best in geology, and came under the tutelage of the Welsh-born professor Edgeworth David, who helped secure a position for Mawson as a geology lecturer at the University of Adelaide. The sorry spectacle of his father had made a deep impression upon Mawson; he was determined to achieve the fortune and social standing that had so eluded his father. An expedition to the Antarctic provided him with an opportunity to earn both fame and fortune, and quick promotion at his university. For the rest of his life, Mawson would have an absorbing interest in science, and an unrequited desire to make his fortune from it.

The leader of the expedition, Ernest Shackleton, shared Mawson's interest in making a fortune. His father had also left Yorkshire, becoming an unsuccessful farmer in Ireland before training as a doctor and returning with his large family to England. Young Shackleton was a restless go-getter who was acutely conscious of his relatively low social standing. He joined the merchant marine as a boy, and rose through the ranks to become a master mariner before volunteering to join Robert Falcon Scott's first expedition to Antarctica in 1901. He so impressed Scott that he was chosen to accompany him and Edward Wilson on a dash with dog sledges toward the South Pole. As it happened, they wouldn't even get off the Ross Ice Shelf, but they would set a new record for traveling farthest south at 82°15'. It would come at a cost. All were starving and affected by scurvy, and Shackleton was coughing blood. To maximize the distance, they abandoned the dog food and used a scalpel to butcher the dogs, one by one, to feed to the surviving animals. Long after they should have turned back, and with his relations with Shackleton souring, Scott insisted on pushing farther southward. When they did finally stop, Shackleton was ordered by Scott to remain behind while he and Wilson continued for an extra few miles to claim the record. The relations between the two men worsened beyond repair when Scott sacked the ailing Shackleton and sent him home with the relief ship. As a weeping Shackleton sailed out of Antarctica's icy grip, Scott stayed on for another year.[3]

Shackleton's sacking proved to be a blessing. In the absence of Scott, whose expedition was being attacked and derided as an expensive adventure in some sections of the British press, Shackleton became somewhat of a celebrity in Britain. He even stood unsuccessfully for parliament before becoming secretary of the Scottish Geographical Society. That position allowed him to enlist wealthy Scottish patrons for an expedition of his own. With his recent celebrity, and after his experience with Scott, Shackleton was determined to be the leader and to reap all the spoils. He would do what Scott had been unable to do: he would find a way off the Ross Ice Shelf and onto the polar plateau and beyond to the South Pole. If he was the first to reach the South Pole, the feat would set him up for life. It would also satisfy Shackleton's desire to overshadow his former commander and avenge his treatment by Scott.[4]

Although Shackleton wanted celebrity, and the wealth it would bring, he needed to protect himself against those critics who were dismissive of so-called "pole hunting" expeditions. Such critics argued that it was not a good use of public money to finance an expedition with no serious purpose other than to reach the South Pole. While racing to the South Pole might amuse readers of the popular press, others wanted polar expeditions to have a scientific purpose if they were going to be financed by the British government and by scientific institutions. They should settle some important geographical question, collect valuable specimens, or gather important observations about polar phenomena. Shackleton belatedly pandered to these critics by employing a handful of scientists to provide a veneer of science for the expedition. He took a biologist and geologist from England, and, when he reached Australia in late 1907, offered jobs to local scientists. This had the added advantage of increasing his chances of getting financial support from the Australian federal or state governments. Shackleton agreed to a request from the politically well-connected professor Edgeworth David to go south on the return voyage of the expedition ship, *Nimrod*, with the forty-nine-year-old David helping to convince prime minister Alfred Deakin to contribute £5,000 to the expedition.[5]

Mawson had already met with Shackleton in Adelaide, and proposed that he go on the relief voyage of the *Nimrod* in 1909, when Shackleton was being collected from the Antarctic at the end of the expedition. Imagine his surprise then, when he received a telegram from David appointing him as the expedition's physicist, departing within weeks. Mawson was bemused by the offer, but accepted nonetheless. He had no family obligations, and needed only to get leave from the university. Although he would have preferred being appointed as the expedition geologist, that position had already been taken by the young English geologist Raymond Priestley. Mawson went on the understanding that David was not staying in the Antarctic and that Mawson could therefore consider himself as the most senior scientist. It was only after sailing to New Zealand to join the *Nimrod* that Mawson discovered that David was going to stay for the entire expedition. Mawson was not amused. Any scientific work that he did was likely to be overshadowed by David's. But he could hardly complain to his former professor and mentor, whose support had been crucial in getting him the job in Adelaide.[6]

Shackleton had no interest in the scientific results of the expedition. He just wanted to be lauded as a polar hero by becoming the first man to reach the South Pole. He was also on the lookout for any valuable deposits of gold or precious stones that might be found. After his experience with dogs on the Scott expedition, Shackleton would rely on horses to pull the sledges, and took an automobile to pull sledges on the Ross Ice Shelf. However, neither mode of transport would perform well in the extreme cold: the automobile quickly shuddered to a halt, while his horses had all died by the time Shackleton found a way up the Beardmore Glacier to the polar plateau beyond. There were still another 375 miles to the pole, and 1,125 miles to return, during which Shackleton and his three companions would have to manhaul the sledges.

With the pole almost in sight, Shackleton realized that they would run out of food before they completed the return journey. So he turned back, claiming that the pole was just 97 miles away. He would later say that it was better to be a live donkey than a dead lion. It has since been argued that Shackleton was farther from the pole than he let on, and chose the figure of 97 miles because it was less than 100 miles and therefore had more public appeal. He was right about that. It turned out not to matter that he failed to reach his goal. As an imperial power confronting its relative decline, Edwardian England needed heroes, and the rough-and-ready Shackleton would have to suffice until someone better came along. He would be showered with riches and a knighthood.[7]

While Shackleton was slogging his way toward the South Pole, David and Mawson were doing likewise toward the South Magnetic Pole. Although their journey is often overlooked by historians, their accomplishment was arguably greater than Shackleton's. In March 1908, as their first summer in the Antarctic was coming to an end, Mawson, the fifty-year-old David, and the Scottish doctor Alistair Mackay tested their mettle by climbing to the summit of the 13,300-foot-high Mt. Erebus. It was one of two volcanoes looming over Shackleton's base at Cape Royds. The men had a support party of three, including the aristocratic Sir Phillip Brocklehurst, who had paid for his passage. Although the support party was only meant to go as far as they could take the sledge, they ended up leaving the sledge on the mountainside and also ascending to the top during the week-long adventure. At the summit, amid the swirl of sulphurous fumes, they all enjoyed the magnificence of the view into the active crater and out to the surrounding panorama of ice. For Mawson, there was the satisfaction of having his physical stamina tested successfully in Antarctic conditions. But they could not linger at the rim. With Brocklehurst having suffered severe frostbite, which would cost him one of his big toes, they wasted no time getting back. Instead of climbing down the way they had come, they wrapped their gear and rolled it down the icy slope. Then they followed on behind, glissading their way down the cone, using their ice axes to slow their descent on the slippery surface.[8]

The following six months were spent largely in the hut preparing for the summer sledging season. There was much that Mawson could have learned, particularly from the other expedition doctor, Eric Marshall, who believed that fresh food was the best protection against scurvy. The disease often defeated even the best-equipped expeditions, because no one knew that it was caused by a deficiency of vitamin C. Indeed, the existence of vitamin C was not known at the time. However, it had been surmised that the absence of fresh food in the diet would bring on the disease. That was not something that Scott had accepted, and his expedition had been stricken by scurvy as a result of his obstinacy. Marshall, though, was a believer in the protective benefits of eating fresh food, and took preserved fruit and tomatoes from New Zealand, and had the men eat lightly cooked seal meat, which was rich in vitamin C, as a regular part of their diet. As a result of his efforts, Shackleton's expedition was free of scurvy.[9] Time would tell whether Mawson learned from this experience.

Other experiences on the expedition were best forgotten. Shackleton's use of horses and neglect of dogs was a misbegotten failure. He also neglected to adopt methods from societies whose everyday existence involved living with snow and ice. Rather than taking an automobile, Shackleton would have been better served by taking snowshoes and training the members of his expedition in the use of skis. Either would have been of great value on the soft snow of the Ross Ice Shelf and for crossing crevasses. Shackleton did realize, though, that his journey would be expedited by the establishment of food depots along his planned route. When the light returned after the winter, Shackleton sent small parties out on reconnaissance journeys, taking stores forward in preparation for his attempt to reach the South Pole. One food dump was established 100 miles from the hut. However, it contained mostly the bulky food required for the horses, and his method of marking the depots would make them difficult to find in conditions of low visibility. Rather than having a line of flags at right angles to the food depot, as Roald Amundsen would do, he had just a single flag erected atop the snow cairn on which the food was stored. Such food depots were easy to miss when the sky was overcast and the snow was blowing.

It would be a steep learning curve for the Antarctic novices, David, Mawson, and Mackay. In October 1908, they were sent out by Shackleton to find the South Magnetic Pole, which lay inland from the western shore of the Ross Sea. What a triumph it would have been if Shackleton's southern party could reach the South

Pole, and David's northern party could reach the South Magnetic Pole, both within the space of a single summer. There would be nothing left for his rival Scott to do. Even reaching one of the poles would produce a great public splash, and ensure success for the expedition. Ever the fortune-hunter, Shackleton also wanted David's party to prospect for valuable minerals during the return journey from the magnetic pole. Prospecting particularly interested Mawson. The glaciated coast of the Ross Sea was also of scientific interest to Mawson, who was keen to see the action of glaciers on the landscape. He had no interest in the South Magnetic Pole.[10]

The three-man northern party left Cape Royds on October 5, man-hauling two heavy sledges, taking one at a time and doubling back to get the other. It was a laborious method, but there seemed to be no alternative. There were no food dumps along the Ross Sea coast, and they had not thought of living off the seals and penguins that were there in abundance. It was a big challenge for fifty-year-old David, whose physique was not up to it. Mackay was younger and fitter. He had been a soldier in the Boer War and a surgeon in the Royal Navy before joining Shackleton. But he also had a fondness for whisky, and was reputed to have become mentally unbalanced after being kicked by a horse. Nevertheless, he was better suited than David to the tough physical labor and harsh conditions.

The young and physically fit Mawson was even more so. But they were hamstrung by having none of the advantages that Shackleton reserved for himself. The dogs and horses would be kept for the expedition's primary purpose, to reach the South Pole. There would be no preestablished food depots. Neither would there be support parties to accompany them or to establish food depots along the route of their return. Everything necessary for their survival had to be carried on their two sledges, which they had to haul themselves, other than for some initial assistance from the motor car, which carried some of their stores for the first ten miles and towed their sledges for just three miles. After that, it was all up to them, other than those occasional days when the wind and the surface was suitable for raising a sail on the sledges.[11]

The trek would be no easy task. The two sledges were so overloaded with food and equipment for the long journey that it took all their strength to haul them. Each weighed about half a ton. Hauling one of them at a time, and then returning to bring the other one forward, meant that they had to travel ten or 12 miles a day just to progress about three or four miles. Yet they were hauling food across the sea ice on a coastline that teemed with food. Although catching fish might have unduly delayed them, there were plenty of penguins and seals that they passed without attempting to add them to their larder. On October 10, the three men were woken in their tent by the cries of three Emperor penguins. As the men ate their breakfast, packed away their tent, and sledged off, Mawson noted that the largest of the world's penguins went back to sleep. Over the following days, the men would pass large numbers of seals, many of them pupping on the ice. Despite Marshall's prescription about the eating of fresh meat to stave off scurvy, the overloaded men struggled past with their sledge-loads of processed food, leaving the wildlife undisturbed.[12]

From the first, Mawson was scathing in his diary about David, claiming each day that the professor was dog-tired. David had been taking the lead, hauling out in front at the end of a long rope. On October 18, because of a "bad attack of snow blindness," David asked Mawson to take the lead position. He never asked to take it back, even when his eyes returned to normal. He was implicitly acknowledging Mawson's greater strength and stamina, which might have boosted Mawson's ego. However, it meant that Mawson was forever feeling that he was putting more effort into the hauling than the two who were hauling behind him. That caused part of his resentment toward David. But there was much more with which to find fault. Indeed, Mawson complained about everything, from the fact that David "finds it necessary to change his socks in [the] morning before breakfast," to his methods of cooking, the amount of clothes he wore, and the way he got into the sleeping bag long after Mawson and Mackay had got in and then "sits on everybody."[13]

On October 19, Mawson reported that it was two and a half hours after stopping for the day before David got in the sleeping bag, whereupon "he commenced reading and writing." The following day, he griped that David

> generally comes into tent after we are both in bed and spends ½ an hour on top of bag arranging and changing things. He sits on our legs and faces alternately. Finally, when we have got the chill off the bag, he struggles in all cold and bedaubed with snow. Of course he has the warm middle berth and occupies certainly more than ½ the bag as he wears innumerable clothes.

He was annoyed that the overdressed David kept the toggles of the bag undone, which caused the others to shiver. Mawson also claimed that the "weight of these clothes makes him ill on the march but he cannot see it."[14] This experience made the young Mawson averse to using three-man bags on subsequent expeditions, despite their usefulness compared with single sleeping bags in maintaining the core temperature of their bodies.

Mawson had more important concerns. His primary interest was in geology rather in reaching the South Magnetic Pole. At their painfully slow rate of progress of about four miles a day, they would be lucky to reach the South Magnetic Pole, let alone return in time for him to investigate the Dry Valley,[15] a large ice-free area on the coast near Cape Royds, where Shackleton hoped valuable minerals might be discovered. Although Mawson's physical fitness was making him the effective leader of the expedition, he was unable to shift David from his fixation about the magnetic pole. On October 22, he told David that it would be impossible to reach the pole in the time available and that they should just complete their magnetic and geological survey of the coastline. This way, they could be back at the Dry Valley by the beginning of January. But David and Mackay refused. Mawson was incredulous when the professor argued they could live on half rations during the estimated 500-mile return journey from the coast to the magnetic pole. It was a madcap plan that was not only irrational, but would mean missing out on the Dry Valley, concluded Mawson. Because he couldn't shift them, he let the matter go for the time being.[16]

Over the succeeding days, as they passed numerous seals giving birth, Mawson quietly mulled over their options. Matters came to a head on October 29, when David asked his companions to "give up all else" for the magnetic pole. It would mean no more geological investigations, whether along the coast or in the Dry Valley. It was "ridiculous," replied Mawson, to expect they would be able to get to the magnetic pole and back while living on half rations. Although resigned to not reaching the Dry Valley, Mawson agreed to press on to the magnetic pole provided they could live on full rations. They could achieve this, he argued, by living "on seal flesh and local food." On their return to the coast, they should also plan to "subsist entirely on local food." Lastly, instead of trying to head back to Shackleton's hut, he suggested they wait on the coast, living on seals and other wildlife until the *Nimrod* came looking for them. He was concerned that the melting sea ice would prevent them taking the relatively easy route along the coast. None of the men knew that eating seals and penguins would also save them from scurvy — they just saw it as a means of eking out their limited food supply. Mawson's suggestion was "carried unanimously." It meant that their lives would depend on getting back to the coast in time and having the men on the *Nimrod* see them. In case they weren't found, they all wrote farewell letters to their loved ones and sealed them in an empty biscuit tin, which was left beneath a cairn of rocks on an island connected by ice to the continent. A flagpole was left to mark the spot, both for themselves and the watchers on the ship.[17]

It took two days to find their first seal, with the men "experimenting on cooking the seal in his own oil" before having "a feed of steak for dinner." One reason they had walked past penguins and seals without thinking of killing and eating them was that they had no idea how to butcher them, which parts of the animal were best to eat, and how to cook them. It was also a messy and bloody task to perform in the otherwise pristine environment. They first cut the flesh into a steak, but the next day Mawson minced it and made a broth, and used the leftover steak in the "hoosh," a boiled-up mixture of dried, powdered beef and lard, known as pemmican, that was usually thickened with ground-up biscuits. They also used the seal blubber to fuel a lamp for cooking and lighting. Eating seals wasn't an immediate success. After stewing meat over the blubber lamp on November 2, the others reported they "did not feel too much like pulling [the sledge] on this diet." Mawson felt even worse when he ate some of the seal blubber from the lamp, and was stricken with diarrhea. But he ate some chocolate and "felt all right." Indeed, he declared that he was "now ravenous and delight in blubber though it does not agree with me." It wasn't until November 5 that they tried the seal's liver, when they had "a remarkably good liver fry at lunch." Mawson described how the liver was "put in [the] lamp along with wicks and burning blubber" and eaten "partly charred and partly underdone." On November 28, they "killed an Emperor penguin and took breast and heart and liver," and "then killed a full grown baby seal and took liver." Convinced that seal meat was edible, they halved their normal rations, and made up the difference with seal meat.[18]

After three weeks of killing different seals — young and old, male and female — and eating their various parts, Mawson decreed the dos and don'ts of eating seal. The "steak from loins, liver and blubber" of young bull seals, along with their tongue, was "always good," as was that from cow seals provided it wasn't long after they had given birth. Overall, though, he decided that young calves were best, particularly after they had lost their fur. While the livers of the youngest seals were "excellent" and able to provide a meal for the three of them, he found the older calves had "liver larger, steak tender and blubber excellent. The latter melts in the mouth and appears and cuts like bacon about 1½" thick." He also devised a recipe for minced seal meat, which he recommended as "one of the best forms for expeditions." It involved frying finely chopped blubber for half an hour or more and then adding a sizeable lump of frozen seal blood. Once that had cooked and set, it needed to be broken up with a spoon before a large quantity of seal meat was added, along with salt and pepper. After a farther twenty minutes of cooking, powdered biscuit could be added to soak up the oil.[19]

The party was still on the coast and the hauling across the sea ice was getting "almost unbearably heavy," observed Mawson on November 21, as daytime temperatures caused the snow to soften and the sea ice to thin. The trio resorted to traveling at night, when the temperature was colder and the sea ice less sticky and more solid. By late November, they had been trekking for more than six weeks. As Mawson predicted, there was no way they could reach the magnetic pole and make it all the way back to the hut, let alone do any geological work along the way. David argued that they could complete the inland journey in just five weeks, leaving the coast by December 6 and returning by January 10, which was about three weeks before the Nimrod was due to sail past in search of them. In a burst of optimism, presumably to appease Mawson, David suggested they still might have time to do some geological work. Mawson angrily pointed at the mountains they could see across their inland path, which would slow them down and require more food to be taken. Rather than hauling five weeks' food, Mawson argued that they should carry seven weeks' provisions on their trek to the pole and make no decision about their subsequent plans until they had returned to the coast. Mawson's caution seemed to be borne out the first day, when they covered just three miles on a difficult surface of soft and heavily salted snow, rather than the four miles that David had prescribed. It was not only the sledges that held them back. While Mawson conceded that David was "a fine example of a man for his age," he suspected that David was leaning into the harness more than he was pulling. As evidence, Mawson noted that when he and

Mackay were "struggling heavily with hauling he has continued to recite poetry or tell yarns."[20]

Before they could get onto the polar plateau, they had to cross the massive tongue of the Drygalski Glacier, which was 20 miles across and stretched for a similar distance out to sea. This writhing mass of ice and snow was riven with crevasses and ravines. At times, sheer walls of ice required them to unload their sledges and lower them on ropes. Often they were blocked and had to retrace their steps to find an alternative route. When their first attempt failed, they retreated to the sea ice and tried again farther east. It was all taking time and eating up their food. On December 4, Mackay was sent back six miles to kill some seals, while Mawson and David chased and killed a hapless Adélie penguin that wandered past. Their second attempt to cross the glacier was successful, but it had taken more precious days, and was not completed until mid-December.[21]

They were nearly two weeks behind David's schedule for the journey to the pole. Before leaving the sea ice, they cooked up the choicest parts of the seals and penguins, particularly the livers, for the journey ahead. Taking about 25 pounds of meat and sufficient other food to last seven weeks, they left the other sledge on the north side of the glacier, packed with some of the biscuits and processed rations that had formerly provided a staple of their sledging diet. It would provide a food depot when they returned to await the arrival of the *Nimrod*. Apart from protecting them from scurvy, the animal fats also provided a more nutritious and satisfying food than the sugars that Mawson had previously relied upon to keep him going. After eating the seal meat, organs, and blubber, Mawson no longer felt hungry between meals, compared with the time when he was consuming large quantities of chocolate and having twenty-five cubes of sugar a day in his cups of tea.[22]

Taking their leave of the coast, they headed west to where they thought the South Magnetic Pole was located. It was hard work finding a way up the Larsen Glacier onto the polar plateau. Although they only had to haul one sledge, it was packed with more than 600 pounds of food, clothing, and equipment. To make the climb more manageable, they took up half a load at a time. Mawson doubted the ability of his companions to do the distance. He thought David was incapable of doing his share of the man-hauling, while he berated Mackay as "very lazy ... and very unskilful in ... everything but hard plain manual work." Despite these handicaps, they made good progress. The first two days they covered about 18 miles. The ground was much more difficult to cross on the third day, with the roped-up Mawson falling into one of the many crevasses they had to cross. They covered only four miles that day and two miles the next day, when soft snow and a succession of crevasses slowed their progress until they were completely stopped by a blizzard. Farther time was lost as they backtracked and searched for a better route. And they were hampered by David, who was accused by Mawson of being "in nothing like the condition we are in." Then there was the blizzard "of exceptional violence" that brought them to a halt on December 22 and tore two holes in their tent. By Christmas Day, when they had climbed to 2,120 feet, Mawson thought David "appeared to have lost all interest in the journey" — which may have been, as David confided to Mackay, because he was constipated.[23]

Climbing ever higher, they passed 4,000 feet on December 27, and were covering between eight and 11 miles a day. By the end of December, they reached 6,000 feet, and Mawson was becoming more concerned about David's physical and psychological state. "Something has gone very wrong with him of late," observed Mawson, "as he [is] almost [always] morose, never refers to our work, shirks all questions regarding it, never offers a suggestion." He complained that David was "dreadfully slow now, he does nothing." He seldom helped pack the sledge, and was "content with looking on." Apart from suffering constipation, David had lost his Burberry helmet and was feeling the cold. Mackay would later lend him his helmet, which helped protect David from the cold and the sun. But it could not protect him from the altitude sickness that would have started to affect him as they passed through 7,000 feet.[24] Even though David was doing much less physical work than Mawson and Mackay, he might also have been suffering more from the reduced rations.

On December 31, Mawson noted that they were eating "very little now as original supply had undergone two reductions." To extend the food supply, they were saving a bit more than ten percent of each day's ration so that they might have sufficient for an eight-week journey. Mawson relaxed the ration on New Year's Day, when he made "a decent meal," while noting that the "rest of the week will have to suffer for it." Yet just three days later, Mawson reported they had a surplus of food, and consequently had "a better meal" that evening. The strict rationing had been counter-productive. It had saved food, but they now were "really weak," wrote Mawson, with David the worst affected. The combination of malnutrition and the effects of the altitude took its toll, leaving David "quite prostrated between hauls." Mawson was also concerned that David's "memory seems fainter."[25]

Although the ration was relaxed, their physical state continued to deteriorate as their steady progress on the polar plateau took them ever higher, going past 8,000 feet. After having a substantial meal on January 4, with extra biscuits and thick cocoa, Mawson thought that his stomach was "evidently contracted very much now as could hardly hold all this meal. The cocoa seemed almost intoxicating to me." The sun and wind were affecting their lips, which were "swollen and in an awful state of soreness." He was also affected by frostbite on his cheeks and nose, and by snow blindness after not using his goggles for two days.[26]

Their mental state was not helped by Mawson announcing on January 13 that the magnetic pole was 57 miles farther away than he had originally estimated. This was not good news. David and Mackay were "very glum," with Mackay estimating that it would take an extra four days to reach the new location, and another four days to return. This was too long — it would make it impossible to reach the coast on their remaining rations. Interestingly, it was Mawson who argued that they should press on. He claimed that they could reach the pole in three extra days and have sufficient food on their reduced rations to return to the coast if they could cover 13 miles a day. Mackay dismissed Mawson's plan as "impossible," and only relented when all three men vowed that they would do 13 miles a day on the return journey.[27]

After just two days, when they were about 200 miles from the coast, their instruments suggested that the South Magnetic Pole might be only about 12 miles away. If they went another 13 miles, argued Mawson, they should be at least in "the area" of the pole, after which they could "return with all speed to coast." And so that is what they did, dumping most of their load and racing across the "vast white sea" to the supposed "region" of the pole. It would have taken days to determine exactly where the pole was then located, and they didn't have any days to spare. So, on January 16, the starved and exhausted men simply stopped to set up the camera on its tripod, so that David could capture the scene of them hoisting the British flag and taking possession of the surrounding region. They didn't bother taking a final measurement to ensure they had reached the pole. That was information they didn't want, because it would have confirmed that the magnetic pole was still some distance away — perhaps as much as 85 miles. And there was no possibility of them going in search of it, since they barely had sufficient rations to ensure their safe return to the coast. Instead, as David reported, they "did a right about-turn, and as quick a march as tired limbs would allow, back in the direction of our little green tent in the wilderness of snow."[28]

With good weather and easily located supply dumps, the descent from the polar plateau was made in good time, often achieving 16 miles and sometimes as much as 21 miles a day. Their fast pace meant that they could return to an almost normal ration of food, which included some of the seal liver. The return was also easier because they could often follow those tracks they had made on the inward journey that had not been covered by snow and which led them to each of their supply dumps. On top of this, they had the benefit of a following wind, which allowed them one day to use a sail on the sledge. As a result, it took less than three weeks to reach the coast. Only in the final stage were difficulties encountered with the terrain, after David and Mawson overruled objections from Mackay and opted to take a route that they hoped would be quicker and easier.

They knew the ship was coming to search for them on February 1, and they were desperate to get within sight of the sea in time to signal it. If they missed it, there was a strong possibility that David, and perhaps all of them, would die if they were forced to walk all the way back to Shackleton's hut. But their shortcut down the Larsen Glacier proved a terrible trial. On January 31, when they were just 15 miles from their depot on the Drygalski Glacier tongue, heavy snow made the hauling so hard that Mawson described the experience as "an awful day of despair, disappointment, hard traveling, agonizing walking — forever falling down crevasses." David's Burberry pants were "so much torn as to be falling off," and the professor was "half-demented" from the strain. Mackay became so worried about David's physical and mental state that he insisted the professor hand over the leadership to Mawson. Otherwise, said Mackay, acting as the doctor, he would "pronounce him insane."[29]

Mawson's leadership was brief. On February 4, 1909, just a day after reaching the depot, their little green tent was sighted on the snow-covered slope of the glacial tongue by John King Davis, the first officer on the *Nimrod*. They were lucky to be seen. The ship had already gone past and was returning to Cape Royds when the captain decided to take a closer look at an inlet that had been obscured by snow and was now clear. When he heard the signal rocket from the ship, Mawson was so relieved that he rushed from the tent, only to fall 18 feet down a crevasse and land on his back on a ledge covered with hard snow. Mackay and David were too exhausted to rescue him, and had to wait for Davis to go down with ropes to help Mawson out. When they hobbled aboard the ship, its captain observed how they were all "abnormally lean … the color of mahogany, with hands that resembled the talons of a bird of prey." They were taken to Cape Royds to await Shackleton's return from the South Pole trek. In the event that Shackleton did not return, Mawson was instructed to stay behind for another year with five others to search for him. That proved unnecessary.[30]

Mawson could be pleased with his accomplishment. Without any polar experience, and with no horses, dogs, or a support party, David, Mawson, and Mackay had traversed more than 1,200 miles over almost four months and had returned in relatively good health. The feat would remain for several decades as the longest man-hauling journey without a support party. Their fate might have been very different if they had not been spotted by the *Nimrod* and been forced to traverse the hundreds of miles that remained to Cape Royds. As it was, Mawson could take confidence from his physical performance on the trek, when he had proved himself superior to his older companions. He could also take confidence from the relatively benign conditions they had experienced during the trek, when blizzards were seldom encountered and their progress was rarely impeded by the weather. While crevasses had been a danger, they had not caused them any death or injury, or the loss of any supplies.

Mawson might have sworn off any more polar adventures, but he was hooked. The Antarctic provided him with a challenging environment in which to test his physical stamina, prove his masculinity, and pursue his worldly ambitions. The celebrity that he was accorded on his return to Australia was intoxicating. With Mawson looking on, David told a reception at Sydney University that Mawson "was the real leader and was the soul of our expedition to the magnetic pole. We really have in him an Australian Nansen [the famous Norwegian explorer], of infinite resource, splendid physique, astonishing indifference to frost." Back in Adelaide, Mawson was carried shoulder-high from his train by adoring students, and pulled on a trolley to a reception at his nearby university.[31] The trek to the South Magnetic Pole had demonstrated to Mawson that the Antarctic held no terrors for him, and that even a subordinate position on a British polar expedition could make him a luminary in Australia. The experience would leave him with a taste for fame, and a hunger for the fortune and academic promotion that could accompany it.

CHAPTER TWO

A Leader at Last

The Antarctic had made Mawson's name, at least in Adelaide. But finding fame in an isolated provincial city was of little account in the imperial scheme of things. It was the admiration of London that mattered most to Australians like Mawson. His father had left England hoping to find his fortune in Australia. Now Mawson was intending to leave Australia in the hope of finding fame and fortune in the imperial capital. Following his return from Antarctica in March 1909, he completed his doctoral thesis and arranged six months' leave from Adelaide University to visit Britain. Before he left Adelaide in December 1909, Mawson had a chance encounter with eighteen-year-old Paquita Delprat, the tall and comely daughter of a wealthy mine manager. Her father was of Dutch and Basque ancestry, which gave the dark-haired Paquita an exotic air that helped to pique Mawson's interest. He also was doubtless attracted by the advantages that would accrue to himself as a geologist from being connected to a wealthy and influential mining family. First, though, he had to pursue his more immediate ambitions, and the Antarctic would be the means of achieving them.

While David had garnered most of the Australian public plaudits for Shackleton's expedition, his advanced age and near-death experience decided him against any return to Antarctica. Mawson was different. He was stimulated by the struggles,

25

the adventures, and the dangers, and had proved that he could withstand anything that the Antarctic threw at him. Moreover, his experience had convinced him that Antarctica could be the making of his career and his fortune. Joining another Antarctic expedition was at the forefront of his mind when he left by ship for London in December 1909. It seems that he was also on the lookout for an academic position overseas, or at least to establish links that might lead to such a position. At the time, the fastest path to a professorship in Australia was by way of a prestigious university in Britain. Whatever his other intentions might have been, as soon as Mawson learned that Scott was looking for an Australian scientist to join him on another attempt on the South Pole, he immediately cabled to London, asking for a meeting.[1]

Not that Mawson was interested in the South Pole. He was keen to explore the uncharted coast west of Cape Adare, which had only been seen occasionally and fleetingly by explorers sailing past. It was the Antarctic coast that was south of Australia, and consequently was regarded by Mawson and others as belonging rightfully to Australia. When Mawson met with Scott in London, he asked that he and three companions should be landed at Cape Adare so that a proper reconnaissance could be carried out along the coast to the west. But Scott was focused on reaching the South Pole, which would mean retracing Shackleton's route and then going the additional 100 miles or so that Shackleton had been unable to do. Although Scott offered to take Mawson in the pole party, the Australian explorer had no interest in being a subordinate member of an expedition that had no serious purpose and would discover nothing new. If he was to go with Scott, his view was that it had to be as scientific leader; Scott, however, had already offered that position to his close friend Edward Wilson, so the best he could offer Mawson was to make him chief geologist. When Mawson suggested instead that he would lead an expedition of his own to Cape Adare, Scott brazenly declared that he would base part of his own expedition there and use his ship to do a reconnaissance of the coastline to the west. Scott wanted the entire Ross Sea region for himself, from Cape Adare south to Cape Royds; he was trying to lock Mawson out of the Cape Adare region, and remove him as a potential rival. However, Mawson remained as determined as ever to explore the vast coastline between the Ross Sea and the German discoveries far to the west at Gaussberg. Not even a private dinner on January 26, 1910, with Scott and his beguiling wife, Kathleen, could persuade Mawson to abandon his scheme.[2]

Things might have turned out differently had Shackleton been in London when Mawson arrived. He would have ensured that Mawson kept clear of Scott, and would have enlisted the enthusiastic Australian in his own schemes. But the explorer was in Europe, lecturing about his Antarctic exploits and being lured by stories of rich gold deposits in Hungary. It wasn't until late January that Mawson met the returning Shackleton and outlined his ambitious idea of Shackleton mounting a scientific expedition to the vast unexplored region west of Cape Adare. Such an original and ambitious venture would stand in stark contrast to Scott's more pedestrian effort, which mainly followed in Shackleton's footsteps. Anything that belittled Scott was attractive to Shackleton, who initially suggested that Mawson lead the expedition himself, and generously offered to help raise the required funds. Shackleton allowed Mawson to use his office in Regent Street as a London base so that he could draw up the grand plan in detail. But Mawson was no sooner settled there before Shackleton announced that he would lead the expedition and Mawson could come along as chief scientist. The relatively unknown Australian had no alternative but to agree. He would have no hope of raising the money himself in the face of opposition from both Scott and Shackleton.[3]

In a plan drawn up at Shackleton's request, Mawson proposed the establishment of three bases. Ignoring Scott's cheeky attempt to snaffle Cape Adare for himself, Mawson suggested that one base be established at Cape Adare and the other two along the coast to the west.[4] Mawson's plan was designed to encompass that great swath of Antarctic coastline from 90°E to 158°E, which he proposed to claim on behalf of the recently federated British dominion of Australia. Along with David and Mackay, he had made territorial claims on behalf of Britain to Victoria Land and the area around the South Magnetic Pole during the Shackleton expedition. He had developed a taste for territory and the flag-raising that was an integral part of it. Now he planned to do it on a grander scale than had ever been done before in the Antarctic. Indeed, it would almost be on the scale of Captain James Cook's claiming of the Australian east coast in 1770.

Shackleton thought the money needed to finance the expedition might be found in the Hungarian gold mines, and he sent Mawson off to assess their potential. But, while the gold deposits were certainly there, Mawson was unable to secure their ownership for Shackleton. Meanwhile, Shackleton was continuing his lecturing, this time in America. Anxious to be paid for his part in the earlier expedition, and to pin down Shackleton about his role in the future one, Mawson followed him to Omaha in May 1910. It was there that Mawson extracted a commitment from Shackleton about the money that he was owed and the role that he would play in the proposed expedition: Mawson would be the scientific leader and, if Shackleton decided not to go, Mawson would take over the leadership of the entire expedition. In the latter eventuality, Shackleton still promised to help raise funds for it. This was great news for Mawson, who continued on to Australia, quietly confident that Shackleton was losing interest in the Antarctic and that he, Mawson, might soon be leader of his own expedition.[5] His fame and, hopefully, his fortune would then be made.

Imbued with this confidence, Mawson returned to Adelaide and resumed his courtship of the young Paquita, who agreed to become his fiancée. As for the Antarctic, he was hamstrung by Scott and didn't want to start raising money until Scott had filled his own coffers and left England for Antarctica, which he did in July 1910. Otherwise, Mawson might have been accused of detracting from Scott's fundraising. Mawson was also hamstrung by Shackleton, who continued to keep his intentions unclear. Shackleton talked to the press about another Antarctic expedition, without saying definitely whether or not he would be its leader. It was not until December 1910 that Shackleton finally informed Mawson that he would not be going, but remained committed to supporting an expedition led by the Australian explorer.[6] This was what Mawson had been waiting so long to hear. However, there still remained the massive task of raising the funds for an expedition that was to be led by a relatively unknown explorer from a distant British dominion, who wanted the venture to be known as the Australasian Antarctic Expedition. Although he planned to raise some of the funds in England, Mawson began his fundraising in Australia.

The first contribution came from the Australasian Association for the Advancement of Science after Mawson addressed its conference in January 1911. The donation of £1,000 was a small beginning for a projected budget of £48,000. Other contributions were received in dribs and drabs from wealthy Australians, but there was no firm commitment at all from the Australian Labor government, which Mawson had hoped would give £20,000. His pitch to governments and benefactors in Australia was based on the economic possibilities in the Antarctic, and on the national pride that would accrue to the new Australian federation. With Australians proving stubbornly reluctant to contribute sufficient funds, Mawson went back to London in February to seek Shackleton's assistance in opening English wallets. Some of the men, most of the equipment, and the all-important expedition ship would have to be found there.

It was a difficult task. Scott had already done the rounds of likely benefactors for his expedition, and it was hard to squeeze them for more. Nevertheless, the British government agreed to give £2,000, and the Royal Geographical Society, £500. Donations also came from wealthy individuals — some of it as loans, and some with a promise from Mawson to share any profit he might make from his discoveries. Although he kept stressing that his expedition was "purely scientific" and would be "the greatest scientific expedition of the period," he also assured potential benefactors that there was money to be made in the Antarctic. Mawson said there was "a great probability of a commercial future following upon our discoveries," whether it was from minerals, seals, or whales. He promised "legally to divide with the chief private supporters ... any such advantageous discoveries." Unfortunately for Mawson, there were no individuals prepared to contribute more than one or two thousand pounds. Other contributions were given by companies as goods in kind or at a discount. But the biggest contribution came from the British public, after an appeal was published under Shackleton's name in London's *Daily Mail*. Nearly £8,000 was donated, along with many contributions of goods, including a pianoforte, a gramophone, and a ton of marmalade. So much alcohol was offered that Mawson could only take half an offered £50 worth of strong old ale, which was said by its brewer to be better than rum as "a sustaining cold weather drink." When a distillery offered him as much whisky as he wanted, Mawson settled for just two cases, making clear that it was for medicinal purposes only. Another distillery offered him twenty cases, but Mawson accepted only one. He did, however, take twenty cases of Australian burgundy. As for the money from the appeal, it was sufficient to secure a Dundee whaler, the *Aurora*, as the expedition ship, and to purchase those items of food, clothing, or equipment that companies were not prepared to donate.[7]

One of the donors was the German-born physical culturist Eugen Sandow, who had been dubbed "the strongest man in the world." Sandow had made his name and his fortune performing acts of strength and displaying his muscles in an American circus before establishing Institutes of Physical Culture across Britain. Sculpting his body along the line of ancient Greek statues, Sandow toured Australia in 1902, where packed audiences were treated to the sight of him on a revolving pedestal, rippling his muscles and lifting weights, "clad only in his leopard-skin trunks and sandals." His talks in Australia were published as *The Gospel of Strength*, which played into the British and Australian uneasiness about being members of a declining race compared with the Germans.

Mawson's expedition was intended to allay such concerns about Australian men, which may have attracted Sandow to the strapping explorer. He not only gave £1,050 to the expedition, but took Mawson to the theater during the festivities associated with the coronation of King George V, sitting near the new monarch and Kaiser Wilhelm II.[8] One of the expedition huskies would be named Sandow.

Sandow's support was surprising enough. Even more surprising was the support that came from Scott's wife, Kathleen. She was the eleventh and youngest child of a clergyman and his wife who both had died when she was young, which resulted in her being farmed out to relatives and being left with an unquenchable desire for love and attention. Inheriting a modest income, she was able to live an independent and rather bohemian life after she came of age and studied in Paris to become a sculptor. Attractive and vivacious, and fond of sleeping in the open air, she attracted adoring men, and some women, like moths to the newfangled electric light. They included the celebrated dancer, Isadora Duncan, the French sculptor Auguste Rodin, and the English novelist and playwright Gilbert Cannan. She loved just as passionately in return, albeit often chastely, according to later accounts by her family. She rejected offers of marriage until she met Scott. It wasn't a husband that she had wanted; Kathleen was besotted with the idea of giving birth to the son of a hero, and Scott fitted the bill. A year after they married, among much hoopla in September 1908, the desired son was born.[9] She could now divide her attention between raising this young god and ensuring that Scott embellished his heroic reputation with a successful assault on the South Pole. In a note that Scott took with him, she told him to face any risk or danger that presented itself, assuring him that she and their son Peter *"can do without you."* In falling short of the South Pole, Shackleton said that he had faced the agonizing choice of being a dead lion or a live donkey, and had chosen the latter. In such a situation, Kathleen told Scott not to shrink from danger on her account, or that of their son. "If there's anything you think worth doing at the cost of your life," she wrote, "– do it — we shall only be glad."[10]

Kathleen's desire for him to reach the South Pole made her protective of his expedition's interests and reputation. So she sprang to his defense after Mawson publicly criticized Scott for abandoning plans to explore King Edward VII Land and send a party to Cape Adare, where Mawson had planned to have his own base. Mawson had been so frank about his own plans, he was understandably irate in April 1911 when he learned that Scott had gone ahead with his threat to checkmate him, at least as far as Cape Adare was concerned. When a reporter from the *Daily Mail* woke him after midnight seeking a response, Mawson let his feelings be known, and followed it with a letter to Kathleen Scott in which he wished that "Captain Scott had been franker with me." In fact, Scott had been frank about going to Cape Adare once he knew that Mawson was intent on going there. Mawson was angry nonetheless when Scott's threat turned to reality. Despite his anger, he could not afford an open dispute with the flag-bearer of the British Empire, and tried to bridge any rupture with the Scotts by explaining to Kathleen that he had "been almost prostrated for three weeks with acute influenza, septic throat and worry." She was just as anxious to avoid a breach between her husband and Mawson, and desperate to prevent Mawson from attacking the absent Scott when he gave a lecture about his proposed expedition to the Royal Geographical Society on April 10, 1911. She promptly invited him to lunch on the preceding Saturday.[11]

The lunch went on till 4:00 p.m., as Mawson told Kathleen of his frustration about Scott basing his northern party at Cape Adare rather than on the other side of the Ross Sea in King Edward VII Land. She recorded in her diary, which was meant for Scott to read on his return, how she appeased Mawson's anger and "prevented him saying anything foolish at his lecture." It was the beginning of her bewitching of Mawson, with Kathleen claiming that he "begged me not to associate him in my mind with Shackleton." For her part, she assured him that she "wanted to champion him, but he must play the game better." As a result of their discussion, wrote Kathleen, the Australian departed "very much happier," with the two of them being "excellently good friends." She later attended his lecture and was happy to see him pay due regard to the achievements of her husband and show "a *very* nice" photograph of Scott in his naval uniform. Kathleen was not so happy to see Shackleton also in attendance. Although she shook Shackleton's hand, she refused to speak to her husband's bitter rival.[12]

Mawson was different. Indeed, they became such friends over lunch that she invited Mawson to stay at her house in London "if it would assist [him] in any way." When that offer was apparently not taken up, she urged him to "slip down" to a seaside cottage she had rented near Sandwich, where she was fond of sleeping the night in a tent on the beach. She also urged him to come "for lunch [at her London home] any day or dinner if you let me know before." It's not clear if Mawson visited the cottage during this particular visit to England, but they did attend a dinner together in Yorkshire in May 1911. Although she seems to have destroyed most of his correspondence, copies of some letters are in his papers along with her letters to him. The surviving correspondence reveals that they developed a very close relationship, and may have even become lovers during his visit to London in 1911.[13]

Kathleen's support of Mawson is surprising because of the undercurrent of rivalry between Mawson and her husband. It wasn't open warfare, as it was between Scott and Shackleton, but it was rivalry nonetheless, and she was certainly aware of it. Despite this, Kathleen went to great trouble to get Mawson equipped with an aircraft that was better than the one he was planning to purchase. The alternative aircraft, she wrote, was "infinitely more stable, heavier and more solid and will carry more weight." Kathleen told Mawson not to "talk about it in England," as she would "get into great trouble if I'm caught giving away their secrets." The aircraft had a range of 300 miles, with its manufacturer claiming that it would be used "in the final dash for the Pole."[14] That was over-egging the pudding, as Mawson had not announced any intention to race Scott for the

South Pole, and the plane would not have been able to make the distance or reach such heights. Nevertheless, it would be the first plane to fly in Antarctica, and had the potential to attract public attention in such a way as to possibly overshadow Scott's expedition.

This makes it all the more curious that Kathleen would go to such lengths to ensure her husband's rival had the best available equipment. She also recommended a pilot, Lieutenant Hugh Watkins, to Mawson, and advised Watkins on the terms he should demand in his contract. Only later did she discover that Watkins was a drunkard. Although she felt "bound to tell Mawson," who had left for Australia by then, there is no evidence that she did so. She seems to have contented herself with the thought that Watkins "can't drink much or he wouldn't be such a uniformly steady flyer."[15] Anyway, it would have been difficult for Mawson to find another pilot at this late stage, nor did he have the money to pay for one. The aircraft had cost nearly £1,000, which was money that Mawson didn't have. He took it anyway, adding to the debts that he would have to cover on his return. While the aircraft manufacturer extended credit, Mawson was not so fortunate with the manufacturer of the motorized sledges that he wanted to use. They were the same kind that Scott had taken, but Mawson could not afford to buy three of them, or convince the manufacturer to donate or lend even one. An offer by Mawson to name "an important topographical feature" after the manufacturer went unrequited.[16] So he went without them.

As for the food, clothing, dogs, and other necessities, Mawson followed in the footsteps of Shackleton, using the same agent in London to do the purchasing. Apart from acquiring the aircraft, using wireless, and deciding not to take ponies, Mawson made no significant deviation from the things Shackleton had taken in 1907. Even though Shackleton had made no serious use of the twelve pairs of Norwegian skis he had taken, Mawson still took twelve pairs of Norwegian skis and the same number of Australian ones.[17] Despite the difficulties Mawson had experienced trudging through stretches of thick snow on the Skackleton expedition, he didn't take snowshoes. Other than for horses, they weren't used at all in Antarctica, even though their use would have made travel easier, and safer, since snowshoes allowed a person's weight to be spread wider when walking across a snow-covered crevasse. Such equipment had been used for centuries and was enjoying a revival among snow-trippers in North America, so it is not clear why Mawson (and other expedition leaders) did not consider them necessary. Perhaps it was to save weight on the sledges, or he may have regarded them as an alien method of travel for a British explorer.

The food that Mawson took was the same as that taken by Shackleton, with his London agent approaching the same suppliers for contributions. Apart from a large variety of tinned and packaged food for consumption aboard the ship or in the huts, there was the food specially manufactured for taking on sledge journeys. Pemmican was the core of it. Made in Copenhagen from powdered beef fortified with sixty percent fat, it had been taken on Scott's first expedition and then again by Shackleton. It was believed to be life-saving, a foodstuff that could provide the difference between life or death if one was caught by a prolonged blizzard far from a hut. Since man-hauling was the basis for British expeditions, the weight of the food was all-important. It was also important that cooking be kept to a minimum, which would thereby save on fuel. Pemmican qualified on both counts. Plasmon biscuits were another important food for sledging. The plasmon was dried milk powder, and the almost rock-hard biscuits could be eaten cold or broken up and used to thicken the boiled pemmican — a combination commonly known as hoosh. Chocolate, tea, and sugar were also part of the sledging supplies. Unbeknown to Shackleton or Mawson, however, none of these foods was a preventative against scurvy.[18]

Shackleton was aware of the danger of scurvy, after having suffered from it on the Scott expedition. He trumpeted the fact that his own expedition had been free of it, which he ascribed to his having ensured that "preserved food [was] in a perfectly wholesome condition." The key, argued Shackleton, was to give "the closest attention ... to the preparation and selection of food-stuffs on scientific lines."[19] This was an accepted view among a large part of the medical community at the time, which did not know that protection against scurvy was provided by the consumption of fresh food containing vitamin C. Neither Shackleton nor Mawson realized that their consumption of fresh seal and penguin meat was the real reason for the Shackleton expedition having been scurvy-free. Of course, in making his comments about scurvy and the importance of preparing food "on scientific lines," Shackleton was having an implicit dig at Scott for being more of a pole-hunting adventurer than a scientist. Mawson would continue the refrain, as he tried to differentiate his scientific expedition from Scott's headline-grabbing adventure.

One way for Mawson to distinguish his expedition was to explore and claim a large part of the continent for Britain. Scott would struggle to compete with Mawson on this score, as his attempt on the South Pole would take him to an area that was already well traveled and had already been claimed by Shackleton. Before leaving England, Mawson asked for "official authority" from the British government to raise the flag and claim any part of the Antarctic coastline that he explored and surveyed. His request was denied, since there were possible international implications if Mawson claimed the coastline that the French explorer Dumont d'Urville had claimed back in 1840, or the coast that the American explorer Charles Wilkes had sailed along that same year. However, Mawson was told that he could go ahead and raise the Union Jack regardless; it just wouldn't be official. Once he returned, the government would decide whether it would give its support to any territorial claim that he happened to make. This was enough for Mawson, who ensured that an adequate supply of both British and Australian flags were packed among his supplies for all the claiming that he planned to do.[20] He was determined to make his mark on Antarctica as no other explorer had done before him.

CHAPTER THREE

Choosing a Team

The success of the expedition would depend on the caliber of his team, five of whom were chosen by Mawson while he was in England in mid-1911. He recruited a young English soldier, Lieutenant Belgrave Ninnis of the Royal Fusiliers, who had been recommended to him by Scott. Ninnis's father had been in the Royal Navy and had taken part in a surveying expedition to northern Australia. He made his name as a surgeon on HMS *Discovery*, one of the two ships of the British Arctic Expedition of 1875, which had attempted in vain to reach the North Pole and been forced to winter in the frozen ocean. Despite the navy's experience with scurvy over the centuries, and the success of explorers such as James Cook in countering the disease, the sailors on the *Discovery* were beset with scurvy, from which two of them died. The efforts by Ninnis's father had helped to limit the death toll, which was later blamed on a lack of lime juice. Had the sick sailors been fed fresh seal meat, the disease could have been totally averted.

Although the expedition had failed in its purpose, and almost ended in disaster, Ninnis's father was among those honored with the Arctic Medal. His stories of that expedition seem to have drawn his son to the Antarctic. Young Ninnis was keen to emulate and even exceed the deeds of his father. He had wanted to be Mawson's pilot, although he had no flying experience, and was disappointed when he was appointed instead as a cartographer. Nevertheless, he thought Mawson was "a splendid fellow ... and a scientist all over."[1]

Also recruited by Mawson was a twenty-nine-year-old Swiss mountaineer and ski champion, Xavier Mertz, who traveled especially to London to seek a place on the expedition. Unlike Ninnis, Mertz did not want to emulate his father, but to escape from him and the prospect of a life running the family factory in Basel. Mertz's controlling father owned a large engineering plant in which Mertz had labored from the age of fourteen, gaining practical skills in carpentry and metalwork, before running the company for two years while his father was ill. Now that his father was well, Mertz wanted to get as far away as possible. Antarctica fitted the bill perfectly. In a letter to Mawson from the Waldorf Hotel, the German-speaking Mertz claimed he had climbed "all the highest mountains of Switzerland without a guide," and also the several peaks of Mont Blanc. Indeed, wrote Mertz, "I am entitled to say that ... I know as much about mountaineering, of glaciers & ice as any first class guide." But it was his proficiency on skis that he believed particularly qualified him, telling Mawson that the Norwegian explorers Nansen and Amundsen had "proved [them] so good for the purpose," and that Swiss skiers were now as good as the Norwegians.[2]

It is not clear what motivated Mawson to hire Mertz. It is likely that it was more than just his skiing ability. Mawson had wanted to have a team mainly of Australian men in their early twenties, with the odd Briton or New Zealander thrown in. A German-speaking Swiss could dilute the message that Mawson was trying to send about his expedition being an effort by British subjects of the newly federated dominion, whose efforts on the ice would disprove the widespread fears about the supposed physical decline of the British race and the rise of the German race. Despite this, Mertz would have recommended himself as a man of independent means who possessed all the practical skills required for survival in the Antarctic. Mawson later told Mertz's mother that one of the reasons he hired Mertz "was that he was well-to-do and had no one depending upon him." Once recruited for the expedition, Mertz provided his own skis and boots, and brought donations of goods from several Swiss companies. Mertz returned to Switzerland to find suitable alpine ropes, crampons, and ice axes, before going on to Monaco to learn the techniques of water sampling and deep-sea dredging from an oceanography institute. Back in London, he arranged for his Savile Row tailor to send his measurements to the expedition office so that his cold-weather clothing could be made.[3]

It presumably came as somewhat of a shock for Mertz then to be given responsibility, along with Ninnis, for the care of the forty-nine dogs that Mawson had bought from Greenland, and which were loaded aboard the *Aurora* in late July for the long voyage from England.[4] There was no public farewell as the ship slipped its mooring and sailed down the Thames. They left at midnight, wrote Ninnis, "with no soul to see us go, or wish us luck. It was one of the most dismal things I have ever taken part in." Mawson went separately, traveling first class on a P&O liner. He was wise not to go on the *Aurora*, which encountered a storm in the English Channel that saw the cabins awash with water, and Ninnis trying to entertain the crew with a singalong accompanied by his accordion. Some of the crew were so disgusted with the ship that they left it at Cardiff when it stopped for coal, and engaged a solicitor to sue Mawson for damages.[5]

Two other recruits from Britain were the pilot, Hugh Watkins, whom Kathleen Scott now described as "horribly vulgar," and the well-connected and more cultivated mechanical engineer, Frank Bickerton, who had just returned from an expedition to the Cocos Islands and become a member of the Royal Geographical Society. Bickerton took charge of the aircraft that Mawson hoped would give his expedition an unbeatable advantage over his rivals. Mawson also instructed Bickerton to take some surveying classes before leaving England, so that he could be of more value on one of the treks. Money was so tight, though, that he would have to pay for his own passage to Australia, and would not start being paid until he arrived there.[6] Also recruited was Frank Wild, a fellow Yorkshireman, who claimed to be a descendant of Captain James Cook, and took a costume of Sir Walter Raleigh with him on the expedition. Wild had more Antarctic experience than any of them, having been on Scott's first expedition and then as part of Shackleton's three-man assault on the South Pole, which he was lucky to survive. He was about 30 centimeters shorter than Mawson, had a penchant for hard drinking, and hankered to lead an expedition of his own to the South Pole. Like Mawson, he had rejected an invitation to join Scott's expedition.[7] There was a risk for Mawson in having such an experienced polar explorer on his expedition, in case he overshadowed anything that Mawson might achieve. But the risk was minimal and was worth taking. After all, Mawson would control the flow of news from the expedition, as well as the subsequent official history, films, and lectures, and he needed someone of Wild's caliber to lead the second base that he wanted to establish in Antarctica.

Mawson had most of what he needed for the expedition. But he still lacked the most essential element — money. The many wealthy Australians who had flocked to London for the coronation had not been as generous as he had hoped, and some of Shackleton's supporters had not extended their largesse to Mawson. He was so short of funds that he had to take out a mortgage on the *Aurora*. Mawson would have to find the shortfall in Australia. However, when he returned in July 1911, he found that the federal government was only willing to contribute £5,000, rather than the £20,000 he had been hoping for. State governments were more generous, stumping up £18,500 in total. It still left him well shy of the funds he wanted, and he had to sell some of his own assets to finance the expedition.[8] He was still short, which meant that any money he made at the end of the expedition would first have to cover his debts and recoup the money he had contributed himself. So desperate was Mawson for additional funds that he organized exhibition flights of the aircraft when it reached Adelaide. It was an ill-advised move that cost him dearly. Watkins went on a drinking binge the night before the flight, and was apparently still affected the next morning when he crash-landed the aircraft, leaving its wings damaged beyond repair. With no prospect of the wingless aircraft flying in the Antarctic, the injured Watkins was sent back to England. Undaunted, Mawson decided to take the broken machine anyway, describing it now as an "aerial tractor" that could be used to pull a sledge.[9]

It wasn't just a public relations exercise. Mawson hoped that the machine might still provide one of the keys to his expedition's success. Shackleton had taken a car along with his ponies and dogs in 1907, and planned to use it to move men and stores across the hundreds of miles of the Ross Ice Shelf. Mawson had seen its possible potential when the car towed the sledges of the Northern Party several kilometers before being brought to a halt by a snowstorm. If his "aerial tractor" could be made to haul sledges on the polar plateau, he might use it to reach the elusive South Magnetic Pole. After all, Scott was taking a mechanical sledge in the hope that it might give him a winning edge, shifting men and stores across the Ross Ice Shelf more successfully than Shackleton's car had managed to do. If they worked, the machines of Mawson and Scott would signal the advent of the mechanical age in the Antarctic. Only the Norwegian Roald Amundsen and the Japanese explorer Nobu Shirase were in the Antarctic without mechanical assistance, relying entirely on dogs.

Apart from the aircraft, Mawson had another major advantage over his rivals. He would be taking a wireless set to the Antarctic. Like the aircraft, this was cutting-edge technology for the time. Because the range of wireless sets was relatively limited, it would require the establishment of a wireless station on Macquarie Island to act as a repeater station for the messages received from the main base in Antarctica.[10] It also would require masts about 30 meters high to be erected at both places. If that could be achieved, Mawson could maintain constant contact with the world. He appointed a press agent, Conrad Eitel, to work from Hobart, where he would receive the messages and dress them up for publication, while also writing articles of his own to keep the expedition in the news. It was a brilliant idea by Mawson. He would keep his expedition in the headlines while his rivals were left to operate in silence for a year or more. Whatever their relative achievements, Mawson's was likely to be regarded as the preeminent expedition. Just as importantly for Mawson, his wireless messages could be sold to newspapers around the world, which could be the key to rescuing the expedition, and Mawson himself, from possible bankruptcy.

Money would also come from the photographs and films taken during the expedition. Again, Mawson planned to use the latest cameras and techniques to achieve the greatest public impact. A London firm provided eight cameras with a variety of excellent lenses, while a French firm provided four hundred of the recently invented color autochrome plates, which would allow innovative color photographs to be used later in his expedition book and magazine articles, and his illustrated lecture tour.[11] The real crowd-pleaser would be the films taken by the moving picture camera, known as a cinematograph, which would bring the Antarctic and its wildlife to life for the delight of paying audiences around the world. Shackleton had taken one on his expedition, and Mawson had used the resulting film to raise funds for his own expedition. The cinematography was likely to be the most lucrative money-spinner of the expedition, allaying any concerns about the device's whopping weight of 60 pounds.[12]

All this equipment taken south by Scott and Mawson was designed to show the technical superiority of their expeditions. But the motorized sledges and the aircraft were never meant to replace men for the main sledging journeys. Both Scott and Mawson were intent on having man-hauling as the centerpiece of their expeditions so as to showcase the physical prowess of British and Australian manhood. Mawson wanted young men who were fit, smart, and resourceful. He wanted men like himself, who would perform as he had performed on the Shackleton expedition. However, there was one important difference: he wanted the men on his expedition to follow orders and not pose a threat to his leadership. Apart from anything else, it was crucial to the success of the expedition and his own future career. The public wanted one leader and one hero to dominate the story of the expedition. Mawson was determined that it be him, but how could he be sure that someone would not emerge from the expedition party and do to him what he had done to Edgeworth David? Certainly, there were several who were well suited to doing so.

Most of the Australasian members of the expedition were recent graduates from Melbourne, Sydney, and Adelaide universities, with the majority being just twenty-two or twenty-three years old — about seven years younger than Mawson. An oddity was John Close, one of the oldest of the men. He claimed to be thirty-three, but once he got to Antarctica admitted that he was forty. Most suspected he was even older, and wondered how he was ever recruited as an assistant collector of biological specimens. Close claimed to be a veteran of the Boer War and to have served as a mounted policeman in South Africa. He was a follower of Eugen Sandow's exercise methods, and ran physical-culture classes in Sydney, which could have been the factor that recommended him to Mawson.[13] The youngest recruit was nineteen-year-old Percy Correll, a science student from Mawson's Adelaide University whose spirit for adventure saw him cycle from Adelaide to Melbourne by way of the Coorong a few months before joining the expedition as a mechanic and physicist.[14] Others included Archibald McLean, the expedition's chief medical officer and bacteriologist, a graduate of Sydney University who had been jilted by his girlfriend and hoped forlornly that service with the expedition might rekindle the romance.[15]

The chief biologist was John Hunter, who had followed Mawson through Fort Street School and Sydney University before being recommended to Mawson by Edgeworth David.[16] From New Zealand came the young magnetician Eric Webb, whose skills and experience were essential if Mawson was to reach the South Magnetic Pole and provide proof of his feat. Also from Sydney came Frank Hurley, a brilliant young photographer who was so keen to go that he cornered Mawson on a train trip to the Blue

Mountains and made a convincing case about his qualifications. Mawson took him on, despite a letter from Hurley's worried mother falsely claiming that her son suffered from ill health, and imploring Mawson not to take him.[17] From Melbourne came Lieutenant Robert Bage, a strapping young army officer imbued with a liberal dash of imperial patriotism and a great appetite for derring-do. John Hunter would later describe him as "an untiring worker" and the "best liked man on our expedition."[18] Also from Melbourne came the twenty-three-year-old Frank Stillwell, an honors graduate in science from Melbourne University, who joined three other geologists appointed by Mawson to the expedition.[19]

One of the most qualified, both physically and intellectually, was twenty-two-year-old Cecil Madigan, a science student, sharpshooter, and champion rower recruited by Mawson from Adelaide University. At 190 centimeters in height and physically fit, Madigan towered over most of the others, being as tall as the lanky Mawson. He would later be described by one of his fellow explorers as "a magnificent specimen of an Australian." Indeed, Mawson might well have recognized much of himself in his young student. Madigan, though, had done better academically after being awarded a Rhodes scholarship to Oxford. Now he was torn between taking it up or joining the expedition. Arguing against the latter choice was his widowed mother, who worried that her eldest son might ruin his life chances by going to Antarctica with an expedition leader who she regarded as reckless. Madigan had also fallen in love with a woman from a well-connected Adelaide family, so it was not only his education and career that was being put on hold. He was persuaded to go nonetheless, clearly hoping that the expedition would establish his reputation in the same way that Mawson had made his reputation with Shackleton.[20]

And then there was the most colorful recruit of all, the thirty-two-year-old Herbert Dyce Murphy. He would keep his companions entertained during the Antarctic winter with a great fund of incredible stories, most of which were true (albeit embellished), and some untrue. The problem was knowing which was which. Murphy had been born to a wealthy pastoral family in Melbourne, before completing his education in England and going off to sea as an apprentice sailor. It was the Arctic that attracted him, and he was soon aboard a Dundee whaling ship hunting for whales among the ice before taking up a place at an Oxford college. From there he was recruited by British military intelligence to spy on the railway systems of France and Belgium, which he successfully did by dressing as a woman. Resourceful, adventurous, and well connected, Murphy talked his way into going south with Mawson by listing his multitude of achievements and capabilities — from boat-handling and photography to map-making and dog-driving — although it was probably his three voyages to the Arctic that particularly recommended him. Older and more intellectual than Mawson, and experienced in the Arctic, Murphy was the sort of person who could make Mawson feel insecure as leader. It was perhaps for this reason, as much as for his age and Arctic experience, that Mawson intended to have Murphy at arm's length, appointing him as leader of the third base that he intended to establish on the continent.[21]

With the staff recruited, and a final burst of fundraising completed, Mawson's budget was still £9,000 short. That was a lot of money to make up, and it was far from certain that he would be able to do so. The wireless messages and newspaper stories would certainly help. But he also would have to return with a stirring story of achievement calculated to capture public attention. That would be no easy task, as there were several other expeditions in the field or planning to go south. There was Scott with his plan to reach the South Pole; his story would be hard to counter. And Scott was not alone. Also heading for the South Pole was Roald Amundsen, who was just as desperate as Mawson to capture public attention and reap the resultant financial rewards. For Amundsen, reaching the South Pole would be the means to raise money to finance his real goal, which was to drift his ship in the Arctic ice until it passed over the North Pole. Also in the field was the Japanese expedition of Lieutenant Nobu Shirase, which was headed for the Ross Ice Shelf, but was not equipped to reach the South Pole. Lastly, there was the German expedition of Lieutenant Wilhelm Filchner, who was perhaps the most direct threat to Mawson. He was heading for the Antarctic coastline south of Africa, a region that had been previously explored and claimed for Germany. Like Mawson's, his expedition claimed to be a scientific one concerned with determining whether Antarctica was a single continent or two large islands.[22]

As with Filchner, the coastline, rather than the interior, was the particular focus of Mawson's attention. At the time, most of the Antarctic coastline had still not been seen, and its outline on maps was mostly guesswork. Mawson explained to Madigan in November 1911 that the expedition's activity "would be confined to a strip of coastline about thirty miles wide [and hundreds of miles long]. To Mawson, the coast was the most interesting and useful region for his purposes, since the geology of the interior could be ascertained by an examination of the moraines spread about on the flat between the sea and higher land."[23] But it wasn't just about geology. Despite having five geologists, including himself, Mawson told a newspaper reporter that his primary purpose was geographic, to map as much as possible of the hitherto-unseen Antarctic coastline south of Australia. He also hoped that his meteorological observations would help with the forecasting of weather in Australia, while the "enormous number of seals and whales down there" might bring "great gains" to Australia. There was also the possibility of making valuable coal and mineral discoveries.[24] In sketching out a picture of the possible profits to be had in the Antarctic, Mawson was trying to satisfy the Jeremiahs who had dismissed the expedition as a waste of money.

As the members of the expedition arrived in Hobart in November 1911, they were put to work re-packing and color-coding the supplies. Some crates were marked for Macquarie Island, some for use on the ship, and the rest were marked with different colors for the three bases that Mawson was planning to establish along the Antarctic coastline.[25] Mertz and Ninnis were kept busy elsewhere. They had arrived aboard the *Aurora* on November 4 after an eventful voyage during which the cook had come down with syphilis and thereby become, wrote Ninnis, "singularly unsuited to toy with our food" and was relieved of his culinary duties. After leaving Cape Town, they had experienced a rough crossing of the Southern Ocean during which eleven of the dogs had died. Six were shot by Mertz and Ninnis when one dog went mad and began biting at everything and everyone; they mistakenly killed five dogs before the offending dog was correctly identified. Five other dogs were washed overboard during heavy seas. The surviving dogs were placed into quarantine just outside of Hobart, where two more died soon after landing. Mertz and Ninnis looked after the dogs, spending a relaxing fortnight on the beach and sailing on the Derwent in the *Aurora*'s lifeboat, with Mertz flying a Swiss flag from its mast.[26]

It wasn't until November 21 that Mawson and Madigan arrived in Hobart after having traveled by ship from Melbourne to Launceston, where they clambered aboard a reserved first-class carriage with the premier of Tasmania for the short train journey to Hobart. Wild was waiting on the platform to meet them. Despite the experienced polar explorer being "a small man," the lofty Madigan was "glad to see a capable looking member at last." He would become less disdainful of his companions as he got to know them, but the observation shows that Madigan, unlike most of the others, was relatively unrestrained in the comments he wrote in his diary. And he was already starting to have some reservations about Mawson. Although he still had great confidence in him "as a leader," Madigan thought Mawson was "quite below par" as a businessman. Mawson was still learning the ropes of organizing an expedition, he thought, and complaints were being made about his "forgetfulness," because Mawson "tries to do everything himself, which is quite impossible for any man."[27]

Mawson had a serious problem: his ambition exceeded his means. The *Aurora* could not fit all the supplies that he had assembled in Hobart for his three Antarctic bases plus the base on Macquarie Island. Just the coal required for heating the four bases, as well as for powering the ship, was taking up much of the space in the hold. Mawson recalled his experience on the Shackleton expedition, when a similar problem had been solved by having a steamship tow the *Nimrod* as far as the ice pack to save on the consumption of coal. And Shackleton had only had one hut to heat. Mawson wouldn't have wanted to be towed again across the Southern Ocean, which had been both uncomfortable and dangerous for the men on the *Nimrod*.

He tried to charter a ship to take some of the men and supplies as far as Macquarie Island, but then seems to have decided that a simpler solution was to reduce the number of bases. The supplies for each base had been sorted and marked, so it would be easy to identify the supplies destined for the third base and to simply leave them behind, along with the eight men led by Murphy. Even without the third Antarctic base, Mawson reckoned, it would still be the most ambitious expedition ever sent south. But Murphy hadn't come all this way to be left behind on the Hobart wharf with the discarded supplies. If Mawson went ahead, said Murphy, he would buy a ship himself and take the men and supplies to establish a base of his own. This could pose a real threat to Mawson, not only because of what Murphy's party might achieve, but also because of the impression of disarray it gave to the Mawson expedition before it had even started. So he assured Murphy that he would proceed with the third base after all, and go ahead with chartering another ship to take some of the men and supplies as far as Macquarie Island. He also commandeered four of the six freshwater tanks on the *Aurora* to hold some of the stores.[28] The problem had been solved for the time being, but it gave Mawson an inkling of the challenges he might face from subordinates who had ambitions of their own. It was also an added expense that his indebted expedition could have done without.

Most of the expedition members attended a special service at Hobart's St David's Cathedral on November 26, where the progressive Bishop John Mercer lauded the expedition's "spirit of adventure" as "a tonic to the whole community." With the cathedral draped with the flags of Britain and Australia, Mercer told the congregation how it was the "spirit of adventure and the taking of risks which made the British race." He paid particular attention to the place of courage in the advance of human society, noting how those who "survived, and made history" were those who "were endowed with the greatest amount of physical courage."[29] In case they failed, and died in the trying, Mawson had allowed an insurance agent to visit the ship to offer life insurance to any who wanted to take it up.[30] The following day, Mawson gave an illustrated lecture to a packed audience at the Hobart town hall, many of them school children, with Madigan and Webb appearing on stage in their Antarctic gear. Despite the summer heat, they had walked from their hotel dressed in their expedition clothes, which caused "quite a stir in the streets." To amuse the crowd before Mawson rose to speak, the pair "played about with the sledge and ice axes on the stage," while cinematographic film from Shackleton's expedition concluded the evening. The lecture was so successful, and so many missed out on getting a ticket, that Mawson repeated it the following night.[31]

In the last days before leaving, Mawson received good wishes from Prime Minister Andrew Fisher and from the captain of Scott's *Terra Nova* in New Zealand, wistful farewell letters from Paquita, and a brief note from Kathleen Scott, who wanted, she wrote, to "wish you good luck — I often wonder how you are faring … Best of good wishes now & always." They were hectic days of packing and organization of the stores, and it was not until December 2, the day of sailing, that Mawson met all the members of the expedition when he invited them to the Orient Hotel for lunch. After telling them something of his plans and expectations, they sang "For He's a Jolly Good Fellow." Madigan walked to the Hobart post office to send farewell telegrams to his fiancée and his worried mother, before all the men made their way to the wharf in the late afternoon. The Hobart *Mercury* assured its readers that the risks of Antarctic exploration were much less than hitherto and would be reduced still farther by Mawson's innovative use of radio. Nevertheless, opined the *Mercury*, every man going on the *Aurora* "takes his life in his hands," and there were still "quite sufficient [risks] to try the nerves and the courage of even the stoutest heart." As for Mawson, he told the press that he was "leaving Australia to hoist the Australian flag in a land which geographically should belong to Australia," and he promised to "uphold the prestige of the British race."[32]

Ninnis was certainly aware of the danger, telling a friend with a terrible sense of premonition that he might end his "blighted career down a crevasse." He took the risk so seriously that he wrote a letter to be handed to his family in the event of his death. At the same time, he was so excited by the expedition that he told the same friend that he would often "lie awake simply hugging myself for joy."[33] If the men had last-minute nerves, they tried not to let on as they pressed their way through the crush of sightseers and wellwishers being entertained on the wharf by a military band. It was a strange sight. The ship's deck was stacked with lumber for the huts and a ten-meter-long crate containing the "air tractor," while some sheep were confined at the stern, their legs tied to avoid injury. As Hurley recorded the scene with his cinematograph, and Mertz climbed the rigging to take photographs from the crow's nest, the Tasmanian governor gave a formal farewell to the expedition. With that, the sailors tossed any remaining coins into the water to avoid ill luck on the voyage, and the heavily laden ship drew away.[34] Once Ninnis and the dogs had been loaded aboard at the quarantine station, the *Aurora* continued its way downriver, accompanied by a flotilla of gaily decorated small boats that dropped away one by one as the ship headed closer to the open sea. There was a lot to occupy Mawson's mind as the eucalyptus-draped slopes of Tasmania receded in the distance.

CHAPTER FOUR

Into the Southern Ocean

Despite the cheering crowds, and the band playing "God Be with You Till We Meet Again," the omens were not good when the *Aurora* steamed out into the wide Derwent estuary on December 2, 1911.[1] With the barometer falling and the estuary's protected waters splattered with whitecaps, Captain John King Davis was fearful of what might be waiting for them in the open ocean. The vessel was crowded with men and supplies, its deck stacked high with crates and a creaking conglomeration of sledges and boats. There were also the thirty-six surviving Greenland dogs that Ninnis and Mertz had brought on board from the quarantine station and chained across the deck, trying to ensure they were out of biting distance from each other and from the tethered sheep. As if on cue, the enveloping darkness and the worsening storm hit the ship simultaneously.[2]

Mawson's diary has no entries for the nine days it took the ship to reach Macquarie Island. Later, he would tell an audience at London's Royal Geographical Society how "a violent gale was weathered off the Tasmanian coast without any more serious consequence than the loss of half the bridge and slight damage to the motor launch."[3] In a letter to Paquita, he described how he tried to sleep on a couch through the constant rolling of the ship, only to find himself repeatedly thrown onto the floor into water that was sloshing back and forward. Madigan's diary was more descriptive.[4] Unlike Mawson, who was closeted below deck with his head in a bucket, Madigan was housed in a tiny, three-berth cabin on deck and was on watch with his cabin mates, as well as Hurley and McLean, when the first storm hit. Protected by sea boots and oilskins, Madigan found himself wading through two feet of water as he rushed in the darkness to lash down the cargo that was being shifted about by the wash of the water and the fearful roll of the ship. With the massive seas also causing his cabin mates and McLean to become seasick, and the sodden dogs to howl "most hideously and mournfully," Madigan shifted the suffering animals to the top of the stacked-up timber. Then he helped the first mate to pump out nearly a meter of water that had got into the hold, where it was damaging their precious cargo and threatening the ship's stability.[5]

It got worse. Despite Madigan's efforts, the motor launch shifted during the night and ended up lodged against his cabin door, trapping him and his cabin mates inside, as waves continued to surge "against the door and come in at the cracks." When he was finally released, Madigan found that even the dogs atop the stacks of timber were being soaked by the waves. The success of the expedition might well depend on their health, so he put them even higher, carrying about twenty of them up to the forecastle head, only to be bitten by one frightened dog for his trouble. Seawater, mixed with dog excrement from the deck, also contaminated one of the tanks of freshwater supply, leaving only about 50 gallons of fresh water on board, and that water was in the cooling tanks for the engine. The risk that Mawson had taken by using four of the freshwater tanks for supplies had come back to bite him and to anger the men who had to go without freshwater baths and limit themselves to one cup of tea per meal. Even worse was to come. After a couple of brief periods of calm, the Southern Ocean resumed its former fury.[6]

Madigan was rather bemused by Mawson succumbing to seasickness and disappearing into his cabin for most of the voyage. Despite his own bravado, Madigan was not immune to seasickness.

By the time he climbed into his cramped bunk on that first stormy night, Madigan confessed to "not feeling very well." And he remained "very seedy" the next morning, when he could only manage biscuits and apples for breakfast. His condition was not helped by the ship's "rotten" cook, who served up "fearful greasy hash" for dinner, which Madigan vomited overboard. He went back to eating biscuits and apples that he could consume on deck rather than eat among the mess of spattered food and sloshing water in the wardroom, which anyway could only accommodate eight men at a time. By December 4, the sea had calmed sufficiently for the sails to be set and for Madigan to face eating bacon and eggs for breakfast, albeit while perched on the lashed-down motorboat enjoying the fresh air. That evening, he braved the wardroom once again and was carving a roast joint of beef when a roll of the ship sent him flying into a shelfful of jam tins that crashed to the floor while the beef flew into the third mate's cabin. Madigan described how he "scraped it up off the floor and carried on as if nothing had happened." The rescued beef was followed with canned plum pudding and peaches and coffee, which constituted "a good square meal" in their constrained circumstances.[7]

After five days at sea, Madigan reported that most of the expeditioners were now able to eat, although it was not easy in a wardroom that had a fearful roll in the persistent big swell, with the now hungry diners "struggling for food and being hurled around the cabin." Even Mawson was "recovering [and] was about a bit today," although Madigan noted on December 8 that they "still see very little of him." Yet Mawson was a seasoned sailor who had crossed the Southern Ocean before and sailed to London and the New Hebrides. As Madigan gobbled down a can of sardines, the fact that he was doing better than the expedition leader was not lost on him. He proudly noted in his diary that, despite the continuing rolling of the ship, he "never felt better." Indeed, after a week at sea, he described how he had enjoyed the first week of the voyage "very much, would not have missed the experience for anything, learning all about a ship: can now tighten a weather brace, slack away a buntline, belay with great alacrity ..." As for Mawson, he made only occasional appearances on deck, although he did unpack a bottle of whisky so all the men could drink a traditional toast to "sweethearts and wives," with one wag adding "may they never meet." Mawson also came on deck to investigate when Madigan and a dozen or so others were firing away with their revolvers at a sauce bottle being towed behind the ship. Madigan reported with some satisfaction that Mawson had appeared just in time to witness him hitting the bouncing bottle. He also came on the bridge when Madigan was taking a turn at manning the wheel, apparently earning the leader's unspoken approbation. Captain Davis was less restrained, telling Madigan on another occasion he was "a first rate helmsman and better than most of the sailors who had been at it all their lives." It left him "very bucked up," wrote Madigan.[8]

Most days, Mawson was wedged into his bunk to stop himself being thrown about. As he surfed the successive waves of nausea, he must have wondered why he had ever embarked on such a wild undertaking. He had more than the rough seas to worry him. The expedition had a long list of debtors who would somehow have to be paid when he returned. Worse than that, he was already incurring additional costs. He had had to charter another small ship, the *Toroa*, to go as far as Macquarie Island, where some of the men and equipment would be off-loaded and bags of coal trans-shipped to the *Aurora*. The stop at Macquarie Island would also allow the supply of contaminated water to be replaced for the onward voyage to Antarctica, and Mawson, his men, and the dogs to get back on solid land for a time.

Macquarie Island was Australia's most isolated possession, set about 1,500 kilometers southeast of Hobart and administered by the Tasmanian government. About 35 kilometers long and just five kilometers wide, it has steep cliffs rising to a plateau about 150 meters high. The rugged island runs roughly north–south, with much of its western coast being pounded almost constantly by the giant swell of the "Furious Fifties," while its eastern coast is more protected and provides several possible landing places. Macquarie is one of the newest islands in the world, having been pushed up from the seafloor about 700,000 years ago. As I can attest after a visit there in 2013, it also is one of the most beautiful wildernesses in the world. The treeless island is made more remarkable by the variety of flora and fauna that has acclimatized to its almost constant wet and windy weather. Over the centuries, among the megaherbs and tall tussock grasses, and along the beaches of black shingle, four species of penguins and four species of seals, including massive oil-rich elephant seals, had made the island their home in massive numbers. Many types of petrels and other birds also bred there, safe from most predators other than each other. Its isolation from the world was their saving until the arrival of nineteenth-century whalers and sealers. Much to Mawson's disgust, the unregulated killing of the wildlife was still continuing, although now it was the penguins that were being targeted for their oil.[9]

When the *Aurora* anchored off the island's southwestern shore on December 11, the lifeboat was lowered, and Madigan and Hannam rowed Mawson and nine of their fellow expeditioners ashore. Once on the shingle beach, Madigan found himself "in a wonderland. Words cannot describe it. To have had this day is worth all the trouble entailed by undertaking the expedition." There were thousands of inquisitive royal penguins on the beach, rockhopper penguins on the rocky slopes, nesting giant petrels, and seals of several descriptions on the beach and up among the tussock grasses. There were the elephant seals, the dangerous leopard seals, and the smaller fur seals. Madigan and his companions "drove them about" for the convenience of Hurley's cinematograph camera and the amusement of the audiences who would eventually see the film of the expedition. Grabbing their tail flippers, the men pulled the seals around to face the camera, before Madigan saw a petrel on the water some 80 meters away and "shot it dead to the astonishment of everyone," including Mawson. They "then caught a few penguins as specimens and killed them by driving needles into their skulls," so their appearance would not be spoiled for the taxidermist. Later that day, Mawson sent Madigan back to shoot landrails, a small bird endemic to Macquarie (and now extinct). Madigan managed to shoot ten, and also came across a pair of large king penguins, which were "almost extinct" after huge numbers of them had been boiled down. That didn't stop him from taking one of them. It was one of six penguins he took back to the ship, although conceding: "don't know quite what for." Frank Wild promptly took them and gave the men "a lesson in bird skinning."[10]

Despite its isolation and punishing climate of wind, fog, and rain, the island was not unoccupied. For some years, a New Zealand businessman, Joseph Hatch, had sent men each year to kill tens of thousands of the king penguins and boil them down for their oil. Elephant seals were also exploited. Large iron "digesters," about three meters high, were set up adjacent to the several penguin rookeries around the island, with about six thousand of the unfortunate penguins being crammed each day into the digesters to be reduced by steam to their constituent parts, with the prized oil being drawn off, producing about a pint per penguin. Mawson was opposed to the unbridled killing in the mistaken belief that Hatch did not pay anything to the Tasmanian government for permission to kill the penguins, and also because the scale of the killing was unsustainable. He didn't want the killing to be stopped; he just wanted it to be controlled. Madigan's reaction was similarly conflicted. While he regarded the island as "a nature lover's paradise," he proudly reported on his accurate shooting of the island's birds, which he clearly saw as a sign of his manliness.[11]

To house his Macquarie Island party, Mawson intended to erect a hut on the northern point of the island, where a low, narrow isthmus was connected to a rocky bluff. It was on the bluff that Mawson planned to set up the aerial for his wireless telegraph station, which was a crucial part of his scheme to get public attention. Madigan was kept busy unloading the gear for the wireless and its hilltop mast, along with a supply of coal. He also took the dogs ashore to recuperate for the nearly two weeks that it would take to build the hut and erect the mast. It gave Madigan an opportunity to hose the dogs' excrement from the deck, which hitherto had been a constant feature of their lives. "Thank the Lord," he wrote, as it disappeared over the side. Much to his chagrin, a valuable coil of rope also disappeared over the side and sank to the depths as he was using a sling to lower it into the motor launch. After the praise he had received for his marksmanship and his helmsmanship, Madigan found himself being "cussed at by everyone." He couldn't take the harsh criticism, which made him feel "very sick about it" and gave him "the blues."[12] He was prone to depression, and particularly took criticism to heart. He does not mention whether Mawson was one of those who cussed at him, but he would have found criticism from the expedition leader particularly hard to take. Much later, he would note Mawson's propensity for profanity, and his harsh and sometimes unjustified attacks on the men. When Madigan was the target of Mawson's attack, it could take days to relieve his consequent depression.

The day after dropping the rope, Madigan stayed out of harm's way, and perhaps Mawson's as well, by going ashore and helping with the landing of the wireless gear from the *Aurora*. He didn't even go back to the ship for lunch, but simply killed a penguin and fried its flesh, describing it as "very nice." On December 15, Madigan's mood lifted as he used the motor launch to transfer coal and butter from the *Toroa* to the *Aurora,* and was praised as its helmsman, although not by Mawson. Madigan could only watch in envy as several of the other men dropped cans of benzene or butter, only to have them float and be recovered. "Wish I had some fellows luck," wrote Madigan, who was still smarting at the criticism he had copped two days before. Mawson quickly forgave Madigan his clumsiness with the coil of rope; by December 18, he was calling him Maddy, which Madigan thought, presumably tongue-in-cheek, was "beastly familiar."

Privately, he was quite pleased at this apparent sign of approval from the normally reserved Mawson. Perhaps to celebrate, after rising the following day, he dived into the very cold sea from the deck of the *Aurora*.[13]

It was mainly the men of the expedition who now remained on the island. The *Toroa* had sailed away with six of Hatch's men, along with the eight-man crew of a small ketch, the *Clyde*, that had been wrecked on the coast while attempting to pick up Hatch's men and their six hundred barrels of oil. Only two of Hatch's men remained. As Madigan and his companions labored on, erecting the two 90-foot-high wireless masts atop the hill and making them secure, there was an opportunity to become more familiar with the other members of the expedition. It was during this last week on Macquarie, while doing what he described as the hardest work of his life, that Madigan began his close friendship with Mertz and Ninnis, along with several others, including Frank Bickerton, Alexander Kennedy, and Frank Wild. The Swiss ski champion, who "sings and jokes all day," wrote Madigan, "amuses me immensely," describing him as "a gentleman, a sport, a humorist, a scholar, a light hearted friendly fellow." Ninnis, who was a couple of centimeters taller than Madigan, was "very nice" and "very English," and was intending to visit Madigan when he went to Oxford. Madigan's own competence was acknowledged once again when he was put in control of completing the erection of the mast; "things went much better" as a result, according to his diary.[14]

There was some mayhem in their final days on Macquarie Island, as the weather worsened and the *Aurora* kept dragging its anchor before losing it completely. It took hours to fashion another. Madigan and some of his companions found themselves stuck on the island, along with the dogs and some fifty sheep that had been put ashore. Madigan had taught himself Morse code, and was able to read a signal from the ship that instructed him to kill fifteen of the sheep to take on board. It was left to Hatch's men to do so. They were practiced at butchering, but strangely proved incompetent at the task. It was only then that Madigan "seized a knife and killed ten in half as many minutes in most approved style!" Earlier, he helped Mertz feed the dogs by shooting an elephant seal with his revolver and butchering it. With the men, dogs, and live sheep loaded on board, along with the sheep carcasses and the men's gear, the ship still had to have its supply of fresh water replenished.[15]

This was done with some difficulty back at Caroline Cove, where they had earlier seen a small stream coming off the plateau. Although the cove was "fairly open," a "large pile of rocks right in the middle" made it somewhat precarious. It was, after all, named after a ship that had been wrecked there, and it was responsible for several other shipwrecks. Before the *Aurora* was taken in closer, Mawson and Madigan were rowed toward the shore to ensure that there were no hidden rocks, with Madigan taking frequent soundings with a lead line and Mawson scribbling the measurements down in a notebook. After it was deemed safe to take the ship closer, the men filled 100-gallon casks with buckets of water from a small stream; the casks were then towed back to the ship and emptied into the tanks. They also took back the meat from an elephant seal, which Mertz had shot to provide feed for the dogs. Back on board that evening, the ship remained anchored near the rocky shore. They intended to get more water the following morning, which was Christmas Day. But the ship was dangerously close to the rocks, thought Madigan, who hoped "no wind comes up as our anchor has a habit of dragging."[16]

Madigan's fear was borne out in the middle of the night, when they were rudely awoken by the ship bumping broadside against the rocks in the slight swell and freshening wind. When it began to "bump with some force," wrote Harrisson, it was "the most horrible feeling imaginable."[17] Hastily pulling on his underpants and coat, Madigan emerged from his cabin to see "Mawson calling hands to the winch" to raise the anchor, while Davis prepared to steam off from the rocks. They were lucky to escape unscathed. The expedition could easily have ended before it really began. Some expected the worst, and began frantically packing their blankets and clothes to go ashore. But Madigan claimed to be more sanguine, declaring in his diary: "I never seem afraid in circumstances like that, I always seem to take it for granted that we can get out of any difficulty. I never doubt it till a thing is very apparently impossible." With the ship secured, Mawson and Davis decided to head south rather than risk their luck by returning to the cove to collect more fresh water. The 400 gallons they had collected would have to last them the 1,500 miles or so to Antarctica, which would mean keeping the men on a strict ration of just a quart of water a day. Madigan went back to bed, where he opened the Christmas parcel given to him by his fiancée, containing a "little bit of Edelweiss," "three little books and best of all, the sweetest of notes." He went back to sleep, "thankful for our safety and happy."[18]

Those first three weeks aboard the *Aurora* did much to confirm Madigan's confidence in himself. Now that he was back at sea, he returned to spending some hours at the helm each day, trimming and raising the sails, and also being taught by a sailor how to tie various knots. Madigan then taught some of the other members of the expedition how to do so. He also agreed to teach Mertz how to write in English, while Mertz agreed in return to teach him how to write in German. There would be no time for the light novels that Madigan's fiancée had given him. Instead, he applied himself to studying the science of navigation after Mawson told him once again that he would be in charge of finding the way during their proposed journey on the ice. The urgency of his study was emphasized by the sighting of the first icebergs on December 29 and later, when Madigan had climbed the mast with two of the sailors and saw in the distance the first of the floe ice that would soon slow their progress.[19]

The sighting of icebergs was the first intimation of the Antarctic continent. But it was crossing the Antarctic Convergence on December 30 that gave them their first real feel of Antarctica. That was where the ship crossed from the prevailing westerly current of the Southern Ocean to the colder easterly current surrounding the continent. The meeting of the currents is marked by a sudden drop in temperature of a few degrees, and often by mists or fog. Without realizing its cause, Madigan noticed the suddenly colder temperature as the *Aurora* probed its way through the fog. He remarked on the weird sound of whales blowing in the mist and the "awful roaring rumbling sound" that was ascribed to waves crashing into the caves of an iceberg that was hidden to view. Emperor penguins were sighted on the floe ice, and snow settled gently onto the ship. A flurry of excitement occurred when a seal was seen on the ice and judged by Mawson, using his binoculars, to be a "new kind of fur seal." Mertz, Madigan, and Wild got their revolvers ready as the ship turned about to get it, only to have the seal slide away into the water. The presence of the penguins convinced Madigan that they were "within one hundred miles of land."[20] Although the penguins' range is much greater, he was right about the ship's proximity to the continent.

Because of their Antarctic experience, Mawson and Wild might have been relatively unmoved by their surroundings. But the others were certainly impressed. Bage thought the colors of their first iceberg were "absolutely past description," while the pack ice they encountered soon after was the "most wonderful sight I have ever seen."[21] From the vantage point of his bunk, Madigan looked through his deck-cabin doorway to the pack ice that the *Aurora* was passing. "My poor pen cannot describe it," he wrote. But he gave it a shot anyway, noting

> its quietness, its perfect whiteness with that marvellous cobalt blue in the hollows, and green where it can be seen through the water: a dull sky, dark threatening clouds, a few penguins on the ice, and now and then a beautiful snow-white ice bird flying across my small field of view.[22]

Mertz was another who was entranced by the sight of the ice and snow, and "sang with great pleasure some Swiss songs." On

December 30, he decided to sleep on deck in a sleeping bag "to get accustomed to cold temperatures," although there was little chance to sleep in the almost constant daylight as they "sailed past some superb ice sculptures and admired them for hours on end." The convoluted shapes of the pack ice, which might have been two or three years old, looked to Mertz "like Egyptian or Roman temples, palm trees, mushrooms and animal pictures."[23]

The pack ice was not the continent, which still lay over the horizon, and successive probes by the *Aurora* were rebuffed by the close-knit pieces of ice. I had a similar experience during two voyages in January 2013, having to return without reaching land at all. There was no certainty that Mawson would have any better luck. At year's end, Davis was still steaming farther and farther west, with a sailor constantly in the crow's nest searching for a break in the pack. Surely the New Year would see them safely through? With icicles hanging from the ropes, the men assembled on the snow-covered deck to welcome in the New Year. With the ship's whistle blowing and the bell ringing out the last eight bells of 1911, those with revolvers fired in celebration, while other men "beat biscuit tins." They watched the sunset at midnight and "then ten minutes later the sunrise." Mertz reflected on how he "would know Antarctica better" by the following New Year, and wondered "what effects will peace, cold and loneliness have on me?" Despite the cold and the snow, Mertz was in his pajamas and got into a sleeping bag when Hurley took a formal photograph of the assembled men on deck. There would be nothing to celebrate if they did not get to the continent. "If the ship were newer we might try to force our way through," wrote Madigan. "When land is sighted I think we will," he added.[24]

Indeed, the extensive pack ice circling the continent can be slow to break up, and can sometimes act as an impenetrable barrier of a hundred kilometers or more. Not only did Mawson need to find a way through, but he also needed a safe harbor in which to off-load his supplies, and preferably a rocky shore on which to erect his huts. There was no way of knowing where such a place might be located, since there were no charts of this extensive coastline. Mawson's plans were greatly hampered by Scott having denied him a base at Cape Adare, where there was usually ice-free access during the summer, and where accommodation already existed in the form of Borchgrevink's hut. Because of his trek to the South Magnetic Pole, Mawson was also familiar with the weather conditions in that region. With Cape Adare unavailable to him, Mawson had to find an alternative base for the eastern party. However, the nature of the Antarctic coastline south of Australia, and its climate, were largely unknown to expeditioners. By early January 1912, the *Aurora* was about 1,500 kilometers west of Cape Adare, and Davis was becoming increasingly concerned about the depletion of his ship's coal supplies. As they edged farther and farther west, it became clear to Mawson that his plan to have three parties explore the coastline from Cape Adare to the limit of the German discoveries at Gaussberg was no longer possible.

When not gazing at the changing panorama, peeling frozen potatoes on deck, killing the remaining sheep, or shooting at seals or penguins that came within range, the men were given the task of sewing their own sledge harnesses from strips of canvas. As Mawson well knew, these harnesses might one day save their lives if they fell into a deep crevasse.[25] Madigan was also preoccupied with helping the crew work the ship. He proudly wrote of being the "first on deck, and the only one of the Expedition men" when the ship's whistle signaled the crew to come up to adjust the sails. Madigan was not shy about lauding his undoubted practical abilities. He several times ranked himself as the best of the expedition men at a particular activity, while at the same time noting that it was "an embarrassing thought that others are to read this." However, wrote Madigan, "a diary must be about one's self."[26] His diary also continued to record his changing view of Mawson.

When Mawson instructed Davis to take the ship into the pack ice to get snow for their depleted supply of fresh water, Madigan and Wild were among the men sent out with shovels. Hurley took his cinematograph machine to record the activity for movie audiences. It was "very badly managed," wrote Madigan. Because there was a swell jostling the ice about, they used an ice anchor to tie the ship to the ice, only to have the valuable anchor pulled out by the drifting ship and then drop to the depths when the line was let go. That left the men marooned on the ice until they could be thrown a rope and hauled back on board. "By this time, Davis and Mawson were both pretty peevish," wrote Madigan, "and the scheme was abandoned; a lot of time wasted and very little water got." In fact, it was about 100 gallons, which Bage thought was "sufficient for the present."[27] It was the shortage of coal that was becoming more of a concern.

They had spent eleven days among the pack ice, unable to find a way through, let alone a landing place for Mawson's main base. The possibility of the coal lasting long enough to find three separate landing sites was looking remote. Mawson's suggested solution to the predicament was to make do with two bases, and to send Murphy and the seven men of the planned third base back to Australia on the *Aurora*. As we have seen, Murphy had argued his way this far south by threatening in Hobart to mount an expedition of his own, but he could not argue against the shortage of coal. In their present situation, when it wasn't even clear that a site for the main base could be found, there was nothing that Murphy could demand or threaten to get his cherished third base. The only thing he could do was to suggest to Mawson that the eight men of the third base be added to the twelve men destined for the main one. After some thought, Mawson agreed, although deciding that two of Murphy's men could be added to the six men of the second base led by Wild, and that Murphy and five of his men would join the main base, where Murphy would be demoted from his former position of base leader to being put in charge of stores.[28]

Their search for a way through the pack ice came to an end early on January 3, when it thinned out sufficiently for watchers on the *Aurora* to see a great cliff of ice about 100 feet tall looming to the south. The sight "caused great excitement," wrote Bage, "as there was no idea of a barrier here," and "a new discovery like this is a great thing right at the beginning." The so-called barrier formed the coastline of the continent, and was actually the front edge of the ice cap as it slid slowly but inexorably to the sea. Now that the barrier was in sight, they did as Madigan predicted, and "barged straight into the pack" and quickly reached the clear water beyond. By lunch time, as the ship slowly steamed westward, the pack ice disappeared altogether, and the ship was able to get close to the barrier, which Madigan described as "a great wall of compressed snow, perpendicular and slightly irregular, rising back in a smooth white surface."[29] As a first-timer to the Antarctic, Ninnis described how the place had "an extraordinary fascination" and that he was "already gripped thereby." Although Mawson had seen it all before, he was ecstatic at getting through. Until then, "failure appeared to stare us in the face," he wrote in a letter to Paquita. It had seemed that the impenetrable pack ice might prevent them getting to the continent at all. Now that they had done so, it was as if Providence had come "forward at the eleventh hour and made a heaven for us."[30] But he still had to find somewhere to land and establish his base.

CHAPTER FIVE

The Windiest Place on Earth

Mawson's elation at finally reaching the continent in January 1912 was short-lived. It was a very different coastline to that of the Ross Sea, where Mawson had operated with Shackleton. Instead of the ship being able to pull alongside sea ice to unload, he was confronted by an almost continuous ice barrier of great height, and there seemed no place to make a landing. Nevertheless, Mawson was excited by his discovery of the barrier, because it showed that the American explorer Charles Wilkes was wrong to claim in 1840 that no such thing existed. It would be something for Mawson to trumpet when he got back and reported on his expedition to the Royal Geographical Society in London. His name might stand alongside those of Wilkes and other great explorers. As he exulted in a letter to Paquita, they had now "made important discoveries and, Oh my Dear, I am beginning to live again after a period of several days of impending evil and disaster."[1]

On January 4, 1912, as the ship sheltered behind an iceberg to escape the wrath of the men's first Antarctic blizzard, Madigan managed to buttonhole Mawson and question him about his plans in light of their present difficulties. All Mawson would confide was that they would try to make a landing at Adélie Land, which was just 60 miles away. Of course, Mawson had no way of knowing whether there would be a suitable landing place there — the only people to have seen Adélie Land were the French explorer Dumont d'Urville and his companions in 1840, and they had only been able to land on a small offshore islet. With the ship's coal being steadily depleted by the fruitless cruising among the ice, Mawson needed quickly to find a site for his main base. He would also have been concerned that five of the dogs had sickened and died on 5 January. Another had died previously, apparently from being kicked by an angry sailor, and a seventh dog had been left behind on Macquarie Island after biting one of the men. An angry Mawson had wanted to shoot it, but Madigan and Ninnis had tied up the dog and asked the men on the island to tame it. Now there remained just twenty-nine of the thirty-six dogs that had been loaded on board in Hobart.[2] It added to the urgency of their need to find a suitable site.

Mawson's decision to abandon plans for a third base had implications for Madigan. Shortly before learning this, Madigan had collected the signatures of all the expedition team. Alongside their signatures, Madigan wrote down the roles they were expecting to perform. While Mertz was listed as the "ski expert" and Ninnis as "Surveyor and in charge of dogs," he listed himself as the sole "Navigator" in the main eighteen-man party, which would be led by Mawson. This group would be the first to land. The second party was led by Wild and comprised just eight men. With eighteen men at the recently expanded main base, it would be that much harder for Madigan to make his mark in the group. Wild wanted Madigan to join his group, but Madigan predicted that Mawson would not allow it. Anyway, Madigan calculated that "Mawson's party is the best place for me."[3]

A site for the main base was found finally on January 8, 1912, after circumventing the tongue of a gigantic glacier that stuck 60 miles out to sea. (It would later be named after Mertz.) Beyond the glacier tongue, they chanced upon a relatively sheltered bay with areas of bare rock on which to erect their huts. "It is a wonderful place," wrote an exultant Madigan in his diary, providing "a natural Boat Harbor, rectangular with only one side open." The excitement was all the greater for them being "the first human beings to land at Adelie Land!" But was it the continent? Bage was not completely sure, describing in his diary how they "stepped on to (we hope) genuine Antarctic Continent." There could not have been a better introduction to the place. "It was a perfect day," observed Madigan, "not a cloud and beautifully sunny."

The calm conditions turned out to be very misleading. Before the day was out, the weather suddenly deteriorated into a blizzard, which blew up as Madigan and several companions took the first boatload of equipment and supplies ashore. They were not adequately dressed for the drastically changed conditions. Madigan was in the front of the boat, and described how "the spray froze on the boat and on our boots and clothes; it is a wind that makes this place feel bitterly cold, we were nearly falling off the boat." There was a slope of a thousand feet or more that rose up from the harbor, and snow was being driven down the slope by the wind until it "covered the boats and their occupants." Two of the men suffered frostbitten fingers, and the motorboat was nearly lost in the choppy waters.[4]

It was no better the following day, so the unloading had to be suspended. "Wind continued with fearful violence all day," wrote Madigan, "the sound of it in the shrouds and running gear was awful." It was whipping up two-meter-waves topped with white-caps, with the combination of wind-driven snow and sea spray limiting visibility to 100 meters. The temperature had plummeted to 19°F, causing the *Aurora* to be shrouded in ice. It was not until the late afternoon of the third day that the unloading could be resumed. They were fortunate that the wind had died away, since the ship was out of fresh water, and the collection of ice had become almost as important as the unloading of supplies. The improved weather persisted, and the place became a hive of industry in the rush to unload. On January 11, Madigan rose to "find the weather perfect, the sea like glass and the air still, the sun shining." With the temperature near freezing, Madigan described how he sometimes "positively perspired while working," with the cold being "quite bearable, almost unnoticeable."[5]

The good weather did not last long. The barometer began

falling again on January 12, with the wind strengthening during the day until all work was suspended. Madigan and several companions were caught ashore by the "howling blizzard," and spent the following day or so in their hastily erected tents. They tried to resume work on January 13, but the wind remained so strong they were "almost blown into the sea" and "had to crawl on hands and knees." The following day, it had abated sufficiently to allow Madigan to collect rocks with Mawson, although the wind still made walking "very difficult." The rocks would be sent back to Australia on the *Aurora*. They would be a down payment on the scientific collection that Mawson expected to amass by the end of the expedition. It was gradually dawning on them that the place they had chosen was subject to frequent, severe weather events. Mertz noted on January 16 how "blizzards seem to blow constantly in this area." Madigan found this out for himself when the weather was sufficiently calm to allow the whaleboat and motorboat to take a load of supplies ashore. Madigan loaded the whaleboat with a ton of coal briquettes "when up came the wind again. I never heard of such a place." Despite the drenching spray, he had to quickly throw the briquettes back on board the *Aurora* and haul the whaleboat on deck to protect it from the gale.[6]

The suddenness of the weather changes was outside of their normal experience. A drop in the wind could catch them just as unawares as the onset of a gale. After blowing strongly in the morning of January 18, the wind suddenly died away around lunchtime, and "the sun shone bright and warm." As he worked frantically to get the final load of stores ashore, as well as the dogs and the aeroplane, Madigan "got quite sunburnt" and "suffered badly with snow blindness." Mertz, though, was in his element, watching with awe as "gigantic broken blocks" fell off the face of the advancing glacier into the sea, sounding "like a thunderclap." The following day, he and Mawson were aboard the *Aurora* as it prepared to depart. Mawson brought out an old bottle of Madeira that had been on the *Challenger* voyage in 1872, with the company drinking the health of the *Challenger* crew, and Mawson making a farewell speech. They said goodbye to Wild and his party, who were going farther westward "to an unknown area," while Ninnis and Mertz said a poignant goodbye to the crew they had worked alongside ever since leaving England. "The handshakes were very warm and tears were not far away," wrote Madigan. All hands then manned the capstan to raise the anchor, while the whaleboat was lowered to take Mawson and his companions ashore to where they would spend the next twelve months. As Madigan took up his oar to begin the long row to shore, "there was cheering from ship and boat till out of hearing."[7]

As the overloaded whaleboat with its eighteen occupants was rowed ashore, they were "cheered and cheered" from the ship. Then the *Aurora* steamed off "full speed ahead westward," with the landing party watching till the ship slipped over the horizon. On board the *Aurora* were letters from the men, most of them written with a mixture of excitement and foreboding. "I am vanishing for a time into the unknown," was the final line in Frank Stillwell's letter to his family, while Madigan also wrote final letters to his fiancée and his mother.[8] On board the *Aurora* was a collection of rocks and other specimens that Mawson was sending home. Madigan noted that it included "some pretty rock specimens to send back per ship; mica schist full of big garnets." Mawson had interrupted the unloading and the construction of the huts to collect them. It was meant to differentiate Mawson's expedition from Scott's by providing early confirmation to the world that he was engaged on a serious scientific enterprise and not a publicity-seeking adventure.[9]

The men at Commonwealth Bay lived for a week in their tents as they blasted holes in the rock for the foundations of the hut. They were blessed with mostly fine weather as they nailed down the floorboards, then put up the sides and roof, complete with skylights. Little did they know that they would soon be using a skylight to gain entry as the hut became buried beneath windblown snow. Within the main hut, a small room was made for Mawson, while the rest were allocated bunks built along the walls. In fact, Mawson's room was more like a cubicle, with an area just six feet square, but at least he had some privacy; the rest of the men had none. The hut was 24 feet square, and had been meant for twelve men. It now had to house eighteen, which made it that much more claustrophobic, particularly when the men were confined inside for days or weeks at a time during the dark winter. A second, smaller hut that had been intended for the second base was tacked on to the main hut and used as a machine shop and laboratory. In having a private space, Mawson was following the example of Shackleton. Unlike Shackleton, though, the more reserved Mawson did not keep the library of books in his room, which therefore gave no excuse for any of the men to wander in and engage in casual conversation while browsing them.[10]

In a corner of the hut made by the wall of Mawson's room, Madigan, Mertz, Ninnis, and Bickerton made their home of four bunks. Their alcove was called "Hyde Park Corner," as an allusion to the English origins of two of them, with Mertz decorating his space with a picture of his mother and a colored view of the Matterhorn. There was no memento of his father, who he had defied by going to the Antarctic. The four inhabitants of Hyde Park Corner became particularly close friends. Madigan described in his diary how

> Ninnis is a cheerful idiot, a fearful pessimist and yet withal very humorous. I feel a thorough idiot when with him. I simply laugh all the time.
>
> Ninnis and Mertz provide most of the amusement. Ninnis by his absurd manner of speech and gloomy ways, Mertz by his funny English and undying cheerfulness.[11]

Doubtless, the friendship of Mertz and Ninnis provided a welcome antidote to Madigan's occasional gloominess.

Mawson's views during these early weeks, and his reaction to the unexpectedly fierce weather, are not recorded in his diary. Indeed, from January 8 to 19 there were no entries at all, as he worked like a navvy to get the huts erected and organized, and the stores sorted. It was left to others to make occasional observations about Mawson and to describe the scene of frantic activity. But the seventeen other men were also preoccupied with the business of building and getting the place secure and relatively windproof before another blizzard swept down from the polar plateau. Although Madigan and a few others diligently maintained their diaries, Mertz had no time or energy to write in his diary until January 29, when the interior of the hut was sufficiently complete for their occupation to begin:

> Mawson unpacked lots of crates. The cutlery and the kitchen utensils appeared. We built the darkroom, the furnace and the area for the instruments ... "Hurrah!" Peace and leisure. It was about time because some of us were tired to death.

Mawson helped cook a special meal to celebrate, with courses of soup, rabbit, blancmange and jam, nuts, and black coffee. It was a "fine feast," wrote Stillwell, and was followed with a walk outside to enjoy the "beautiful calm evening" before they settled back in their bunks to listen to gramophone records.[12] Then the real business of the expedition began.

Mawson instructed Madigan, with help from Mertz and Ninnis, to erect the two meteorological screens on nearby rocky outcrops. Madigan would become the principal meteorologist of the expedition and would have to make daily excursions to read the instruments, whatever the weather. Ski instruction also began, although it was hard for the men to take it seriously. After tea on January 31, as the first of the Adélie penguins began to leave their summer rookery, Mertz got out his skis and gave a demonstration. Mawson had brought him along for this skill, in the expectation that it would prove vital when traveling on the polar plateau. "It looks grand," observed Madigan, as he watched Mertz glide past. "He is wonderfully graceful." However, there was more ice than snow on the ground, which made it unsuitable to teach beginners.

When the following day brought a fall of snow and a pleasant day, Mertz went out again to teach Madigan and others the art of skiing. Madigan likened it to "roller skating, mostly falls at first," and he was only able to "manage about one hundred yards in an erect position." They tried again a couple of days later on a longer slope, by which time Madigan judged his skill on skis to be "fair." He kept practicing whenever he could. By February 3, he reported that he was "much braver and did quite big slopes. Turning is the difficulty, can't turn at all yet, simply go till I fall."[13]

Only a minority of the men tried their hand at skiing. Moreover, they do not seem to have done so at Mawson's direction, nor did Mawson take part. There is no sense in the diary that Madigan thought of himself as learning a skill that could prove vital when out sledging. Biologist John Hunter described how it was "most amusing to see us all get going on the skis for a few yards and then suddenly fall on the hinder part of our anatomy." Nevertheless, wrote Hunter, "we all enjoyed it very much and it will prove one of our best amusements."[14] Bage also referred to practicing skiing in terms of a sport, rather than for sledging. He noted how Hurley planned to film them "before we get too good (if ever. Not too hopeful at present)." Work on completing the huts often intervened. Although there were three calm days in a row, there were only three skiers out and about on February 5, with the remainder of the men continuing to work on the construction and other tasks.

On February 6, Madigan wrote of his regret at missing ski practice that day, noting that he was "going to try to have one every night. We are lucky to have the champion of Switzerland to teach us." With new snow falling on February 7, the surface was more suited to skiing, and Madigan reported that he felt "quite confident on the straight, and can do a curve to the right, and stop without falling about 50% of the tries. Went up much higher and did runs of about a mile. It is a glorious sensation." This time, it was Bage who didn't have time for skiing. The following day, Madigan and others posed on their skis for the cinematograph, with Hurley getting them to ski down a small bank so that they would fall at the bottom, for the amusement of cinema audiences.[15]

On several days, skiing was impossible due to the wind. It was so strong one day that it blew their best sledge out to sea, never to be retrieved.[16] The following day, Madigan measured the wind's strength at 70 miles an hour. That made life difficult enough, but it soon began snowing as well. Madigan had never "imagined such a snow fall; it was impossible to see ten yards. What ho! sledging on the plateau. From what I have read and seen of the Antarctic, sledging is a fearful game." That same day, Mawson announced that he was planning to send out four sledges during the current summer so the men could gain experience and establish food depots for the following summer. This had become the usual procedure for Antarctic expeditions, but no other expedition had had to confront the weather conditions of Commonwealth Bay. Mawson said that he would lead a three-man party that "would make the longest trip." Over tea the following night, he told the assembled men that "the real work had hardly begun, and we must hurry on to get away and do some sledging before the summer is over." He chose Madigan and Bage to join him on a three-day sledge designed "to look around and see in what direction to start the big journey this summer." Bage thought that would be "jolly nice." Mawson told him that one of the parties would only be out for two or three days, another for seven or eight days, and the other two parties for a month. "All will get experience," noted Bage, "& the shorter journey sledges will lighten loads for the farther ones & also will enable depots to be laid. All will go straight inland." Mawson's own diary gives no clues as to his intentions, but it seems that the one-month trek was to be preparation for an assault on the South Magnetic Pole the following summer, which he would lead, with Madigan doing the navigating and Bage in support. But a five-day blizzard of unusual ferocity forced Mawson to postpone his departure, and then to delay it still farther so he could raise the Union Jack over the hut.[17]

Prior to the flag-raising ceremony, Mawson conducted their first divine service, with prayer and hymnbooks placed "on a cushion covered by a Commonwealth flag, the blue Australian ensign." A "rather nervous" Mawson read from the books, and added a prayer of his own for the safety of the expedition. With Stillwell playing the pianoforte, they sang "Nearer My God to Thee" and "God Our Help in Ages Past." The rather devout Madigan found it all "very comforting." With most of the men dressed in their Burberrys to guard against the cold wind, they went outside to watch Mawson raise the British flag atop the pole on the roof of the hut. "With rousing cheers," wrote Madigan, "we annexed Adelie Land to the British Empire." At a celebratory dinner that night, the hut was festooned with flags as Mawson handed out cigars and summed up their position. While they were "snug and comfortable" in the hut, he told the men that they

> were in a much worse place than any Antarctic expedition had ever landed in, the weather was far worse, it looked as if these winds were constant and sledging would be most difficult. No other expedition had been game to land here. Perhaps it was a terrible region; we were going to prove it.

In other words, the terrible weather would be another way in which their expedition would be distinguished from those of Scott and others. Wrapping himself dramatically in an Australian flag, he implored the men to put their "shoulders to the wheel in the coming fight & uphold the honor of Australia and the British Empire." While Mawson lauded the value of their meteorological, magnetic, and biological work, it was the "geographical work" that was most important. "We must *explore,*" declared Mawson[18] This was easier said than done.

Mawson had intended setting out on February 26 for an initial reconnoiter of three days' duration, but delayed it till the following day. A renewed blizzard caused a farther delay, with "snow and wind to beggar description," prompting Madigan to predict that they wouldn't get away till the next summer. Mawson told Bage that the intensity and persistence was much worse than any weather he had experienced on the Shackleton expedition. In this instance, Madigan's instruments measured gusts of 76 miles an hour, with the strongest wind on the Beaufort wind scale being 77 miles an hour.[19] It wasn't until the late afternoon of February 29 that the wind moderated sufficiently to allow Mawson, Bage, and Madigan to set out with a sledge-load of provisions, which they planned to deposit several miles from the hut. Mertz, Bickerton, and Hurley helped haul the sledge up the icy slope behind the hut. Even with six men, it was almost more than they could do to haul the sledge in the face of drift snow "blowing low on [the] ground like a river." They traveled little more than a mile before they secured the sledge and returned to the hut for the night, there being little chance of pitching a tent in such conditions. It was a fortunate decision. Back at the hut the next morning, another ferocious blizzard brought cyclonic winds and blinding drift snow — the snow was so thick that the hut could not be seen at a distance of ten meters. Nevertheless, Madigan still had to go outside to take his meteorological observations. The lack of visibility made it particularly difficult, and the freezing wind made it much worse, with his Burberry helmet filling with ice, and his eyelashes freezing together. He had to resort to crawling and being blown along the ice by the wind.[20]

Setting out again the following morning, Mawson, Madigan, and Bage collected the abandoned sledge and took it about five and a half miles from the hut, climbing to a height of 1,750 feet. It was slow going, because of the steepness of the slope and the strong wind into which they were walking. And it was all done by man-hauling. On the third day, a blizzard forced them to remain in their tent for most of the morning. When the wind abated, they decided to go no farther up the slope, which they estimated would extend for another 35 miles. The sledge was left there unprotected, along with its rations, clothing, and sleeping bags; it would provide a supply cache when serious sledging became possible. During their return to the hut, Madigan was leading the way when he fell forward into a deep crevasse, and was luckily able to throw his upper body onto the snow edge to save himself from falling any farther. It would be months before anyone returned to the abandoned sledge. In the meantime, Madigan would often wonder about "the state of the sledge and flag and thermograph we left up on the plateau," and feared that it would be "almost worn away with drift."[21]

Any farther thought of sledging was stopped by the wind. "Will it never stop?" wondered Madigan. But it only got worse. It reached 70 miles an hour on March 5, and 80 miles an hour the following day. Mawson described in his diary how the men "are now getting reconciled to our weather and shall be surprised only should a fine day greet us."[22] "That is probably a world's record," thought Madigan, who was now convinced that Commonwealth Bay was "without doubt the windiest place in the world." Although there were still occasional days of fine weather, Madigan was under no illusions that the good weather would last. Far from it being the "most pleasant and harmless land," which they had presumed it to be in January, Madigan now thought it was "terrible, inhospitable, unearthly. It seems as though nature is trying to keep man out of this, one of the last of her untrammelled fastnesses." And so it went on. "Will the wind never cease?" asked a frustrated Madigan on March 11, who was concerned that sledging in such conditions would be "absolutely impossible."[23] Despite the difficulties of working in the wind, they were becoming used to it and, according to Mawson, "even get some exhilaration in going out and fighting with the elements."[24] There was no indication that Mawson's plans were being shaped, or even influenced, by the frequent and sudden gales they were experiencing.

There was one aspect of the expedition, though, that suggests that Mawson had learned something from his experience on the Shackleton expedition, when he had resorted to eating seal and penguin meat. He accepted the mistaken medical opinion that scurvy could be caused by food that was not scientifically prepared, with canned meat often being blamed by explorers when their expeditions were afflicted. However, the scurvy in such cases was ascribed to a fault in the canning process rather than to the nutritional deficiency of a diet limited to canned meat. Because Mawson had taken six tons of canned meat with him, he could not dispense with it altogether without offending some of the expedition's generous donors. In February, he instructed that canned meat only be served as the main course for dinner once a week. In place of canned meat, Mawson ordered that seal meat be served for dinner twice a week, penguin meat twice a week, fresh mutton once a week, and "variables" on another day. Because "we shall not have much tinned meat," observed Hunter, we "will be rid of that great polar scourge — scurvy." Mawson and Hunter only half-understood what had kept scurvy from the Shackleton expedition. They didn't realize that it was the plentiful fresh meat that was important, rather than the avoidance of tinned meat.[25]

If Mawson had understood what had really saved him from scurvy on the Shackleton expedition, he would have made more effort to store sufficient seal and penguin meat to last them through the winter. On February 28, Hunter counted 164 seals basking on the ice. Only one of them was killed for fresh meat, and much of the carcass was left for scavenging birds. Although there were still numerous seals seen on the shores of Commonwealth Bay in March 1912, the men made little attempt to kill them. Consequently, they had run out of seal meat by early April, when there were few seals to be found. They might have made it up with penguin meat, but they were short of that as well. When a penguin hunt was organized in late March, the birds had mostly left for the winter, and only about two dozen could be caught and killed. Instead of having fresh meat four or five times a week, the expeditioners were reduced to having just penguin meat twice a week. With no seal meat left for the dogs, they also were fed on penguin meat twice a week, supplemented by biscuits on other days. As a result, noted Madigan, they were looking "a good deal thinner."[26] It was different with the men, who were all putting on weight because of their inactivity and a diet that was rich in sugars and fats.

It was not good preparation for the coming summer of sledging. Other preparations for the sledging season were also neglected. Mawson seems to have given a low priority to dog sledging, even though practicing with the dogs on different surfaces was important preparation for both the dogs and their handlers. It was not until mid-June that Mertz put two of the dogs in harness so they could pull a sledge on several practice journeys near the hut, which was now buried by snow up to the roof. Mertz did this in the face of a 70-mile-an-hour wind until the rough, icy surface caused one of the dog's paws to bleed. Mertz and Ninnis had the same two dogs back in harness two days later, and took men for a ride to and from Webb's magnetic hut for the price of four squares of chocolate. Madigan thought it was "great to see their little feet pattering over the snow, and their strength is wonderful."[27] It was "amusing," wrote Hunter to see Ninnis and Mertz "sitting on the sledge and giving the dogs a little of the lash now and then."[28] Such a jaunt was hardly the sort of preparation that was required to support a summer of sledging across snow and ice.

After nearly four months of wild weather at Commonwealth Bay, Mawson had little to show for their presence. And they knew little of their surroundings. Madigan conceded at the end of April that they had "accomplished nothing beyond obtaining magnetic and meteorological records." They hadn't ventured more than a few miles from their winter quarters, and they didn't even know whether there was land beyond the circumference of their closed-in existence. Indeed, wrote Madigan, "we might, for all we know, be on a large island." They hoped for weather in winter or spring that would allow them to sledge, but they had had "three continuous months of the worst weather ever experienced on earth," and there was no telling when it might improve. By mid-May, they had become convinced, correctly, that the bad weather would last till October. As the meteorologist, Madigan had to venture outside each day to check his instruments, often having to go on his hands and knees to do so. Many of the others spent days on end cooped up in the hut, which was now lit even during the day by artificial lighting.[29] "The constant stopping inside the hut makes one feel awfully tired and sleepy," complained Hunter, "especially at meal times & the only exercise we get is a little bit of skipping and boxing."[30]

There was a vain hope that the gales and blizzards were a feature of the Antarctic autumn, and that the following seasons would be better. Mawson assured them that this had been his experience on the Shackleton expedition. But Commonwealth Bay was very different from the Ross Sea. Hard as it was for Mawson to believe, the weather worsened as they descended into the darkness of winter. On May 17, Madigan reported that the wind gusts were "making the Hut tremble." The following day, he described the weather as "like hell let loose." The gusts were so strong that they began to fear whether their hut could withstand the onslaught. On May 20, there were "some fearful gusts, which struck the Hut like a blow, and made our ears sing with the pressure; we had misgivings re the roof." The interludes of calm were increasingly brief. Although Madigan greeted May 21 as "a fine day!," the wind cranked up by 4:00 p.m. and soon became "the usual terrific blizzard." Two days later, Madigan's anemograph recorded winds of 100 miles per hour for the first time.[31]

The gales came suddenly, and could just as suddenly abate into an eerie calm. When that occurred, the men were quick to take advantage of the calm to work outside. But they could never tell how long the calm would last. When the wind dropped away one night, Madigan described how he and cartographer Alfred Hodgeman took the opportunity to put some oil on the hilltop anemograph, Mawson and Bage went to repair the tide gauge, Hunter and taxidermist Charles Laseron went dredging for sea life, and magnetician Eric Webb and wireless operator Walter Hannam took a time shot on a star. Madigan did not bother donning his protective Burberrys, confident that he would have time in the clear moonlight to complete his work and make his way back to the hut. However, as he was preparing to apply the oil, he looked up the icy slope to the south and "saw a wall of snow approaching down the slope: when I say 'approaching' it was doing about 60 [miles per hour]." As they rushed to finish their work, the blizzard hit with its full force, snatching from their hands and sending "the hurricane lamp, screwdrivers, oil bottle, brushes, all over the place." There was a mad scramble by the various parties to get back to the safety of the hut, with the snow-covered Madigan resembling "a young Father Christmas."[32]

Just as the gales could come and go, so too could the bouts of gloominess that plagued Madigan. On April 5, his depression was caused by some harsh words from Mawson, which Madigan conceded he "should not have taken to heart." Two days later, he reported that his "mental atmosphere cleared wonderfully well under the influence of the innocent sleep." On May 26, he was gripped by another of what he called his "hideous unreasonable moods," which again was brought on by Mawson questioning what Madigan and one of the other men "had been doing all day." The moods were "a blight on my otherwise pleasant existence," wrote Madigan, acting as "a kind of malignant blues, which render me morose, rude, unsociable, peevish."[33] Yet Hunter considered Madigan to be "one of the best & with Bage shares the honor of being the best liked members of the expedition." He described Madigan as having "a jovial spirit" and being "always willing to lend a hand."[34] Hunter's comments suggest that Madigan was successful in keeping his dark moods relatively hidden from his companions in the claustrophobic circumstances of the hut.

Closeted away in his room, as he often seemed to be, Mawson lived a lonely life. He had no deputy to whom he could unburden his concerns. Nor did he make much use of his diary to do so. Yet he was burdened with many worries. He was consumed by the need to cover the debts of the expedition. That meant returning with a gripping story and important achievements. With Scott also in the field and expected to return with the South Pole in his bag, Mawson had a formidable challenge to capture public attention. His Australian lecture agency was already trying to advise him when and how he should return to maximize publicity for the expedition. In early April 1912, the agent urged Mawson to return as early as March 1913 so that he might preempt the return of Scott. Although Scott was not expected to do a lecture tour in Australia, his "custom of giving so freely to the press, must discount somewhat any other Antarctic celebrity who comes after him." His agent provided Mawson with a secret code to indicate where he intended to land so that a lecture tour could be booked before any details of the expedition had leaked out. He urged Mawson to arrive with two prepared lectures, both committed to memory, so they could be presented rather than read, as Shackleton, Scott, and Amundsen were inclined to do.[35] This advice went unheeded. There was no communication with the outside world, as the frequent blizzards prevented the erection of the wireless masts.[36]

Mawson could only wonder about the activities of his Antarctic rivals. He had no way of knowing that Amundsen had reached the South Pole in mid-December 1911, when Mawson was still at Macquarie Island, or that Scott's five-man party was about four weeks behind him. By March 7, 1912, Amundsen had returned to Hobart and announced his feat to the world. Mawson wouldn't learn of this for another ten months. Neither would he know until then that Scott's party had failed to return from the pole, and that its fate was unknown. The race between Scott and Amundsen had captured the headlines and the public imagination, and its tragic end would do so even more. As for Mawson's other rivals, Filchner's German expedition failed to reach the continent, let alone get anywhere near the South Pole. As his ship became trapped by ice, Filchner had to be content with the limited scientific observations that could be undertaken from his vessel. At least the Japanese expedition of Nobu Shirase made it ashore on the Ross Ice Shelf in January 1912, but Shirase was not equipped to compete with Amundsen or Scott. After a short dash to the south using dog sledges, he made do with raising the Japanese flag and claiming the now well-trodden area for Japan. It was enough to have him hailed as a hero when he returned to Tokyo in June 1912, although he was largely ignored by the rest of the world. Mawson might face the same fate if he did not return with an exciting story of achievement and adversity overcome.

The silence from Antarctica alarmed Mawson's press agent in Hobart, Conrad Eitel, who thought Mawson's wireless set must have been underpowered. Eitel began a furious dispute with the Australian wireless company for selling them such a weak set, and frantically planned to charter a ship to take more powerful ones to both Macquarie Island and Antarctica. The plan was only canceled when the first messages began to arrive from Macquarie Island, where the wireless was operating successfully.[37] However, with no messages coming from Antarctica, it could not fulfill its function as a relay station. The lack of wireless communication from Mawson had serious implications for the financial success and public profile of the expedition. It also left Mawson in the dark as to what his rivals were doing. His hopes for the aeroplane were also fading. It not only had no wings, but had been left buried under snow for months before being finally moved into a specially constructed garage where Bickerton could work on it.

Mawson was struggling to fill the role of expedition leader. On the Shackleton expedition, he had been reluctant to take over from the exhausted Edgeworth David. Now that he was in charge of seventeen men, with no deputy as a sounding board, Mawson failed to provide the leadership that was required in their challenging circumstances. He tried to rouse them with occasional inspirational talks, with after-dinner readings from his books, and with special dishes concocted in the kitchen. But mostly he remained relatively aloof, and relied too much on hectoring them into making a greater effort rather than using gentle encouragement and praise for their work. Madigan and the denizens of Hyde Park Corner referred to him privately as *Dux Ipse* (Latin for "the leader himself"), which was meant disparagingly. Mawson was also remarkably reluctant to inform them of his plans, let alone discuss them or ask for suggestions. It was hard for Mawson, shut away in his room as he listened to the men lying in their bunks enjoying friendly banter. He was also on notice that his leadership was under scrutiny, after Madigan and Ninnis read out extracts from their expedition diaries, with Ninnis declaring to all and sundry that he aspired "to outdo Pepys."[38] A copy of the seventeenth-century diary of Samuel Pepys had accompanied the expedition, providing inspiration for those who might be intent on emulating Pepys by providing a "warts and all" account.[39]

Mawson had taken some precautions by having the men sign a contract preventing them from publishing any information about the expedition for two years.[40] But there was nothing to prevent them doing so after that time, and no telling what they might be writing about him. Interestingly, his perfunctory diary entries come to an end the day after Ninnis and Madigan read from their diaries, with Mawson starting a new notebook on February 28. He now began to write much more extensive entries. And as winter wore on, Mawson ensured that the men were fully occupied, with no time formally set aside for private activities. He tried to channel their writing into a monthly expedition magazine instead. It was partly as a "memento," noted Hunter, "but mainly to keep us all interested & busy for there is no doubt that we are getting very lax owing to the lack of outdoor work & exercise." Although contributions were submitted, no magazine was ever published, much to the chagrin of Madigan. When the men persisted in writing their diaries, Mawson would make sneering comments about their idleness.[41] As the darkest day of the year approached, their relative idleness was about to come to an end.

Mawson laid on a special dinner for mid-winter's day, June 21. For the first time, he permitted them to have a day free of work. It marked the gradual return of the sun and a sign that the summer sledging season was approaching. Not that they ever experienced a day of complete darkness — Commonwealth Bay is too far north for that. Madigan described how "half the disc of the sun is visible for about an hour, and for two hours we get beautiful sunset effects." To celebrate mid-winter, the gramophone was kept going all day, they walked the dogs, and explored the neighborhood of the hut in the relatively benign weather. A few of them went up the slope toward the polar plateau in an attempt to see even more of the sun. They returned in time for the feast, which had specially printed menu cards: penguin with peas and potatoes was the main course. During the dinner, Mawson proposed toasts to British royalty and to the Australian government, although he couldn't stop himself from having a dig at the Labor Party, berating it for having no affinity for Antarctic exploration. Later, Madigan and McLean dressed as Romans and performed Shakespeare's dialogue between Caesar and Brutus, with Madigan playing the role of Brutus.[42] Some of them would wake with a hangover the following morning. At least they could look forward to the greater activity that the approaching summer would bring. The end of their self-imposed exile was in sight.

CHAPTER SIX

Preparing for the Unknown

There was little to show for Mawson's first six months at Commonwealth Bay. The party had done meteorological and magnetic observations, collected rock samples and some marine specimens, killed and skinned birds, penguins, and seals, and explored their immediate surroundings. But they had done little preparation for the summer sledging, which would determine the success or otherwise of their expedition. The successive blizzards had kept the eighteen men largely confined to the cramped hut, other than short forays outside during brief spells of calm weather. During those first six months, Mawson organized only one desultory sledging journey to lay down a depot of food and supplies. And that was on February 29, when Mawson, Madigan, and Bage had taken a single sledge of clothing and food just five miles from the hut and left it there. Originally having intended to take three days and go farther, Mawson had headed back to the hut after two days. Plans to take more food up the slope were abandoned.

The initial sledge journey was meant to be the first step in a program of depot-laying to provide secure stepping stones for the coming summer of treks along the coast and south toward the magnetic pole. However, nothing more had been done over the subsequent four months. They didn't even return to inspect the condition of the exposed sledge with its valuable contents, including reindeer sleeping bags and wolf-skin mitts.[1] The almost constant gales and snowdrift meant they had done little training for sledging. Mawson also had been unable to test the modified aircraft to see whether its engine would work in the extreme cold, and whether it was capable of hauling a sledge in the windy conditions. These deficiencies in their training, and the loss of fitness caused by their confinement, would have serious implications for the coming sledging season. The dogs had also lost condition from being on a diet mainly of biscuits. Madigan noted in his diary on July 10 how they were now "simply waiting for the spring and praying for a cessation of the terrible ceaseless wind." He was worried that their failure to establish a great store of food up on the plateau during the autumn would mean that their "summer sledging will be greatly hampered."[2]

The dogs were finally hitched to a sledge on July 16, when good weather allowed Mawson, Mertz, Ninnis, and Madigan to go two miles up the slope, where a flag had been left as a marker from their abortive journey. This brief foray was done as preparation for a longer trip to retrieve the sledge that had been left higher up the slope. Madigan's diary entries now became more sporadic as the men grew busy preparing their gear for sledging, altering their clothing to suit the colder and windier conditions, and measuring and packing rations.[3] On July 27, as the wind howled outside and the drift snow fought to get inside the hut, everyone was sitting at the table sewing, making alterations to their clothes and equipment. Madigan thought they were making a lot of "unnecessary alterations, but Mawson seems keen on them." It was a frustrating time, with the men being anxious to start sledging. "Oh that we were on the trail!" wrote Madigan. "It is the most earnest wish of everyone. We thought there was going to be a let up in the weather, but the last two days have been worse than ever." Mertz described how they "feverishly prepared our clothes for the sledging expeditions." When they "would start, only the Gods knew."[4] In preparation, Mawson handed out a bottle of cod liver oil and malt extract to each of the men "to fatten us up for sledging."[5]

The darkness of the winter could not come to an end too soon. Not seeing the sun was getting on their nerves. Mawson was becoming more critical of the men, which was causing some justifiable resentment. The part of the hut dubbed Hyde Park Corner, where Mertz, Ninnis, Madigan, and Bickerton slept, was now dubbed disparagingly as "Sleepy Hollow" by Mawson, who accused them of laziness.[6] He expected them to work seven days a week, and set aside little time for leisure activities, and was angered if he noticed them reading or writing in their diaries. Madigan took criticism hard and was becoming increasingly disillusioned with Mawson. One evening, when Mertz was talking to Madigan about Switzerland, Mawson came out of his room to ask whether Swiss women were as attractive as those portrayed on the tins of Nestlé condensed milk. Although Mertz makes no mention of the exchange in his diary, the rather strait-laced Madigan thought that "Paquita would not like to hear him sometimes."[7]

Mawson was under pressure. The unexpected severity of the weather at Commonwealth Bay was threatening the success of his expedition, which had to outdo the achievements of the other expeditions that were in the field. Mawson's advantage over his rivals had been eroded by the failure of the wireless, his inability so far to prove the worth of the aeroplane, and the loss of the whaleboat, which ruined his hopes for the biological program. The wind also was testing the worth of their equipment, with "calico depot flags being torn to pieces by the wind." When Stillwell tried a flag made of tin, it "tore and bent the tin as if it was plain calico."[8] How were they to safeguard their lives if they couldn't clearly mark their food depots? It was particularly frustrating for Mawson that he had no way of knowing how his rivals were faring. He had planned it so well, by equipping his expedition with wireless and having a repeater station on Macquarie Island. The system was designed to keep the world informed of his achievements and to learn news of his rivals, who did not have wireless sets of their own. But the weather had prevented the erection of the requisite aerial masts at Commonwealth Bay. For all he knew, Scott or

Amundsen might have already reached the pole and been feted by the world.

On July 31, another attempt was made to erect one of the radio masts, but it had to be abandoned when the wind returned in force. They were all "very anxious," wrote Madigan, "to get the wireless in action." They wanted to get the *Aurora* back early so that there would be more time for exploration by ship and to ensure that Wild's party could be picked up before access was blocked by the ice. They also wanted to know what their rivals were doing, particularly Scott and Amundsen. "Speculation and betting are rife," wrote Madigan. He thought both of them had "good chances" of reaching the pole, while Filchner's expedition was "not reckoned to have much chance of the pole, but the Germans are sure to put up a good scientific show." And they wanted to receive news from their loved ones. The lack of news made their life in the hut seem "dreadful," and they longed to start sledging. "That will pass the time," wrote Madigan, "and we will feel we are doing something."[9] But they couldn't start sledging until the weather improved, and that was unlikely to happen any time soon. When Ninnis and Mertz tried to take a few bags of supplies to an ice cave just half a mile from the hut, set up by Webb for magnetic observations, they were brought to a stop every hundred yards by the wind, and knocked over "many times." As a result, Hunter thought their "sledging prospects ... do not look very bright." Mawson was similarly concerned, noting that the calmest days in July were equal to the windiest days on Shackleton's expedition.[10]

Madigan continued to enjoy a close relationship with Mertz, Ninnis, and Bickerton in Hyde Park Corner, where they shared stories of loves won and lost. Ninnis confided to his companions about a "rather dreadful" affair that "worries him a good deal," apparently because he had been jilted, while Mertz talked of his latest love, a woman he had met at the Winter Sports. He had brought a photo of her and a pillow that she had embroidered, while he had presented her with "a brooch in the form of crossed skis." Although Mertz would not admit to loving her, Madigan was confident that "Frëulein Betli Kupferschmidt has a good chance of becoming Frau Dr. Mertz." The four men discussed plans for meeting up in Britain and Switzerland, with Ninnis inviting Madigan to stay with him in London and "do a boating trip from London to Oxford," while "Mertz is going to take me all over Switzerland and up Mt. Blanc and the Jungfrau."[11]

As the sole German speaker on a British expedition, during a time of increasing tension between Britain and Germany, Mertz was in a peculiar position. As we have seen, Mawson had been particularly keen to have expedition members drawn exclusively from within the Empire, and had only made an exception for Mertz because of his skiing prowess. Nevertheless, despite his nationality and somewhat rudimentary English, Mertz had endeared himself to many of his companions. Madigan and Ninnis were particularly close to him. And he made more friends when he put on a special Swiss dinner for his companions on August 1, with Madigan judging it "a fine menu, the best dinner we have had." It concluded with cigars and "a long and very interesting and moving speech … in his pretty foreign English." With both the Swiss and British flags draped above the table, Mertz lectured them on the "topography and history of Switzerland." Mawson responded with "the best speech I have heard from him," wrote Madigan. Then it was the turn of Ninnis, "who loves Mertz and has known him longest."[12] Mertz was overwhelmed, noting that "the signs of sympathy from my comrades were so warm that I have never lived such a 1st August until now."[13]

Despite the regard in which Mertz was held, Madigan thought that his nationality would probably debar him from being leader of any of the treks. Not that Mawson had even decided on where he intended to trek, let alone who would go on them. And they had made no reconnaissance to get the lay of the land in any particular direction, nor had they established the line of food dumps that would allow them to lighten the load on their sledges and increase the chances of their survival. Although Mawson was keen to start sledging, he had not experienced much sledging in the face of a strong wind. Stillwell thought Mawson "would not be quite so keen after he has been out a little." There was much discussion within the hut about the "great journey, or journeyings" that were in prospect, with Madigan suggesting that he, Mawson, and Ninnis were "going out." On 3 August, Madigan fitted up one of the sledges with "a cooker box, Nansen cooker and straps." But Mawson had still not announced "what the parties will be, beyond that one will go East, one West and one inland, and I think he and I are on the inland journey."[14]

Two days later, Madigan went sliding on the ice and crashed into rocks, hurting his knee. His chances for sledging looked slim. However, he worked hard to reduce the swelling, and satisfied a worried Mawson that he was up to the task. Mawson wanted Madigan to take a leading part in the sledging during the spring, since "he would have to be at the Hut a good deal if the wireless worked." But the wireless was still not working. So Mawson left with Ninnis and Madigan on August 9 for the first proper sledging journey. At least, that was the plan. Although the wind had been blowing about 50 miles per hour for the previous two days, it would not be allowed to stop them from sledging "in our dire necessity," wrote Madigan.[15] There was relief in the hut when they left and Bage took over as acting leader, with Stillwell feeling that the experience would be "the best treatment for [Mawson's] impatience." The others were happy to see the back of him. Stillwell noted the "marked improvement in the cheeriness" of the hut when Bage was in charge.[16] They set to work with a cheerful willingness, erecting the second mast for the wireless and grinding up plasmon biscuits for the summer sledging parties.

Mawson was so impatient to get away that he forgot to pack two vital pieces of equipment — a lamp and his watch.[17] They would have to set up camp in the dark, and could have difficulty determining their position without a watch. After just three miles working their way up the icy slope, Mawson called a halt and pitched their tent in a 50- to 60-mile-an-hour wind. They fed themselves and the eight dogs, and got into their three-man sleeping bag. Without a lamp, this all had to be done in the dark. The wind was still blowing on the following day, which left them exhausted by the time they reached the abandoned sledge at the five-and-a-half-mile depot. Despite going such a short distance, they again pitched camp, and the following day decided to construct a permanent camp and food depot beneath the ice. During the short daylight hours, Ninnis and Madigan dug a sloping shaft to a depth of two meters and then created a small room at the end, which they subsequently extended. The activity was preferable to the fourteen hours they had spent in the sleeping bag in the tent during the long Antarctic night, when Madigan complained of not being able to sleep much and suffered "aching joints from the hard ice mattress, and worst of all old Mawson made it very uncomfortable for us; he would crawl up against me for warmth and I gradually forced Nin against the side, so only half the bag was used and we could not move." As soon as the cavern was complete, they promptly occupied it and named it Aladdin's Cave. Their new home was warmer than the tent, and the "walls scintillated beautifully from the ice crystals by the light of the primus and an occasional match." Mawson thought it was "a truly magical cave," where "perfect peace" coexisted with the "roaring blizzard" above, and they could hang their clothes up "by spitting on them and pressing them to the wall."[18]

Ninnis and Madigan wanted to press on farther inland, but Mawson took some convincing to continue. To Madigan's annoyance, he then criticized his two companions for being slow starters. Madigan was taken aback, since Mawson was "far worse," with Madigan being "surprised at his unwillingness to get out of the [sleeping] bag." When they did get going, they headed into a wind that Madigan estimated to be 60 miles an hour. The dogs pulled on regardless, while the men struggled to keep pace. Their chances of doing a decent distance were dashed when Mawson declared after little more than three miles that they should "turn round and go right back to the Hut that night." Madigan and Ninnis "were dumbfounded; you could have knocked me down with a feather," wrote Madigan. They had wanted to go on to the ten-mile mark and pitch camp, hoping to do 50 miles before turning back. But Mawson was alarmed by the threatening weather, and insisted on returning.[19]

Madigan reported how they "stuck a flag in a small crevasse, dug a hole in the ice and cached the six tins of pemmican, left the pick and shovel, and turned round." With the wind at their backs, they made quick progress. It was too quick at times. The three men all rode on the sledge, which built up such momentum on the ice that it often crashed into the dogs. It also had a tendency to slide along sideways, and then have a runner get caught in a small crevasse. This would cause the sledge to topple and send the men flying. "We got shot from it time and again," wrote Madigan, "and severely shaken, and the cooker came off, also the cover of the sledge meter, every time, and had to be chased." Eventually they released the dogs from their harness, and allowed the sledge to slide down by itself, with Mawson and Ninnis riding on top and Madigan running along behind with a rope attached to the sledge to keep it straight and stable.[20]

They managed to reach Aladdin's Cave just after dark, and stayed the night. The following morning, stores were stashed away in the cave, and the men readied for their onward journey to the hut. Madigan reported that Mawson took fright when snowdrift cut the visibility to about ten feet, judging that it was too unsafe to try to reach the hut in such conditions. Madigan was aghast. He was accustomed to collecting his meteorological observations in such weather, and wanted to press on. Instead, the sledge was unpacked and the cave reoccupied, with snow covering everything and then melting when the primus was used. Ensconced in the sodden cave, they lifted their spirits with raisins and chocolate and, for Ninnis and Madigan, by smoking their pipes. It was "another long night," wrote Madigan, with the three men crammed into the one sleeping bag.[21] It's likely that Madigan was prepared to take his chances in the snowdrift if it meant avoiding another night in the bag with Mawson.[22]

When Mawson saw that the drift was still blowing the next morning, he wanted to stay in the safety of the cave until visibility improved. He had good reason to be cautious. The final five miles of icy slope down to the hut had to be done carefully. Either side of the hut were sheer ice cliffs 200 feet high, while around the hut were rocks that were best avoided by men on a fast-moving sledge. However, Ninnis and Madigan had had enough, and insisted on going regardless. Madigan was confident of finding his way. Despite Mawson protesting that it was "against all Antarctic principles to move in a blizzard," Madigan and Ninnis packed the sledge and fed the dogs before prevailing upon a reluctant Mawson to accompany them. Even though the weather worsened, they pressed on. Mawson kept hold of the sledge to prevent it being toppled by the small crevasses, while Madigan and Ninnis were harnessed to a tail rope to keep the sledge from sliding away on the ice. They had traveled a quarter of a mile before realizing that they had forgotten the dogs sleeping in the snow. Mawson decreed that it was too difficult and dangerous for one of them to go back in such conditions, and too hard for them all to return with the sledge. So they continued on down the slope, leaving the dogs to find their own way to the hut or be collected later.[23]

Tentatively finding their way through the blinding snow, Mawson and Madigan argued fiercely over which direction they should be taking. Madigan was concerned that Mawson was steering the sledge too far to the west and was heading for the ice cliff. After going "crook" at Madigan, he allowed the younger man to take over the steering. It was Mawson who now feared they were going too far east and were in danger of going over the cliff. So they made another change in direction and, soon after, waited for the weather to clear sufficiently to recognize some local landmarks. Familiar icebergs were sighted, and then the rocks near the hut. "We are a little too far West," wrote Madigan, "but safe." They reached the hut just after lunch, and were warmly congratulated by their companions in the mistaken belief that they had covered the 50 miles that Madigan and Ninnis had wanted to take on. Rather shamefacedly, they related what Madigan called their "miserable tale," while plans were made to rescue the dogs and deposit more supplies at Aladdin's Cave. According to Stillwell, the men had enjoyed Mawson's absence, noting that "the joyful period of hilarity and much work is probably at an end, though [Mawson] seems a good deal better for the outing."[24]

Mertz was anxious to rescue the dogs, and tried to do so the following day. But he, Bage, and Hurley were forced to return to the hut after going just half a mile. The wind was so strong that it sometimes forced them back down the slope of blue ice. They were only saved, wrote Mertz, by "our sharp crampons, and our muscle power."[25] Several days of severe blizzard conditions followed, which meant that the dogs had to be left to their own devices. There was concern among the men about the fate of their canine charges, with Mertz being "in a great state" about it, reported Madigan, rushing out "every time he hears a noise in the dog shelter." Mertz complained in his diary that Mawson was "definitely too cautious," and he worried whether Mawson "would show enough gumption during the sledging expedition." It was six days before Mertz, Bage, and Hurley were able to take a six-dog sledge up the slope to locate the missing dogs. They were away for nearly five days, as blizzards kept them confined to Aladdin's Cave. As for the dogs, six were frozen to the ice and all were in a pitiable condition, not having eaten for six days. Although one was beyond saving, the other seven dogs were taken into Aladdin's Cave and slowly nursed back to health. The needless calamity blighted the remaining regard that Mertz had for Mawson, even though Madigan and Ninnis were just as much to blame for forgetting the dogs.[26] It was not a good beginning for the long sledge journey that lay before them.

CHAPTER SEVEN

Madigan Proves Himself

By August 1912, the dogs were eating the pemmican that had been meant to be used solely as trekking food for the men. Due to Mawson's failure to organize the killing and storage of sufficient seal and penguin meat, the dogs were "eating thirty shillings worth of pemmican per diem," as Madigan bemoaned.[1] It was not until the beginning of September, when they enjoyed a couple of fine days, that the men were able to venture onto the sea ice, where Hurley managed to shoot three seals. "There was great joy at this," wrote Madigan, since it meant "food for dogs and fresh meat for us." A couple of days later, Mertz managed to shoot a female seal that was not far from giving birth. The unborn pup was preserved, and the meat of the seal dragged back to the hut. "Seals are very precious," observed Madigan, "they are wanted for the dogs, especially for dog food while sledging."[2]

Not surprisingly, the abbreviated sledge journey with Mawson and Ninnis had not satisfied Madigan's desire for activity. By August 23 he was confiding in his diary that he was "fed to the teeth with this place, I must admit it, and I long for the return to my course of life; activity will start again if ever we can get away sledging, and at least when we start the cruise on the *Aurora*; but I long, long, long for home again."[3] Madigan's frustration spilled over into criticism of Mawson. Madigan was used to going out in blizzards, and no longer got lost on his way from the hut to his meteorological instruments on Observation Hill. "I know every foot of it and never have to hesitate, except when compulsory, due to falls," observed Madigan.[4] But Mawson had not spent much time out of the hut in bad weather and, as the trek revealed, was not confident moving about in conditions of limited visibility. Madigan's mother had been concerned about Mawson's supposed recklessness, but her fears were groundless, observed Madigan, noting that he and Ninnis had "chafed at [Mawson's] unwillingness to move when within five miles of the Hut."[5] Mawson's leadership ability was also called into question, with Webb telling Madigan that "on most expeditions the leader encouraged the men, [whereas] on this one it takes the men all their time to bear up under the discouragement of the leader."[6]

Mawson's nervousness was seen again on August 27, when most of the men wanted to take advantage of an improvement in the weather to work on the wireless mast. They had managed to erect the second mast during Mawson's absence, and wanted to complete the work so they could get news of the outside world. Mawson was just as anxious, but he worried whether it was safe. He had been grouchy that day, "giving everyone beans; he treats us like children as a rule," wrote Madigan, "and his mood spread to me; polar depression, and I have had the blues all day." The outdoor activity was likely to lift Madigan's mood, but Mawson tried to dissuade them from going out, complaining that they "were wasting time, and ought to be in writing our diaries (sarkassum!), and would kill ourselves." Although it proved too windy to haul anyone up the topmast, they succeeded in making some repairs, and returned in good spirits. Even Mawson became good-humored by evening. It did not last. On August 30, Madigan claimed that Mawson was "in a dreadfully peevish mood of late," with Madigan taking the criticism of himself "philosophically and silently." In his diary, though, Madigan complained that Mawson "scarcely does [anything] himself, but walks about grumbling directly he sees anyone apparently idle for a second."[7]

It was not until early September that Mawson ended his

indecisiveness and announced that he would be sending out reconnaissance treks as preparation for the summer sledging. Madigan was ecstatic: "The great news of the day I have left to the last; the Old Man has pulled himself together, and picked three parties to do a reconnaissance lasting about a fortnight, and each to cover about fifty miles." Webb, Stillwell, and McLean were to track the magnetic meridian south; Mertz, Ninnis, and Murphy were to trek along the barrier to the east; and Madigan, Whetter, and Close were to follow the coastline to the west. Madigan was excited at the prospect of sledging, but could not understand Mawson's choice of Leslie Whetter, one of the two doctors, and Close as his two companions. He considered them to be "the most unsuitable men for sledging here," describing Close as "the most helpless man I have ever seen," and Whetter as "incurably lazy and fearfully careless." Mawson shared Madigan's view of both Whetter and Close, telling Whetter that he was "entirely unfit for an expedition." Mawson picked on Whetter and Close unmercifully. Rather than rotating the unenviable tasks among all the men, he gave the New Zealand-born Dr. Whetter the awful daily job of collecting ice for the hut, and Close the task of emptying the rubbish into the sea and clearing the hut entrance of snow. Mawson would then continually carp at them if he ever them found reading or sleeping. His attacks on Whetter became even worse when the doctor dared to question Mawson about the amount of work he was expecting them to do. The poisonous relationship between the two makes Mawson's choice of Whetter all the more curious.[8] It may have been done as a punishment for Close and Whetter, whom he regarded as shirkers. Then again, Mawson may have been setting Madigan up to fail. Stillwell looked on in dismay. He was worried that Mawson was premature in sending out sledging parties, and had "got cocky with the good weather," which Stillwell was "fully convinced is purely freak."[9] He would be proved right in his premonition.

The short treks would provide some sledging practice for the nine men, but there was no certainty they would be the same men embarking on the long summer treks, or that they would be in the same sledging parties. Whetter and Close were particularly unsuited to be participants on a long trek. They left early on the morning of September 12, with Mawson giving Madigan some farewell words of encouragement along with a bottle of port and some chocolate to celebrate Close's forthcoming birthday. Hunter watched with amusement as Close took an hour longer than the others to get ready, being "as slow as an old draught horse." Madigan was keen to set out and to be doing something. However, he found that "the two deadly weeks … were the hardest, most dangerous and most uncomfortable I have experienced." After 15 miles of man-hauling the sledge across blue ice, they encountered "terrible sastrugi," ice formations shaped by the wind, which continued for the next 35 miles. The wind was 70 to 80 miles an hour, and the temperature averaged -20°F, which showed up the inadequacies in their equipment and made frostbite a constant problem. The rheumatic Close was particularly affected by frostbite, with his hands in such a state that Madigan had to help dress him. Madigan had problems of his own. His hands and feet were frostbitten, as well as an eyelid that caused his eye to close for two days.[10]

All the men were out of condition, having been largely confined to the hut for so many months. Even Madigan, whose duties took him outside each day, found that he had put on about six kilograms since leaving Hobart.[11] The other two parties fared much worse. Mertz, Ninnis, and Murphy were forced to return with a torn tent after covering 18 miles and fearing that they might be swept away in their sleeping bags by the wind, while Webb, Stillwell, and McLean had given up and returned after covering just 11½ miles. "Sledging now looks [more] off than ever," observed Hunter.[12] When the first two parties returned early with their tents torn, Mawson began to have serious concerns about Madigan's party. On September 18, he worried that they "must be having a bad time as their tent is so frail." Mawson knew the tent well, since he had helped to prepare it for the trek. When they had not returned after twelve days, Mawson wrote in his diary that

"We must try and get out along their trail in a day or two if they don't turn up." He told Hunter that he was particularly concerned because "none of them have had much experience."[13]

It wasn't only their lack of experience that posed a problem. At forty or more years of age and wracked by rheumatism, Close was too old for the challenges of even a 50-mile trek at that time of the year, while Madigan's opinion of Whetter as being both lazy and selfish was borne out by his behavior on the trek. "Whetter disgusted me," wrote Madigan. "I knew Mawson's opinion of him before we started but I had made the best of him; we all knew him to be lazy, indifferent and selfish, but I thought he would be all right sledging." According to Madigan, Whetter "hardly pulled at all, it was difficult to get him to do anything, he ate greedily and … he got no frost bites as he hardly ever took his fingers out of his mitts." They were lucky to survive the experience. Madigan was determined to achieve the objectives that Mawson had set him, and drove his two companions hard. When they stopped for lunch, he only allowed them to eat dry pemmican and plasmon biscuit in the lee of the sledge, rather than erect the tent so they could melt ice and have a hot drink.[14] While this helped to increase the distance they covered each day, it left them seriously dehydrated.

Madigan had never known such a thirst, and took to eating small amounts of ice in the afternoons, even though "only a little can be taken at a time and it reduces the vitality greatly and is condemned as a sledging practice." Through a supreme effort by Madigan, the hapless trio did reach the 50-mile mark, where Madigan set up a depot flag and left a cache containing a week's provisions for three men and a gallon of kerosene. Then they pitched their tent for the night, only to find the next morning that there was "a furious blizzard raging." They were forced to remain in their wet sleeping bag for a day and a night, with Madigan praying for the weather to clear as they had only two weeks' food to last the return journey. "This was the worst time," wrote Madigan, "shivering cold, fifty miles from the Hut, the tent likely to go any moment, tearing in several places."[15] Had the tent been torn to shreds, they might not have made it back alive.

Madigan's prayers were answered. The weather cleared, and they could make a start back. It was a testing time, with the tent badly torn by the wind one night, and a shortcut finding them among "serac ice, all tumbled and crevassed and very difficult to negotiate." They eventually reached the sanctuary of Aladdin's Cave, where they restored their spirits with food and hot drinks. "I never felt so relieved and content," wrote Madigan, who had experienced just one "calm day and night" on the two-week trek. "We were safe, we had done our reconnaissance, laid a depot, taken hypsometric heights; all was well."[16] But the experience had taken a toll on Madigan's self-assurance. His daily excursions to Observation Hill had given him the confidence to move about in blizzard conditions. Now he was "sick of the wind and snow, and afraid of it, and wished never to go sledging in such weather again." However, once he resumed his daily observations, he regained his confidence "in this dreadful region, or what of it I had, for truly it is a god-forsaken country."[17]

The success of Madigan's party was celebrated by Mawson with "a great oration at the Hut and a special dinner and toast." Strangely, though, Mawson made only the most perfunctory mention of the three treks in his diary. He had been expecting, perhaps even hoping, that Madigan, Whetter, and Close would fail due to the strength of the wind and the frailness of their tent. Instead, Madigan's party was the only one to fulfill his instructions to the letter, and the tent held together until the second-last night, when a strong wind finally tore it to pieces. The treks had been a sobering experience for Mawson. According to Madigan, it "postponed any chances of early sledging," and ensured that "no farther attempts on long journeys will be made for some weeks."[18]

Preparations for the sledging season went on nonetheless. By early October, all the sledging rations had been divided up and packed, with most of them taken to Aladdin's Cave. The expeditioners had done about as much as they could in preparation, and most were exhausted. Mawson had driven them hard, although not always effectively, and frustrations were boiling over. Mawson had not taken them into his confidence, some were tired of him acting as a martinet, and a few were sick of the whole expedition. Whetter brought matters to a head when Mawson criticized him for knocking off work to read a book. According to Stillwell, it was Mawson's behavior, rather than Whetter's, that "came to a crisis." Indeed, the argument could just as easily have been started by Close or Murphy or Webb, or one of the other men to whom Mawson had taken a dislike. In Mawson's view, it was Whetter who was at fault. Whetter had tackled Mawson back in June, complaining over breakfast that they were working too hard and should have the afternoons to themselves. Mawson had allowed those comments to pass, but he became increasingly upset about a few of the men who he believed were taking longer than necessary to do their allotted tasks so they would not be given more work. He had been unable to change their behavior.

After Mawson instructed Whetter to dig the ice out of the air-tractor hangar, the simmering tension boiled over into a raging argument, with Mawson and Whetter accusing each other of being "a bloody fool." Mawson was "wild" and called Whetter into his room, hoping to persuade him to back down. But it was Mawson who caved in. Whetter told him that the discontent with his leadership was universal and that there was "not a man on this expedition who would come with you again." In the wake of these home truths, a temporarily contrite Mawson told the assembled men after dinner that he was "sorry if at any times he had ruffled our tempers," and announced they could now have Sundays off work and be free each day after 4:00 p.m. to do what they liked, whether it was reading or writing up their diaries. It was something that "he ought to have done long ago," observed Madigan, who had always felt guilty writing up his diary "knowing that the Old Man is worrying round and hinting that I should be doing something else." Mawson also assured them that he would not personally profit if the expedition made a surplus and, unlike the men on Shackleton's expedition, they all would be paid.[19]

Despite some reservations, there was a great sense of anticipation about starting the treks. It would get them out of the confines of the hut, and the daily routine of domestic tasks, and into the wilderness, where they would have to rely upon their physical prowess in the battle against the elements. The routine was broken up by special occasions, whether it was a mid-winter dinner or a celebration of someone's birthday. On October 6, it was time to celebrate Mertz's birthday, and Madigan was cook for the day. Although the main course of the dinner was boiled cans of jugged hare and vegetables, Madigan topped it off with mince pies and trifle. "The trifle was the 'piece de resistance,'" wrote Madigan, "it consisted of Vienna brusks, a biscuit affair, as ground mass, with [a fortified wine] liberally poured over it, and then a custard of the ordinary type." Mawson contributed a pudding made by Paquita, which was followed by chocolates, caramels, biscuits, and cheese, and then port and cigars. "It was a most enjoyable evening," observed Madigan, "and bucked us up tremendously."[20] Several days later, a grand opera entitled *The Washerwoman's Secret* was staged, with McLean playing the female role. "We roared the whole time," observed Madigan, "for it was excruciatingly funny."[21]

On October 8, Mawson called Madigan into his room to discuss his tentative plans for the summer sledging. If the air tractor worked, Mawson planned to have charge of it and to take Hurley and Bickerton with him on a march to the south, presumably to the South Magnetic Pole, which he had failed to reach on the Shackleton expedition. The innovative air tractor, the presence of Hurley as photographer, and the redemptive struggle to reach the South Magnetic Pole would ensure that this trek was the one that captured public attention. Although Webb was the expedition's magnetician, and the obvious choice to lead the southern trek, he had fallen out of favor with Mawson after challenging his authority and questioning his ability. According to Madigan, Webb was the least liked of all the men. Hunter described Webb as "somewhat peculiar; at times he is almost arrogant & bombastic & bad tempered, yet at other times he is most obliging and good natured

— a queer mixture." Mawson now proposed that Webb take charge of the eastern trek with Ninnis and Mertz rather than go south, while Bage, Whetter, and Stillwell also would go east but take a more coastal route. As for Madigan, he would take charge of the western party with Correll and McLean, while the six remaining men would make short coastal forays from the hut. It all depended on the air tractor working. If it didn't work, then the southern journey wouldn't be the great success that Mawson was hoping for. In that case, Webb would take charge of the southern party with Hurley and McLean; Mawson would go east with Ninnis and Mertz; Bage would lead the eastern coastal party with Whetter and Stillwell; and Madigan would go west with Bickerton and Correll. Mawson agreed with Madigan that no long treks would be possible "till the weather greatly improves, and God alone knows when that will be."[22]

The omens didn't look promising. Rather than the conditions improving, the men began to experience some of the worst weather they had ever had at Commonwealth Bay. Wind was combining with dense snowdrift to tear at the hut and push over their equipment. With wind gusts measured at 200 miles an hour, the main wireless mast came crashing down, and was left "a mass of wreckage." Mawson's hopes of getting the story of his expedition out to the world seemed doomed. And it did not bode well, either, for the long sledging trips that were planned to start within weeks. "The wind gets worse and worse," moaned Madigan, "will it never cease? Anyone out sledging today would certainly have been utterly destroyed."[23] Moreover, the dogs were not in a good condition, due to the lack of seal meat. Mertz suspected that the dogs, which were often let loose, had begun to hunt down the few penguins that were starting to return to Commonwealth Bay. Because there was "no more seal meat for the dogs," wrote Mertz, "they are hungry and eat everything they find in their path."[24]

However, things soon improved. The first Adélie penguin was sighted on October 12, leaping onto the ice "in a furious hurricane." McLean saw it behind a rock, sheltering from the wind and making frequent forays into the open, only to be deterred each time by the wind. When McLean approached, the penguin immediately launched an attack on him. With a block of chocolate being the prize for the first penguin captured, McLean carried the hapless bird to the hut to be "pithed and skinned," and its entrails examined for parasites. More penguins and the first of the seals appeared over the following days, with Mawson reporting on October 19 that "Adélie Penguin skinning was in full swing." Although he noticed them copulating in their rookery, it was to be *coitus interruptus* for a good number of them. The return of seals and penguins to Commonwealth Bay was regarded as a sign of better weather to come. When a single Emperor penguin turned up among the thousands of Adélies, the first Emperor they had ever seen, it was quickly pinned down by three men, then pithed and skinned. Madigan fried some of the flesh for dinner, "rolling it in flour and onion powder first."[25] Despite the penguins' arrival and their breeding, the wind was still too strong for sledging, reaching 85 miles an hour on October 16, and "shaking the Hut in an alarming manner."[26]

Final adjustments were made to the sledges, with Mawson letting it be known that they should be on the trail by the first week of November. Considering the prevailing weather, Stillwell was doubtful, noting that the men now regarded such statements by Mawson "with incredulity. He says so much that he apparently doesn't mean."[27] Mawson was so intent on getting the parties away and having a full two months' sledging before the return of the *Aurora* in mid-January that he wanted them to set out almost regardless of the weather. The success of the expedition depended upon it. Only if the conditions remained too terrible would he contemplate any delay. This would be "a serious mistake," thought the normally loyal Bage, who was convinced that it would be wiser to limit their summer journeys to a month at the most if the conditions did not improve. If Bage had his way, they would not leave the huts until mid-December. He also harbored other misgivings about Mawson's plans. During the winter, Bage had been helping Bickerton repair the air tractor so that it would be ready for the summer trekking. Now he was dismayed to hear Mawson suggest that the machine might not be used at all. Mawson was concerned that the weather had to be almost perfectly calm before it would work, and he didn't want to leave "3 men waiting behind for absolutely good weather." However, Bage and Bickerton were confident of the air tractor's potential, with Bage arguing in his diary that "a few days good weather with the [air tractor] will do infinitely more than 2 months bad weather with man haulage." Not wanting to challenge Mawson, both Bage and Bickerton kept their thoughts to themselves.[28]

Despite the reservations of Bage and Stillwell, Madigan could hardly wait to get out of the hut. After his 100-mile reconnaissance trek with Close and Whetter, he had been lucky to escape with just the loss of the toenail on one of his big toes and a bad case of exhaustion. Had his tent not held out, Madigan and his companions might well have lost their lives. It was more than a week after his return before Madigan felt sufficiently confident to venture outside again. By October 6, in the relative comfort of Hyde Park Corner, Madigan heard Ninnis explain how he was counting down the one hundred days until the arrival of the *Aurora* on January 15. That thought gave Madigan an added boost. By October 11, he was writing of being "keen as a knife to get away sledging again. It will make those ninety-five days pass so much more quickly." The arrival of the *Aurora* would bring long-awaited news and the beginning of their return home. Madigan thought that "the happiest moment of the Expedition will be when the Hut is sighted after a long and successful sledging journey, especially if the ship is in the Bay; this would be supreme, just to tumble on board and read letters." He was already packing his belongings for the trip home.[29]

Before they set off on their treks, however, Mawson decided to ditch his original plan to lead the southern party. He had lost confidence in the air tractor, which he had wanted to use on the southern journey. Without the tractor, the southern journey was unlikely to achieve its aim of reaching the South Magnetic Pole, so Mawson decided instead to take the dogs and to lead the eastern party with Mertz and Ninnis. He calculated that the use of the dogs would ensure his journey was the longest and most noteworthy. The southern party would be led instead by Bage, with Hurley and Webb, who Madigan feared had "gone a bit off his head." The western party would be led by Bickerton, who would take the air tractor if it could be got to work. If it didn't, Bickerton would man-haul the sledges with Whetter and Murphy. Instead of going west, as Mawson had originally planned, Madigan would lead another eastern party along the coast, "but not to go so far [as Mawson], and take a dip circle and do magnetic work." Madigan was happy to do the scientific work, but was frustrated by his trek not being longer. Rather than announcing the change of plan generally, Mawson took some of the men in turn into his room to have what Stillwell disparaged as a "solemn secret conclave."[30] It meant that the hut was awash with rumors for several days, which didn't help their morale.

Although the plans were still not definite, Madigan set about practicing his latitude and longitude observations. On one longitude observation on October 23, Mawson acted as his assistant. Madigan was scathing about his competence, reporting that he "tried to work it out tonight, but does not seem to know the first thing about it." Although Madigan helped Mawson with the calculations, Mawson gave up in frustration and retired to bed after making several mistakes. Nevertheless, Madigan now claimed that he got on "very well with the Old Man, I like him very much, though very few do, I fear."[31] Despite their apparent feelings toward Mawson, Madigan thought they all supported the final changes to the plans.[32] Stillwell, however, certainly didn't. All through winter, he had been led to believe he would be navigating on one of the longer journeys, only to now find himself relegated to one of the short supporting parties. Webb was also disappointed not to be leading the southern party, after earlier having been assured he would be doing so.[33]

The three principal journeys would comprise the southern party of Bage, Webb, and Hurley; the eastern inland party of Mawson, Mertz, and Ninnis; and the eastern coastal party of Madigan, Correll, and McLean. The two eastern parties would be supported during the initial stage of their treks by Stillwell, Close, and Hodgeman, who would take some of their load for the first week. Bage's southern party would be supported for the first two weeks by Murphy, Hunter, and Laseron, who would take some of their load and establish a depot for Bage's return journey. Murphy had to be back in time to join a fourth journey at the beginning of December, which Bickerton would lead along the coast to the west with Murphy and Whetter, and making use of the air tractor. They were instructed by Mawson to wait until December, ostensibly because the wind was expected to be sufficiently moderate by then to allow the use of the tractor. But the late departure put Bickerton out of contention for covering the longest distance. Apart from Bickerton, the other parties were expected to start out "for better or for worse" by November 6, with the men wagering pieces of chocolate as to which party would go the farthest. As part of the preparation, and to save weight, Mertz and Ninnis began grilling the seal meat they planned to take as food for the dogs. According to their calculations, only two dogs were expected to make it back alive, with "the rest [being] killed for food for the others as the load gets lighter."[34]

Once again, the weather intervened, and the first departure didn't occur until November 7. Murphy's support party was the first to get away, adjusting the sledge straps around their hips as they put their heads down into the strong wind. Bage's misgivings about departing in November were immediately borne out. After just three miles, the wind was too strong for Murphy's party to go on. Abandoning their sledge on the slope, they picked their way back to the security of the hut, from where they left again late the next morning, followed soon after by the parties of Madigan and Stillwell. For Madigan, it was an emotional farewell to men he might never see again. They were also ambivalent about leaving the hut on a day when sledging conditions seemed less than ideal. However, after some pressure from Mawson, Stillwell reported that they "yielded and decided to start and it really did fine up considerably and was not at all bad at start."[35] Their caution was understandable.

The two-week reconnaissance trek in September had alerted them all to the risks they would be taking and the possibility that one or more of them might not return. On the earlier trek, Madigan had pushed himself and his companions to the limit to ensure they reached their goal of 50 miles. Now, on this longer journey, Madigan intended to be "much more cautious" and to take care about keeping his clothing dry. "I don't mind tackling wind," he wrote, "but blizzards are beyond the pale." It was presumably because of the risks he was facing that Madigan found the farewell in the hut strangely affecting. He was annoyed with himself when he "could not keep tears back" as he said goodbye to Bickerton. In his diary, Bage kept his emotions in check, simply assuring his loved ones in a farewell letter that "a trip like this is a great thing & an experience that I wouldn't have missed for anything."[36] It was the sentiment of a soldier heading into battle, and it was not only going to be waged against the elements. There was also an unspoken battle between the younger men, such as Madigan, Mertz, Bage, and Ninnis, and the experienced Mawson. Both battles would be played out on the ice over the following two months.

CHAPTER EIGHT

Into the White Wilderness

The morning of November 8, 1912, didn't look good for sledging, with the wind blowing a white wall of snow off the plateau. But it improved as the day wore on, and three parties managed to depart for the unknown. First off were Murphy, Hunter, and Laseron, whose abortive departure the previous day had seen them abandon their sledge halfway up the icy slope toward Aladdin's Cave when the snowdrift made it impossible to go farther. Now they were off again, to set up food depots for Bage's southern party. Murphy's support party was followed soon after by the eastern coastal party of Madigan, McLean, and Correll and the eastern support party of Stillwell, Close, and Hodgeman. Looking on with his camera was Frank Hurley, who filmed Madigan finishing his farewells and Mertz harnessing a dog team to take Madigan's sledge up the difficult first two miles. Temporarily released from the task of man-hauling their own sledge, McLean and Correll assisted with the hauling of Stillwell's sledge while Madigan went out in front with Bickerton, who had come along for the walk.

Having someone walk out in front of a dog sledge provided a guide for the dogs. But Stillwell became annoyed when Madigan continued to walk in front "in a high-handed fashion," rather than taking a turn in the sledge harness. It was an early sign of the stresses that could poison relationships on sledging trips. Stillwell became even more annoyed when Bickerton returned to the hut and Madigan continued to walk out in front, and later made a "self-satisfied gloat that he had had the best of it."[1] It was not a good way to begin, as the two parties would have to travel together for the next week or so.

Mawson, Mertz, and Ninnis didn't leave the comfort of the hut until November 10, and it wasn't until the eve of his departure that Mawson scribbled out a page of instructions for the men left behind. Among other things, they were told not to let the dogs kill the penguins and to break open the case of whisky only if there was a "medical necessity." Any emperor penguins that arrived were to be pithed, and any rare seals were to be killed and skinned for museums.[2] Mawson had waited until November 10 for the weather to clear and for the other parties to have time to move on from their first stopping place, Aladdin's Cave, so that he could occupy it. Mertz didn't mind the delay, as three of his bitches were about to give birth and it would be awkward if this happened on the trek. He used the time to collect penguin eggs, which he made into omelettes and feasted on for dinner and the following breakfast. With the morning of November 10 being fine and relatively still, it was time to take their leave. Mertz and Ninnis rounded up the seventeen dogs and strapped them to the three sledges. Before leaving, Mawson scribbled a farewell letter to Paquita, in which he assured her that he had "two good companions, Dr Mertz and Lieut. Ninnis," and that it was "unlikely that any harm will happen to us." However, if it did, Mawson wanted her to know that he had "truly loved" her.[3]

Although Madigan had left two days before him, Mawson expected to meet up with him and a support party at the food depot that had been established by Mertz and Ninnis in September, about 18½ miles from the hut. After that, Mawson and Madigan would go their separate ways, with Mawson intending to "rapidly cross the coastal highlands to the south of the tracks of Madigan's party, and to pick up the coast beyond where they could expect to reach."[4] In other words, he expected to go faster and farther than Madigan, and to return with greater knowledge of the hitherto-unseen region. In particular, he wanted to reach that part of the coast where Scott's *Terra Nova* had recently discovered new stretches of the Antarctic coastline west of Cape Adare. It was about 350 miles away. Depending on what he found, Mawson might then be able to claim that Antarctica really was a single continent rather than two or more landmasses, as some geographers still maintained. It was the world's last great geographic question. If he resolved it, Mawson could well outdo anything that Scott or Amundsen did at the South Pole. At least, that was his plan.

As we have seen, the air tractor and the wireless telegraph had been Mawson's other intended trump cards in the battle for public attention against the competing exploits of Scott and Amundsen. Both innovations had been disappointments. Although he still harbored hopes of overshadowing Scott and Amundsen, his main rivals now were the younger men leading the three other principal treks. Australian army officer Robert Bage was heading south toward the South Magnetic Pole with magnetician Eric Webb and photographer Frank Hurley. Were they to reach it, the trio would divert attention from whatever Mawson managed to achieve. However, it was still generally believed that Edgeworth David and Mawson had already reached the magnetic pole in 1909, although Mawson knew he had not. Unknown to Mawson, Webb knew of his dark secret, after having been told by colleagues in New Zealand who had analyzed their figures and concluded that they "had not reached the magnetic pole's area of oscillation." Webb calculated that they might claim the prize for themselves if they could journey 400 miles, which he estimated would take them over and past the pole, thereby proving beyond doubt that they had reached the elusive feature. They might be able to do this if they had dogs to help with the hauling, since the polar plateau was ideal for dog sledging. But Mawson had reserved the dogs for his own use, which made the task of reaching the South Magnetic Pole almost impossible in the sixty-seven days before the *Aurora* arrived to take them all back to Australia.[5]

The presence of Hurley and his photographic equipment might have given Bage's journey a winning edge if cinema audiences were to see more of his journey than Mawson's. Although there would be no cinematograph on Mawson's sledge, Mawson made sure that Hurley filmed his departure, and he could always adopt appropriate poses for the cinematograph to represent his eastern journey upon his return to the hut. While the 60-pound cinematograph weighed down Bage's sledge and slowed his team's progress, Mawson took a much lighter still camera on his own journey among the mountains and glaciers of the coastal region. He was likely to return with much more dramatic photographs than Hurley could take on the largely featureless polar plateau. Moreover, with Webb taking magnetic observations along the way, and Hurley stopping to arrange set-piece shots of the journey, Mawson could be confident that Bage was unlikely to get very far, and certainly not reach the always-shifting South Magnetic Pole. Mawson's main challenge was not likely to come from Bage's party.

Neither was it likely to come from Frank Bickerton, whose western party was powered by the air tractor that Bickerton had spent so much time tinkering with during the winter. Although it was meant to be Mawson's secret weapon in the race with Scott and Amundsen, Mawson had seen enough of the machine to know that the patched-up vehicle would not accelerate Bickerton's journey. It couldn't operate at all in a strong headwind, and it worked best on a surface of firm snow — conditions that were not often experienced in the region. Mawson added two additional handicaps, instructing Bickerton not to leave the hut until December 1, supposedly because it would allow the weather to moderate sufficiently for the safe use of the air tractor, and appointing the lazy and incompetent Whetter to Bickerton's party. These moves by Mawson effectively ended the grandiose idea that Bickerton had harbored, which was to continue west until he reached Wild's base or was picked up by the *Aurora*. Such a hazardous journey would have eclipsed Mawson's, and Mawson had ordered him not to do it. Forcing Bickerton to wait so long to depart, so that he would have only six weeks to do his journey, made sure that Mawson's written instructions would have to be followed.[6] For the first 50 miles, Bickerton was going to be traveling along the same route that Madigan had taken in September. The *Aurora* had also made one voyage along that coastline when it had taken Wild to establish the western base, and it would be making another such voyage when Wild was picked up in early 1913. As a result, the major coastal features would already have been discovered by a combination of Madigan and the men on the deck of the *Aurora*. So there was little original work for Bickerton to do.

There was always a possibility that Wild and the men of the western base might achieve something sufficiently newsworthy to overshadow anything that Mawson might do. But that was unlikely. Wild was working in an area that had already been looked over by the Germans, and was going there mainly to set an eastward limit to any territorial claims that Filchner's German expedition might be able to establish. Those activities were not likely to capture public attention, particularly as Mawson would have charge of compiling the official account and would ensure that his own journey was seen as the preeminent one. Nevertheless, the success of the expedition depended upon each of the journeys being successful in its own way. On his return to Australia, Mawson would need to be able to declare that the various treks had made the whole expedition the most scientifically significant of all time, which is what he had told Scott it would be. But Mawson also needed to make his particular journey stand out above the others, which is why he kept changing the journey that he intended to make. After initially wanting to head south with Madigan, his final decision to head east put him in direct competition with the man he had wanted as his navigator. Madigan was the one man who had the ability, the physique, the competitive edge, and the motivation to outdo Mawson. In response to this threat, Mawson would rely on dogs to help make his journey the longest and the most scientifically important. This is why he chose Mertz and

Ninnis — the two men who had been in charge of the dogs ever since the *Aurora* took its leave of London — as his companions for the journey.

Of the three sledges on Mawson's eastern trek, one was packed with dog food, made up of seal meat and pemmican, while the other carried the empty third sledge, along with tent bags, clothing, and instruments. He planned to pick up most of the food they would need from Aladdin's Cave, and more from the depot established by Ninnis and Mertz 18½ miles from the hut, where he also expected to meet Stillwell's support party with additional food. Mawson had no intimation that the way in which the food and equipment was divided between the sledges — with dog food on one sledge and human food on another — would have terrible implications for their survival. He was preoccupied with the condition of the dogs, with two of them still heavily pregnant when it came time to leave the hut. Mawson had expected the dogs to have whelped and to do their bit in pulling the sledges. Instead, both had to be carried on the sledges, and thereby added to the total weight of about 1,500 pounds that the other dogs had to haul.[7] Most of that weight was food.

Mawson had put a lot of thought in deciding what to take as the daily rations for each man. According to Hunter, Mawson "sought the advice of all previous polar expeditions," which meant that he copied Shackleton's rations and read the accounts of other expeditions.[8] In Mawson's view, he needed to ensure that the sledging parties had sufficient calories to sustain them when doing strenuous work in the sometimes intense cold. And the calories would be provided by a combination of protein, carbohydrates, fats, and sugars. The main foods were pemmican (dried meat powder and fat), plasmon biscuits, cocoa compound, sugar, butter, and Glaxo. Vitamins not having been discovered, he could, of course, not make any provision to include them. Neither did he make any provision to guard against scurvy. As for the dogs, they would be fed partly on seal meat — which Mertz had roasted to reduce its water content and hence its weight — as well as blubber and pemmican. Mawson packed 700 pounds of dog food on the sledges, but did not specify what proportion was seal meat, blubber, or pemmican. They also would be fed on each other, with Mawson planning to kill the dogs one by one and to feed them to the survivors until there were just two left. He hoped that the last two dogs would be sufficient to haul the then lightly loaded sledge over the final distance to the hut.[9]

Bage, Webb, and Hurley were man-hauling, and left some hours before Mawson. Bage would be assisted for the first fortnight by Murphy, Laseron, and Hunter, who were already ahead of them and would help haul their food and establish one or more depots along the route to ensure their safe return. Although Bage's party was also assisted by Bickerton up the treacherous icy slope, they soon heard the cries of Mawson and his companions urging on their dogs as they scrambled furiously to ascend the difficult surface. In his sledging journal, Mawson reported how Bage and his helpers were "making good progress manhauling," but that he and his companions with their dogs nevertheless "caught up to and passed Bage's party," and arrived at Aladdin's Cave half an hour before them.[10] The cavern had been occupied for the previous two days of difficult weather by the parties led by Madigan, Stillwell, and Murphy, but was now empty. Mertz regarded the calm weather they were experiencing as "a good omen for our journey."[11]

The parties of Madigan and Stillwell had just left together. They had arrived at Aladdin's Cave on November 8 to find Murphy's party preparing to leave for the south to support Bage. Madigan intended to move on himself the following morning, but the worsening snowdrift convinced him that "it was not worthwhile to go on; the crevasses would have been dangerous and the course hard to keep" in a blizzard. Murphy decided likewise, which created something of an accommodation problem. It was solved by the toss of a coin that saw Madigan and four others sheltering in the cavern, while McLean joined Stillwell's party in a tent alongside. It may have been snugger in the cavern, but Madigan and his companions were lucky to emerge alive. As they smoked away on their pipes and took turns reading aloud from Owen Wister's groundbreaking western novel, *The Virginian: A Horseman of the Plains*, the blizzard was quietly dumping a solid plug of snow across the entrance. Only when they had trouble lighting their matches and began to suffer headaches did they notice that the blocked entrance was starving them of oxygen. Luckily, they still had sufficient energy to dig themselves out.[12] The close call made Madigan even more anxious to get away and begin his journey proper.

On November 10, as soon as he had cooked breakfast for the men in the cavern, Madigan left the relative security of Aladdin's Cave for the uncertainties of a region hitherto unseen by human eyes. The day began with a 50-mile-an-hour wind and just a light snowdrift. It was so comfortable for sledging that Madigan didn't don the Burberry hood that he had packed for additional protection against the cold. While Murphy's party headed south to establish another depot and await the arrival of Bage's party, Madigan and Stillwell's parties pulled their heavily laden sledges eastward, with Madigan noting in his diary how Stillwell's group kept lagging behind, and how he and McLean went back on separate occasions to help them haul their heavier load. Stillwell's sledge was packed with food and equipment for his own party's short trek, along with food for the parties of Madigan and Mawson. By the time they halted for lunch, the sun was shining, the wind was abating, and the drift had disappeared. Usually, a tent would be erected at lunchtime so water could be boiled for drinks and food heated up, but Madigan's eagerness to make progress meant that he had no time for such luxuries. He would use the same methods that he had used on the reconnaissance journey, snatching handfuls of snow and eating a small portion of plasmon biscuit in the lee of the sledge. As a result, complained Stillwell, they became "very hungry and thirsty in [the] afternoon."[13]

When it came time to camp, the visibility was so clear that Madigan could see the arrival of another party at Aladdin's Cave, just over five miles away. Grabbing a pair of binoculars, he tried to see whether there were any dogs among them, which would indicate that Mawson's party would soon overtake him. Not being able to discern any, Madigan assumed it must be Bage's party.[14] In fact, it was both Bage and Mawson. Conscious that Mawson had the advantage of dogs, Madigan was anxious to get away early the following morning, and roused a surprised Stillwell out of his sleeping bag at 6:15 a.m. It did Madigan no good, as he had to wait for Close, the oldest man on the trek, to finish getting ready. It could take Close half an hour just to get out of his sleeping bag. Stillwell acknowledged that Madigan's party "are certainly much smarter than we are," and hoped to get his own party "moving more early in future," which meant that he "must wake up first."[15]

Eager to catch up with Murphy and not waste any good weather, Bage only stopped long enough at Aladdin's Cave for a meal, while Hurley took "cinematographic views" of Mawson, Mertz, and Ninnis pretending to set off with their sledges in pursuit of Madigan and Stillwell. The success of the whole expedition could well depend on the stirring story that Mawson was able to weave with words, pictures, and film. But the dogs refused to play their part, and raced off with one of the sledges, damaging the all-important sledge-meter in the process. It was the sledge-meter that kept count on the distance they traveled, which provided an added check on their location. Once the cinematograph was packed away, Mawson went back into the relative comfort of Aladdin's Cave while Bage and his companions hauled their sledges off toward the polar plateau. "Our job is the Magnetic Polar Area if possible," wrote Bage in his diary. And he did believe it was possible, if they had "perfect weather," noting that the magnetic readings at the hut indicated that it was "not more than 400 m[iles]" away.[16]

Rather than taking advantage of the brief burst of good weather, Mawson waited until the following day to pack some of the stored food onto his sledge.[17] He was confident that the dogs would allow him to catch up with Madigan and Stillwell. In the morning, he was away early. He had to find Madigan and Stillwell, since Stillwell's support party was carrying 230 pounds of food meant for him.

The three groups planned to meet at the 18½-mile food depot. Once there, Mawson would take on the food from Stillwell, who would return to the hut by way of the coast, making observations and collecting samples as he went.[18] When that food was added to Mawson's three sledges, they would be weighed down with 1,709 pounds of food and equipment. Mawson had calculated that this would be sufficient food for their anticipated eight-week trek. It was an improvised plan borne out of desperate necessity. Because of the bad weather over the previous ten months, Mawson had been unable to establish more than two caches of food along the route, which left him dependent for almost all the coming journey on what the sledges could carry. He didn't think to use the additional men he had at his disposal from the abandoned eastern base to establish food caches farther along the route of his return journey. There would be no penguins or seals to be captured and eaten on Mawson's inland route. Everything would depend on the weather and the topography allowing Mawson to complete his trek within his anticipated time frame. There would be little margin of safety.

His journey didn't begin well. The wind was blowing at 40 miles an hour when Mawson set out from Aladdin's Cave after breakfast on November 11, and it became steadily worse. Clear skies turned to thick cloud by noon, and the snowdrift thickened. It was a good test of Mawson's navigation abilities, which Madigan had found wanting when he had tried to teach him back at the hut. After a few miles, Mawson concluded that they were going too far to the south, and changed to what he thought was a more easterly direction for "about two miles." In fact, as Mertz noted in his diary, they saw Bage's party in front of them, which meant that they were heading south rather than east. Only one day out, and it seems that Mawson was lost. Moreover, they were now traveling on sastrugi — protrusions of ice of various heights that were difficult to see in snowdrift. The high winds and a fog-like drift made it too dangerous to go on.[19]

The drift only got thicker, and the men spent the next day

in their tent, boiling up food and patching their bedding and clothes. A break in the weather on November 13 allowed Mawson to reach the 18½-mile mark, but there was no sign of the food depot, or of Madigan and Stillwell. Mawson had miscalculated his location and the direction he needed to follow. He was in a difficult predicament. He needed the food from the depot and from Stillwell if he was going to ensure that his trek was the longest. But the weather worsened over the following two days as they waited for Madigan's party and Stillwell's support sledge. This time, the wind became much fiercer, reaching 80 miles an hour, making Mawson so fearful of losing his tent that he took all the valuable items into his one-man sleeping bag. The noise of the wind and the flapping of the tent on his head left him unable to sleep, while the tied-up dogs were buried beneath the snow and had to be dug out. The previous months spent in the hut with little opportunity for exercise was taking its toll on the men. They were "all feeling pretty rotten," wrote Mawson, with "Ninnis quite faint at noon." As for Mertz, he complained of backache because he was "not accustomed to sleeping on hard ice and snow." The days in the tent "makes life unbearable," wrote Mertz. As they waited, one of the dogs had pups, which were promptly "eaten by her or by other dogs."[20]

Frustrated by his failure to find the 18½-mile depot, and by the non-appearance of Madigan and Stillwell, Mawson decided on November 16 to leave his loaded sledges and head back to Aladdin's Cave with the empty sledge to take on supplies that he had been expecting to get from Stillwell. However, his party had barely gone a mile when Mawson saw Madigan and Stillwell's parties in the distance. Hurriedly retrieving their loaded sledges, they went to meet them. Madigan realized that Mawson had gone off-course, which had left him unable to find the depot. Madigan was desperate to go on alone, and did not want to waste time traveling with Mawson. Like Mawson, he and Stillwell had been stopped for days by the blizzards. In fact, as Stillwell lamented, they had been forced to spend five and a half of the first eight days in their sleeping bags, unable to continue their journey because of the weather. Madigan had the added burden of having been slowed down by Stillwell, and was anxious to get away so that he could do his planned 300-mile trek. In the same way that he had led the only party that was able to complete the 50-mile reconnaissance trek in September, he wanted to make his name by being the only one to traverse 600 miles, there and back.[21] But first the weather had to clear.

Although Madigan was desperate to get going, he and Stillwell assumed that the snowdrift would continue the next day. Stillwell explained in his diary how they consequently slept in on November 17 and didn't notice until they emerged from their tents at about 8:00 a.m. that the wind had dropped away and that the snowdrift had disappeared.[22] It was "a real Antarctic sledging day," wrote Madigan, and they had wasted several hours of it. The frustrated Madigan made no mention in his diary of his own responsibility for this, and instead blamed "the Old Man" for being slow to get going. Mawson did take the time to check his watch with Madigan, presumably to discover how he had gone off-course, and he took 200 pounds of food and three cans of kerosene from Stillwell. One of Mawson's party — either Ninnis or Mertz — also shot and butchered the dog that had whelped. With all the extra weight he was taking, Mawson didn't want to carry the dog on the sledge as well. So it was "cut up into about 24 rations," which included its seven pups, only for Mawson to find that the other dogs were reluctant to eat his offering.[23]

While they were together, Madigan may have told Mawson of an accident that had befallen young Percy Correll the day after they left Aladdin's Cave. Madigan was walking out in front when he crossed a crevasse that was "about three feet wide at the top and had a thin ice bridge." He did not think to warn McLean and Correll, who were following on behind, roped together and hauling the sledge. To his horror, Madigan "heard a call from Dad [McLean] and looked round and saw no sign of Correll." He had fallen through the ice bridge and was hanging by his harness six feet below, with the sledge overhanging the edge of the 60-foot-deep crevasse. Madigan and McLean were able slowly to pull the shocked Correll to the surface, but it had been a close call. It seems they had become sanguine about crevasses after crossing hundreds without much incident. "I always test them first," noted a now-chastened Madigan.[24] Even if Mawson was told of this near miss, it cannot be certain whether it would have averted the terrible events that would later befall his party.

On the night before Mawson went his own way, there was another opportunity for last-minute leave-taking and socializing. "Everyone was excited at the prospect of the weeks ahead," wrote Madigan, with the "mystery and charm of the 'unknown' [having] taken a strange hold on us." Madigan's description of that evening, later published as part of Mawson's *The Home of the Blizzard*, implied that Mawson held himself aloof from the others. While Mawson remained in his tent, Mertz and Ninnis went to their friend Madigan's tent for a final merry time, with a German student song by Mertz sounding across the plateau. It was at this late hour that Mawson issued instructions to Madigan. Much to his amusement, they were in the form of a letter delivered by a messenger "from the general's tent." Madigan was ordered to

> ascertain as much as possible of the coast lying east of the Mertz Glacier, investigating its broad features and carrying out the following scientific work: magnetic, biological and geological observations, the character, especially the nature and size of the grains of ice or snow surfaces, details of sastrugi, topographical features, heights and distances, and meteorology.[25]

Whether designed to or not, the detailed scientific program that Madigan was belatedly instructed to fulfill reduced any hopes he had of his man-hauled journey being able to exceed in distance the journey of Mawson's dog-hauled journey.

Yet it seems that young Madigan continued to think that he might still outshine "old Mawson." On November 17, conscious that it was a "very late" start, Madigan decided "to go absolutely on our own from this." Every hour counted if he was to be successful. While Mawson had the dogs to haul his load, which was spread across three sledges, Madigan's massive load of eight weeks' provisions and five gallons of kerosene was loaded onto just one sledge, which had to be man-hauled all the way. The only assistance would come when the winds and the surface were favorable, which would allow the tent floor to be hoisted as a sail for the sledge. According to Madigan, it was "one of the heaviest loads ever taken by a sledge party of three." While seven weeks' provisions was usually "looked on as a maximum," they would be taking eight. Far from being daunted by this, Madigan regarded it as a challenge. He knew it would be a considerable achievement if he could go farther than Mawson and return with greater scientific results and an accurate map of 300 miles of hitherto-unseen coastline.[26]

It was November 17, and they were just over 25 miles from the hut, when Mawson's party veered off, heading east-southeast, while Madigan and Stillwell kept to an easterly direction. Mawson was going "as fast as possible," wrote Madigan, while his own party was "going to keep in touch with the East coast and map it in," which would be "very interesting." The day was perfect for sledging, and Mawson's two dog teams and three sledges "went at a great pace." They were off "into unexplored land, which no human eyes have yet seen," wrote Mertz excitedly. The first sledge was pulled by one dog team, while the other two sledges were tied one behind the other and pulled by the other dog team. As Madigan and his companions trudged away eastward, they watched Mawson sitting atop one of the dog sledges "with cap off, yelling and waving like a boy. He is in his element," wrote Madigan. At noon the following day, Madigan saw Mawson's sledges in the distance once again, before losing them to sight. It would be the last he would see of his close friends Mertz and Ninnis.[27]

Madigan was able to catch up some of the distance, because Mawson was inclined to stop and erect his tent each lunchtime to have a hot drink. In contrast, Madigan stuck to his habit of having little more than a cold snack at lunchtime in the lee of his sledge. This meant that they were desperately thirsty until they camped each night. The first few days were particularly difficult because of the strong sunshine, which made them "*terribly* hot" and caused "extreme thirst." The sunshine made them take off their protective clothing, leaving them "very sunburnt" despite a thick layer of lanolin. But it allowed Madigan's party to cover a greater distance each day. It was because of this that they had caught sight of Mawson in the distance a day after they had parted company. Madigan's speed was helped by attaching the improvised sail to the bamboo sledge pole, which allowed him to cover more than 15 miles on November 18. At times, the sledge ran by itself without having to be hauled.[28] It would have given him some confidence that he might yet exceed the length of Mawson's journey.

On November 19, it was time for Stillwell and Madigan to finally part company. Stillwell's role as a support player was over. With the rheumatic Close slowing them down and not pulling his weight, any longer journey would have been hazardous. They were all suffering from degrees of painful snow blindness, and Close was worst of all after having lost his goggles. Over the following eight days they headed for the coast and back to the hut, investigating several places of exposed rock along the way. Although his sledge-meter was broken, Stillwell estimated that they had made a return journey of 117 miles by the time they reached the hut on November 27. An hour later, Murphy arrived from the south after having traveled a similar distance in support of Bage's party.[29] By helping Mawson, Madigan, and Bage during the initial stage of their journeys, Stillwell and Murphy had helped to compensate for the months of bad weather that had prevented Mawson from organizing a proper program of depot-laying. Now the parties of Bage, Madigan, and Mawson were on their own, and they would all be competing to outdo the other.

CHAPTER NINE

Making Their Mark

Bage, Webb, and Hurley had left the hut on November 10, after first fortifying themselves with an omelette of penguin eggs. Bage's instructions were to head for the area of the South Magnetic Pole, which was an estimated 400 miles away. Helping to haul the Norwegian-made sledge up the steepest part of the slope was Bickerton, who was to be otherwise unoccupied until early December. Bage also had the support party of Murphy, Laseron, and Hunter to help haul supplies for the first week or two of the journey. They were already ahead of him, and Bage was anxious to catch them up. He only stopped long enough at Aladdin's Cave to have a quick meal and for Hurley to film Mawson's dog team in action. Bage, Webb, and Hurley then hitched themselves back in their harnesses and took off "almost at a run over the smooth ice," with Mawson, Mertz, and Ninnis cheering them on. While Mawson settled down for the night in the warmth and security of Aladdin's Cave, Bage hurried after Murphy, hoping to catch him at the 11-mile mark, where a supply cache had been established in another cavern, dubbed Cathedral Grotto.[1]

The going got more difficult as the icy surface turned to snow, the headwind increased in strength, and the crevasses became more difficult to discern in the gathering darkness. About three miles on from Aladdin's Cave, there was a region of crevasses that went on for several miles. Even though some were about five meters wide, Bage reported that they were mostly "well bridged" with packed snow. Hurley described how they "fell through many crevasses to our waists, but without any serious mishap." But it did slow them up. It was nearly midnight before they finally reached Murphy's party at Cathedral Grotto, which was cleared of snow for Bage and his men to occupy while Murphy's men stayed in their tent. After a hearty meal, the exhausted men were able to turn in, "feeling well content with our first day's work." While Mawson and his dogs had covered just over five miles, Bage's party had traveled 11½ miles and had reached a height of 1,900 feet. Webb was just happy "to be out here clear of the boss," as he told the similarly disgruntled Murphy.[2]

Their effort that day pushed Bage and his men to the limit. The months of relative confinement in the hut had left them in a weakened physical condition, which would take some days of trekking to remedy. They were slow to start the following day, not setting out until after lunch, and covering little more than two miles in difficult conditions of "heavy wind and fairly thick drift." The wind and snowdrift worsened so much the following day that it kept them huddled in their small tent, which had been pitched in the lee of Murphy's larger and much stronger one. Even when the wind partially subsided and the snowdrift was light, as it was on November 13, the cloud cover could make the conditions just as difficult for traveling. With no sun to cast shadows, and everything colored a uniform white, Bage complained that it was "easy to bump against a four foot sastrugi without seeing it." After just five and a half miles of hauling the sledges in such conditions, he found that they were "thoroughly exhausted and glad to camp."[3]

Bage was as eager as Madigan to cover the maximum distance each day, as both were competing against Mawson's dog teams. Rather than taking time to erect their small tent so they could have a hot drink and food at lunchtime, they mimicked Madigan and had their meal "al fresco in the lee of the sledge." Bage explained what this meant in practice:

First came plasmon biscuit broken with the ice-axe into pieces small enough to go into the mouth through the funnel of a burberry helmet. Then followed 2 ozs of chocolate frozen rather too hard to taste much, and finally the *pièce de résistance* — 2 ozs of butter, lovingly thawed out in the mouth to get the full flavor.

For fluids, they had to suffice with handfuls of snow melted in their mouths, which was never sufficient and left them desperately thirsty till they could stop and camp for the night. Although a hot drink of tea and some warmed-up hoosh for lunch would have had a positive physical and psychological benefit, Bage initially thought that a frozen meal eaten out in the open had a better effect on their progress, since it was "uncomfortable enough for everyone to be eager to start again as soon as possible." However, he soon found a way of stopping for a brief lunch and eating it warm. Instead of erecting the tent, a sufficient shelter for using the cooker could be formed by digging a hole two feet deep in which there was room for them all to sit beneath the sledge sail tied to a bamboo pole. Experience had taught him that "a warm lunch and a rest" allowed them to go "a good deal farther than would otherwise be possible." The dug-up snow also acted as a marker for their return journey.[4]

The Antarctic weather often dashed Bage's hope of maximizing the distance of his journey. After two days of enduring a fierce blizzard that kept them confined almost constantly to their sleeping bags, they had covered just 19½ miles over the six days since leaving the hut. At that rate, there was no way he would cover his desired 400 miles. Desperate to make up the lost time and distance, Bage decided to store some of their food in a cache atop a six-foot-high mound of snow. The days confined to the tent had seen them consume less than their rationed amounts, and they had eaten less than anticipated when sledging. It was largely this "saved" food that Bage now left behind, along with a heavy thermograph, his heavy boots, and a pickaxe, hoping that the lighter load would hasten their journey. Although this meant there was a risk of their food running out before they reached their objective, Bage was satisfied that the cached food could be retrieved on their return journey, ensuring that they would not starve.[5] But that would depend on the visibility at the time, and their ability to determine their position in relation to the cache. Neither was vouchsafed.

As it turned out, abandoning part of their load was a timely move. Their southward journey was taking them ever higher onto the polar plateau, where the air was becoming thinner. When Bage called a halt and camped on November 16, fearful they were about to be hit with another blizzard, he calculated that they were 3,200 feet above sea level. Hauling the sledge in the increasingly rarefied atmosphere left them "thoroughly tired out," wrote Bage.[6] Remaining in the tent during a blizzard could also tire them out, as the "seething drift" was "like a sandblast" against the thin calico walls of their tent, forcing them to shout if they wanted to be heard. Preparing a meal in such conditions could take two hours, as they donned their frozen clothes to unpack from the sledge the ingredients for making hoosh. It was a race against time, which left all of them with frostbitten hands that had to have their circulation painfully restored. Once their bodies got cold, wrote Hurley, it was "a hard job to warm up again and much of the calorific value of the food is wasted," unless they huddled motionless in their sleeping bags.[7]

When the weather calmed and the sun emerged, as it did on November 18 and 19, Bage and Murphy made the most of it. It felt as hot "as an Australian summer," wrote Hurley, even though it was just 10°F. So the six men took off all their protective clothes and hauled in their underclothes, making good time on the smooth surface. "Soon we were almost naked," wrote Hunter, "all our clothing being open, & still we perspired." After days of difficult weather, their fast progress made them optimistic once again about their chances of attaining their objective. However, when Murphy was badly stricken by snow blindness and Laseron became too sick to haul on November 20, Bage was forced to call an early halt to the day's work. With Murphy's party becoming more a handicap than a help, Bage decided to press on with Hurley and Webb. After eleven days of trekking, they had only covered 67½ miles; at that rate, they were unlikely to cover even half of the 400 miles that Bage aspired to. So he decided to lighten his load even more by leaving behind more food, along with some clothing, books, and equipment. It still left them hauling a weight of 748 pounds. Before the two parties went their separate ways, Murphy helped build a huge cairn of snow ten feet high, with "snow blocks wrapped in black bunting" on top. They also "fitted a special flag vane about 20 feet high" alongside the mound to make it visible from a distance of eight miles.[8]

As Murphy, Hunter, and Laseron turned back, they were confident that Bage's party "will do well." Hunter noted in his diary that they were "good scientists," so "their results should be … better I think than the results of any other sledge journey in Antarctica." Bage pushed on farther south with a renewed determination to succeed, despite the often-punishing conditions. All their protective clothing was donned on November 24, with Hurley describing how they were hauling uphill against "this terrible wind" in "an area of very bad sastrugi and snow ramps." When it came time to camp, Bage was so worried about the 75-mile-per-hour wind ripping the tent apart that he and Hurley spent "two miserable hours" building a protective wall of snow blocks five feet high and 15 feet long. Still Bage pressed on, like the good soldier he was, refusing to erect the tent at lunchtime to allow a hot drink to be made. It meant, as Hurley described on November 29, that they became so "parched and thirsty" that they "tried to quench it by sucking pieces of ice which burnt our tongues and afforded us little relief." It was "the worst day of the journey," wrote Hurley, as they fought "against a relentless and cruel wind with bowed backs and strained muscles." There were worse days to come, however. On December 3, they encountered a succession of wide crevasses, some over "70 feet wide and … spanned by great bridges of compressed snow." To get across these "sledging nightmares," the roped-up Hurley was sent out ahead, "stamping and jumping" on the snow bridges to ensure they were safe for his companions and the sledge.[9]

By December 4, twenty-four days after leaving the hut, Bage had covered 150 miles and had abandoned his original aim of covering 400 miles and reaching the South Magnetic Pole. They still had fifteen days before they had to turn around, wrote Hurley. Although 400 miles was out of the question, he thought that they might reach 350 miles if they maintained an average pace of about 13 miles per day. They had rarely managed to cover such a daily distance, and it wasn't becoming any easier. "Our mitts and Burberrys are frozen stiff," wrote Hurley, while "our feet are wet, cold and tired," and "our appetites are terrific, yet we dare not increase our ration by half an ounce." He complained that the manufactured food on which they relied for their sustenance left them "more hungry at the end than at the beginning of the meal."[10] It would have been better if Mawson had sent them off with seal and penguin meat, which had sustained him on Shackleton's expedition. But the little seal meat that Mawson had was kept for the dogs.

With time running out, Bage was more desperate than ever. He decided that once they reached the 200-mile mark, they would embark on a final, lightly loaded dash toward the South Magnetic Pole. On December 13, they completed their 200 miles and spent the day going through all their gear to remove anything that was not essential for their survival. Ten days' food and a gallon of fuel were cached in a mound of snow for collection on their return, while only sufficient food for seventeen days was taken on the slimmed-down sledge. In the event of bad weather, this provided little margin of safety for what Bage thought would be a fast, fourteen-day journey. However, in their small tent at the end of the first day, Bage was forced to concede to his companions that even his new aim of reaching 350 miles was beyond their grasp. Because of the difficult surface, they had only covered 12 miles that day, and "would be lucky to reach three hundred miles." But that was the distance that Mawson was aiming to do, and Bage had hoped to exceed his leader's distance. What was worse, Webb's magnetic readings had not shown any sign for the last 65 miles that they were getting closer to the South Magnetic Pole.[11]

When they stopped to camp on December 20, Bage calculated that they were 298 miles from the hut. Although they had climbed to nearly 6,000 feet on the polar plateau, and were beset with ever-colder temperatures, Bage's party now were blessed with relatively good weather that allowed them to complete about 15 miles each day. Indeed, it was so warm in the sun that they were hauling the sledge in their shirtsleeves. Now there was just two miles to do on the following day before they were scheduled to turn around. Perhaps hoping that he still might outdo Mawson, Bage made Hurley and Webb go one mile more than that, which gave them a total of 301 miles. Stopping for several hours to take final magnetic and geographical observations, Bage marked the completion of their southward journey by raising the British and Australian flags and giving three cheers for the King in their otherwise silent surrounds. Although they had just pushed past 70°36', they were still an estimated 50 or 60 miles from the South Magnetic Pole and 175 miles from the farthest point reached by David, Mawson, and Mackay on the Shackleton expedition.[12] Just as Mawson had done back then, Bage would have to return home without attaining the South Magnetic Pole. He would have a similarly difficult time getting back alive.

Far to the northeast, Madigan and Mawson were having a race of their own. The young geologist was hoping to make his mark by covering a greater distance than either Bage or Mawson, and combining that with greater scientific and geographic discoveries. As geologists, both Mawson and Madigan were on the lookout for areas of bare rock that would reveal the age and ancient history of the continent and possibly expose deposits of valuable minerals. This is why Madigan was excited on November 20, just three days after taking his leave of Mawson, to see in the distance "a huge mountainous nunatak showing *rock.*" A nunatak is the peak of an exposed hill or mountain, which can be found poking above the ice. Because of the peculiarities of perception in the clear air of the Antarctic, Madigan wasn't sure whether the nunatak was "a small thing a half mile away" or "a huge mountain ten miles away." In fact, it was four miles away, and peaked 1,200 feet above the ice.[13]

Leaving their sledge on November 22, Madigan, McLean, and Correll roped themselves together to climb the imposing nunatak, which was "almost perpendicular in places." Toward the end it became so steep that Madigan had to cut steps with an ice axe. It was a "real alpine climb, and quite dangerous," he wrote, with "an almost sheer drop of 150 feet below us at times." When they reached the top, they found it was a razor-sharp ridge on which it was barely possible to stand, with a sheer drop of 800 feet on the other side. Under Madigan's direction, they collected "typical rock specimens" along with samples of "soil, lichen and moss found in the rock." Rather than carrying these samples with them, they created a high mound of snow in which the samples were stored for collection on their return journey. Also left at the depot was some of their food and fuel. Madigan was going to take just six weeks' provisions and make them last forty-five days, by which time he expected to be back at this newly created depot.[14]

The next day almost saw his carefully calculated plans come undone when Madigan fell down a crevasse. Since leaving the hut, the three men had crossed hundreds of crevasses, mostly without incident. If one or more of them fell through the snow bridge covering the crevasse, they would usually fall just a few feet and scramble out, with only their dignity injured. This time it was different, and it was Madigan who barely escaped with his life. Nearly two weeks earlier, when Correll had fallen down a crevasse, Madigan claimed in his diary to have learned his lesson about crevasses and to "always test them first."[15] But he was in a hurry to make up some distance on November 23, after having spent the morning and part of the afternoon confined to the tent by "dense surface drift." With Madigan hauling on a 24-foot-long sledge rope, they were going downhill at such a fast pace that McLean and Correll had to be roped up behind the sledge to act as a brake.

They could not hold it. As the heavily laden sledge overtook Madigan, and he turned to remonstrate with his companions, he broke through a snow bridge and fell into the darkness of a deep crevasse. Madigan described how his 14-stone body was "almost wrenched in halves by the sudden stop, as my sledge belt caught me after a sheer drop of twenty four feet." The experience left him traumatized and "sore in every limb."[16]

Madigan was crossing what would later be called the Mertz Glacier, and there were many more crevasses to be negotiated. After so narrowly avoiding death or serious injury, he was compelled to spend the following day crossing "nine miles of the worst crevassed country on God's earth." It was the "rottenest day I have ever spent," wrote Madigan, as he was forced to test a succession of snow bridges across numerous crevasses that seemed to be waiting to take his life. With the snow-covered ice presenting a hard crust that his feet would often break through, Madigan could never be sure whether he was about to plunge into another crevasse. As a result, whenever "a bit of pie-crust snow broke under my feet," wrote Madigan, "my heart would leap in a nasty way." He was still sore two days later, and was having nightmares about crevasses, resolving if he got out safely never to go back to Antarctica. When another patch of crevasses was encountered on November 26 in conditions of poor light, Madigan opted to camp and read Thackeray's *Vanity Fair* until the sun reappeared.[17]

Things became easier when they began traveling on "perfect flat hard barrier surface," which was actually sea ice in the bays between two massive glacial tongues that stretched 60 miles or more into the sea. It was on this ice that Madigan encountered an Adélie penguin, which was quickly "caught ... and photographed against the sledge." Rather than being killed and consumed, it was released and allowed to go on its way to a distant region of rocks. Madigan was more interested in consuming the pemmican and other food that was weighing down his sledge, and did not see the necessity of going through the messy business of butchering the penguin to get fresh meat. He was more concerned, when the light permitted, to use a theodolite to measure angles on any visible geographic features so that the first chart of the coastline could be compiled. This work was essential for making a map of their journey, which could well decide whether or not it would make his reputation. Magnetic observations were also taken to add to those being taken by Webb on the southern journey and by the men back at the hut.[18] But he was also aware that every hour spent on scientific observations meant less chance of covering 300 miles.

On December 3, after having traveled just over 150 miles, Madigan lightened their load by leaving a week's provisions and a tin of kerosene on a mound of snow that he hoped would remain visible from a distance. He also left behind a pick and some "perks" — a pound of raisins and a tin of toffee. This meant that they would have 60 pounds less to haul across the surface of soft snow, where their feet were sinking "twelve inches every step and going very tedious." The sun had burnt their faces, and the cold wind had cracked their lips. But they had enjoyed days of good weather, made good time, and their rations were lasting longer than anticipated. Like Bage, Madigan relaxed his earlier intention not to stop for a hot lunch, noting on December 4 that they now "always boil up at noon." As much as anything, this was important for morale. Although the rations were sufficient, the plasmon biscuits and hoosh was not calculated to excite the palate as much as the breast of a penguin was able to do. "This concentrated food does not satisfy," wrote Madigan, who could not stop thinking of all the different meals he had had at the hut. The journey was also starting to drag, with him conceding that they "all look forward to turning back."[19] However, they had covered little more than half the distance that he wanted to cover.

Just when Madigan needed to pile on the miles, several days of bad weather kept them largely confined to their tent from December 6–10, where he was able to finish reading *Vanity Fair*. When the weather did clear, he found the surface on which they were traveling turning to slush just below the crusty surface, while pressure ridges of ice and open leads of water kept them from following a straight course to the east. And despite all the lusting for a square meal, Madigan made no attempt to kill an Adélie penguin that followed their sledge for about 200 meters, nor a young Weddell seal that they encountered on the ice. He couldn't yet see any need for the extra food or the fresh meat. By December 10, when they were just short of 200 miles, Madigan found himself boxed in by a lead of open water and a pressure ridge of ice. To escape, they were forced to climb the ridge and turn south, moving in zigzag fashion. "Only nine more days outward travel in which to make our names," wrote an exasperated Madigan.[20] He would need a good surface, fine weather, and a clear run to make his desired 300 miles.

The weather did improve for the final week of Madigan's outward journey, which he planned to terminate on December 18. On only one day were the three men confined to their tent by a blizzard, and the sea-ice surface also improved sufficiently on most days for them to cover more than ten miles each day. That was not enough to reach 300 miles from the hut. There was also some doubt about the accuracy of their measurements, with the sledge-meter having been damaged by the rough travel. Indeed, the meter had been dogged by "a series of break-downs," with the problem not necessarily being noticed immediately. By December 11, Madigan complained that it had "gone thoroughly to the pack," with it registering half a mile when he estimated they had covered three times that distance. Although the resourceful Correll made running repairs, they found that it still stopped working and would "only go on when the meter receives a good bump." During the day of confinement in the tent, Correll made farther repairs that seemed to correct the problem. However, it called into question the distance that Madigan would claim to have covered.[21]

Not only was Madigan's measurement of the distance questionable, but his scientific and geographical results were also under some shadow. On December 12, while his eyes were "very sore" from snow blindness, Madigan did a magnetic observation that he admitted was unreliable, noting that he "only did dips with one needle as eyes would not stand it." Moreover, to protect his eyes, Madigan wore goggles with iron-wire gauze sides, and was "afraid it may have affected [the results] somewhat."[22] As for his geographical results, it is clear from his diary that Madigan was often confused about the nature of the land across which they were traveling, not being sure whether it was part of the continent, compacted sea ice, or another glacial tongue.[23] He would have to make sense of it all when he got back to the hut.

More than a week beforehand, Madigan had decided that they would turn for home on about December 18. As it happened, the distance they had traveled by then only amounted to an estimated 270 miles, rather than the 300 miles he had wanted to cover. However, Madigan had noticed "a long rocky face, five miles long, showing out of face of plateau," and decided to visit it rather than make a dash for another two days to achieve the hoped-for 300 miles. The cliff face was likely to yield a wealth of rocks and other scientific specimens. But that would require a detour and some time for proper investigation. It would mean sacrificing distance for science — which is what Madigan decided to do on December 18, when they reached the limit of their outward journey. It would have taken another two or three days to achieve the 300 miles that he had wanted to cover, and it just wasn't possible. They had taken thirty-eight days for the 270 miles of the outward journey, and had only twenty-seven days in which to complete the return journey. This would be "cutting things very fine," wrote Madigan. Having made his decision, he looked forward to "one long journey to Home, Sweet Home."[24]

CHAPTER TEN

Crossing the Great Divide

At the time Madigan was turning his sledge around, Mawson was only about 47 miles away. Disaster had struck. Mawson had been forced to cut his journey short, and was heading back to the hut in a desperate race for survival. This was a terrible development in a trek that had started so well. After having taken their leave of Madigan and Stillwell on November 17, Mawson, Mertz, and Ninnis had pushed on strongly in a southeasterly direction. Mertz led the party on his skis, acting as a guide for the dogs, while Mawson and then Ninnis followed on behind, urging on the dogs and either walking alongside or riding on their sledges.[1] Mawson had proved his mettle on the Shackleton expedition, when he had outshone Edgeworth David. But David was a fifty-year-old professor, almost twice Mawson's age. This time, Mawson's two companions were younger than him, and also possibly much stronger. He must have wondered whether they would outshine him in the way he had done with David. Would they write about him in their diaries, using the sort of scathing terms he had used when writing about David?

Mawson was also conscious of the rival journeys by Madigan and Bage, and the concurrent expeditions by Scott and Amundsen, the outcome of which was still unknown to him. Yet he began his journey to the southeast with no apparent sense of urgency. Although he and his companions rose at 7:00 a.m. on November 18, and the weather was ideal for sledging, it was almost three hours before they got going. "Took things leisurely," wrote Mawson in his diary, noting that they stopped for lunch after less than two hours' sledging. It was a "glorious day," with light wind and strong sunshine, which allowed them to spread their sleeping bags across the sledges to be dried out. Despite the perfect weather, Mawson wasted time setting up the tent for lunch, rather than having it beside the sledge. He also stopped for a "boil-up" of cocoa in the afternoon, and camped for the night at just 6:45 p.m. They had covered an estimated 15 miles. During the morning, Mawson had been sitting on his sledge as it was being pulled along by the dogs, watching Mertz, the young Swiss ski champion, move effortlessly across the snow, singing his German student songs with youthful gusto. Mawson seems to have regarded it as a reflection on his own physique and rose to the challenge. After lunch, he replaced Mertz in the lead. Not being adept at skiing, Mawson did a "jog trot" for two and a half miles, noting with satisfaction that he "did not feel it, so am getting into form." He was determined not to be outdone.[2]

They had a long trek ahead of them, and Mawson seemed blithely confident about their chances of reaching their objective on the coast, about 350 miles away. But he had never worked with dogs before, and didn't seem to realize that biscuits wouldn't provide sufficient nourishment for them. The dogs had lost condition at the hut when their seal meat had been exhausted, and Mertz noticed they were "very hungry" at the end of a day's sledging. Mawson, too, wrote of the "dogs getting pretty tired." When a skua was sighted at lunch, Mertz regretted that Ninnis was unable to shoot it, as it "would have been fine dog food" — which suggests that he was already concerned about the food that was available for the dogs. As a mark of their hunger, the butchered dog that had been disdained previously was now eaten "voraciously" by all but one of the dogs. When another dog had fourteen pups, they became food for the hungry adults. A farther dog was shot on November 20.[3] There was a real question now as to whether the dogs would last the required distance. If Mawson was worried, he gave no indication of it. His equanimity was about to change.

Mawson's leisurely pace continued the following day, when he did not get out of his sleeping bag until nearly 9:00 a.m., confessing in his diary that he had "overslept." Yet it was another beautiful day of sunshine and light winds, when they should have been maximizing their daily distance. Instead, they only managed to travel five-and-a-quarter miles for the whole day. Mawson grumbled that it was "extremely hot," with a temperature at 2:00 p.m. of 17°F, which should not have sapped their energy too much, as the dogs were doing the hard work of hauling the sledges. However, they were encountering sastrugi and coming to the edge of a huge glacier, which he would later name after Mertz. This entailed a descent of about 800 feet from their camp of the previous evening. Mertz went ahead on his skis, while Mawson and Ninnis struggled to slow the sledges so they didn't overrun the dogs. They were not always successful. Mawson recorded in his diary how they "got into great trouble [with the] sledges overrunning," with one of the dogs being injured by a hurtling sledge, and another dog running away. When two of the sledges overturned, it seems that Mawson let fly at Mertz, who described how Mawson "complained, believing again that the whole expedition was ruined." The following days, as they crossed the glacier, were even more difficult, with the dogs having to be unharnessed so the sledges could be lowered down precipitous slopes and taken carefully across snow-blocked crevasses.[4]

It was difficult to guard against falling into crevasses, which the unharnessed dogs did more than once, and from which they had to be hauled out. The crevasses could be so difficult to discern that, when they stopped for lunch on November 21, Mawson pitched the tent on the top of a snow bridge that concealed a five-meter-wide crevasse. Only as they were packing to leave and the snow bridge collapsed did the crevasse announce its presence by almost swallowing Ninnis. He only survived, wrote Mawson, by scrambling on the side of the crevasse, which was "very deep." The following day, as they continued to cross the glacier, Mawson reported that the sledge loaded with dog food "fell half into one." And it did the same thing the day after; on the second occasion, the sledge had to be unloaded before it could be hauled to the surface.[5]

They finally got off the glacier on November 23. Mertz calculated they were now 100 miles from the hut, although the distance figures revealed by the sledge-meter were more than a little problematic. Right from the beginning, Mawson complained about the accuracy of the sledge-meter, and was continually making guesstimates of the actual distance they had covered, either adding or subtracting from the measurement shown in yards on the meter. The distance averaged just on ten miles per day for the first two weeks after leaving Madigan, although that did include crossing the massive glacier, when the dogs proved to be more of a hindrance than a help. Another dog was shot on November 26, and another on November 28, and fed to the others. Yet another ran away and did not return, perhaps to avoid the fate of its fellows, while another ate 2½ pounds of their butter, presumably to make up for the seal blubber that he should have been fed. The dogs would have been more useful for Bage on the polar plateau than to Mawson on the coastal edge, with its difficult topography. "Dogs are a curse under such circumstances," he complained. On the other hand, Mawson did enjoy mostly mild and calm weather during those two weeks, which should have helped his progress.[6]

The problem was that Mawson was going much too close to the coast, which would see the trio crossing the two massive glacial tongues with their steep slopes and deep crevasses. The second glacier was encountered in late November. This time, it was the turn of what Mawson called the "tent sledge" to fall into a "very deep clear sheer crevasse" and become wedged there. It was "a most aggravating morning," wrote Mawson, as they struggled to extricate the jammed sledge. At the time, they were climbing steep slopes covered with "very deep soft snow" and "plenty of crevasses."

Snowshoes would have helped in those conditions, but neither Shackleton, Scott, nor Mawson had thought of taking them. Both men and dogs were exhausted, and Mawson was worried about whether they would ever reach the point on the coast that Scott's *Terra Nova* had sighted. "If only we could have a straight-out proposition," moaned Mawson, "instead of these endless snow hills and crevasses." He was traveling blind. And his position-finding was not helped when he forgot to wind his watch, which, as Mertz noted, made it "difficult to determine the longitude." He had to take two "astronomical observations to put the watch right." The region they were crossing had never been explored, and Mawson was relying on the charts made by the American explorer Charles Wilkes in 1840, which had shown two capes on the coast. Mawson now concluded that it was "obvious that we have been deluded by Wilkes' reports of Cape Emmons and Cape Hudson, for it appears that no land exists in that direction."[7]

Mawson's own exploration had left him little the wiser about the true state of the region he was crossing. Partly it was due to the light. When the sun shone, the snowdrift blew; when the wind dropped, the clouds obscured their view with what Mertz described as "an uncomfortable diffused light." They tried to "draw maps of the shape of the region, but nothing is certain, as the light is bad." On November 27, there was sufficient sunshine and lack of drift for them to see "the whole region," which revealed "a huge glacier with crevasses" in front of them. It was the second of the glaciers they had to cross. Mawson began to believe, wrongly, that they were now "off the real continent edge" and suggested, again wrongly, that "Adélie Land may even be severed from the mainland of Antarctica by an ice-filled low-land." However, he was right about one thing, deducing that Madigan's coastal party "must be hard on us from the north." In other words, the two parties were probably traveling on closely parallel lines and in danger of duplicating each other's charts and observations. To avoid this, Mawson noted in his diary that they "must now work to E[ast]." In fact, as he and Madigan subsequently discovered, their journeys over the following ten days or so came closer and closer together, until their routes were only about 20 to 25 miles apart.[8]

The food was holding out better than expected. This was because of Mawson's strict rationing. He made two weeks' rations last for sixteen days, and also didn't eat "perks" that were equivalent to three days' rations. This wasn't because they weren't hungry. As Mertz complained in his diary on November 30, they were "always hungry after a workday and also in the morning." Mawson assured them that it wasn't the degree of hunger that Shackleton experienced. That might have been some comfort to Mertz and Ninnis, allowing them to bear the slow starvation, because that is what it was. When Mertz told his companions about the "terrible dreams" he had been having, Mawson told him that "the reason was because we eat little food in proportion to hard work."[9] But why did he restrict the food so severely when they weren't suffering a shortage of it? It was presumably because Mawson was concerned that the two glaciers had so impeded their progress that it might prevent him from achieving his great aim of reaching 350 miles. As he wrote after "a most aggravating morning" struggling their way across the second glacier, the dogs were "very done" and "things are looking serious for onward progress."[10] At the time, they had barely gone 200 miles. On the objective facts, it was not the right time to start starving his party, particularly as they were taking over more of the hauling from the dogs.

After realizing that he was closer to the coast than he thought, Mawson headed southeast for a few days before turning east again on December 4. When the weather was good enough to travel, they could cover about 12 miles a day. But their average distance was much reduced when strong winds and snowdrift kept them in the tent for three days from December 6 to 8. This limited their average distance to less than nine miles a day for the first thirteen days of December, compared with ten miles a day for the last two weeks of November. On the second day of his enforced confinement in the tent, Mawson wrote in his diary of being

taunted by vivid dreams in half dozing condition, Ninnis the same.
I hear him calling "Hike, Hike" vociferously in his sleep. The noise
of tent flapping, the beat of it on the bags, the short ration, the long
lying down in cramped position etc, all tend to same result. In
addition I have swollen and burst lip and neuralgia on left side.

When they did get going again on December 9, they easily covered
15 miles on the now-flat landscape. Or at least Mertz did. While
he glided across the thick snow with his skis, his two companions
and the dogs had to flounder their way across. Mawson described
how they were "sinking always up to ankles and at times much
deeper." They had a similar experience on December 10, when
they covered 12 miles but could have covered many more if they
had all been on skis. "Mawson gradually realizes how useful the
skis can be in Antarctica," wrote Mertz.[11] It was a bit late in the
day. Mawson had brought along a ski expert and two dozen skis,
but hadn't ensured that he or his men mastered the requisite skills.
The two dozen skis had remained at the hut.

Mawson found that their easterly route was once again taking
them within sight of the sea. On December 10, Mertz saw "a wide
flat area" to their north, which he realized "must be the sea, because
a line of icy islands and icebergs emerged during the afternoon."
By December 12, Mawson found that they were heading for the
continental barrier, and might soon come in sight of Madigan.
That definitely wouldn't do. He tried to determine their exact
location, but had to do the observations and complex calculations
twice. And still he probably wasn't sure. But he turned east-southeast to once again take them farther from the coast and Madigan's
sphere of operations. Mawson and Ninnis were starting to suffer,
with Mawson complaining on December 8 that his "neuralgia
and lip continues a curse," while a whitlow on Ninnis's finger was
"giving him much pain."[12]

Mawson's mention of his swollen lip, which was probably a cold
sore, and the references he made to Ninnis suffering from a whitlow
on his finger, suggest that both men had herpes. One of them had

probably passed the virus to the other, living as they were in such close proximity and eating communally. By December 13, Mawson described how "Ninnis' finger has been very bad during the night." Indeed, it was so excruciating that Ninnis had been unable to sleep for three nights. Doubtless it would have hampered his ability to do his full share of work, which would have slowed them down. Perhaps for this reason, Mawson lanced it that morning in a desperate attempt to relieve his companion's pain. He also spent the morning rearranging the supplies on their sledges, one of which was to be abandoned now that the food for them and their dogs had been partly depleted. The hide straps off the abandoned sledge were given to the dogs, which "straightaway got a taste for hide and ate [the] leather strap off [the] cooker box."[13] It was a sign of how hungry the dogs were and how far their condition had deteriorated over the previous month.

Mawson's diary did not mention the re-packing of the sledges, although it would have dire implications for them all. For reasons that Mawson never adequately explained, the fuel, most of the equipment, and a small part of the human food was packed onto the first sledge, driven by Mawson; and all the dog food, most of the human food, and the tent was packed onto the second sledge, driven by Ninnis. Rather than putting an equal weight on each sledge, Mawson made the second sledge 50 pounds heavier, reasoning that the weight on each sledge would even up as the food was consumed over the following week or two. The second sledge also had the strongest dogs. His decision to put nearly all the food on one sledge and all the fuel on the other is difficult to understand. Mawson argued later that the first sledge with the fuel and the weakest dogs was most at risk of falling down a crevasse, and therefore the one they could most afford to lose. The second sledge with most of the food would only cross snow bridges after they had already been tested and crossed by the first sledge. It was therefore much less likely to be lost to the depths.[14] He and David had done this on the Shackleton expedition, when the second sledge was known as the "Plum Duff sledge," and they had got away with it then.[15]

In fact, it was a stupid decision, dictated by following David's practice without thinking it through, and perhaps also born of complacency after having crossed so many crevasses without coming to grief. But it put all their lives at grave risk. Moreover, the division of fuel and food on the sledges seems to have been done from at least the time when Mawson separated from Madigan and Stillwell. In reality, they could neither afford to lose the fuel nor the food. Losing the food sledge would obviously have dire implications for their survival. But without fuel, they couldn't melt snow for water, or cook their food, anyway. Madigan had eaten snow at lunchtime as a way of saving time, and it had not quenched the terrible thirst he had experienced each afternoon while man-hauling. It would have been impossible for Madigan's party to survive if they had been totally reliant on eating snow. Similarly with Mawson. His party might survive for a few days by eating snow, but not for the several weeks that it would take them to get back to the hut. If they were to lose all their fuel, and thereby their means of heating food or drink, it would have been disastrous for the maintenance of their core body temperature in blizzard conditions.

Less than two hours after re-packing all their supplies on just two sledges, they were on a long downhill slope that took them into an area of "much crevassing." Since the previous evening they had been following a more southerly course in order to escape the crevassed area to the east into which they had been heading. Even the new course, which was roughly south-southeast, saw them encountering "frequent crevasses," wrote Mawson, and they avoided falling into them by "pretty well clear luck." He thought they must be crossing another "great glacier," but it was just the ice of the polar plateau under stress as it neared the sea. After traveling six and a half miles on the more southerly course, Mawson shifted back to a course that was almost due east, noting that he did so because "things looked well," which presumably meant that the area seemed to be clear of crevasses.[16] But it wasn't. Mertz described how the ice beneath them "suddenly cracked a few times," making a "sound [that] was similar to far cannon shots." He had heard such sounds before from glaciers in the Swiss Alps, but noticed that his "comrades were a little afraid, as they never heard before the sound when huge ice masses broke off."[17] In fact, Mawson had heard such sounds on the Shackleton expedition. It's just that he thought they'd got clear of crevasses.

Come what may, Mawson was determined to keep in connection with the coast. His aim was to reach the most western part of the coast that the *Terra Nova* had sighted and implicitly claimed by right of discovery for the British Empire. By reaching that point, Mawson would claim the massive wedge of Antarctica that stretched from there across 2,000 miles or more to where Wild and his party were exploring. He had estimated that point on the coast to be 350 miles from the hut, and he must have realized by now that it was beyond their ability to reach it. When Mawson stopped for the night on December 13, they had been going for thirty-three days, and they had only thirty-two days to get back to the hut, since the *Aurora* was scheduled to take them back to Australia on January 15. But they were less than 300 miles from the hut — although exactly how far they had traveled is still a matter of dispute. Mertz claimed in his diary that the farthest they got from the hut was 265 miles, while Mawson claimed in his diary that they were "about 300 miles" from the hut on December 14. He would later tell the Royal Geographical Society with an unjustifiable degree of precision that they were 311 miles from the hut.[18] He was at the point where he had to make a terrible decision about turning back and conceding that his trek had been a failure. He hadn't reached the point on the coast that the *Terra Nova* had sighted. Nor had he done anything else of significance. He would have feared that his trek was going to be overshadowed by those of Madigan and Bage.

Mawson wanted to do much more. Apart from claiming a large part of the continent for the British Empire, he wanted to ascertain whether or not Antarctica really was a single continent. His diary, which is largely an emotion-free zone, gives few hints of his thinking. It doesn't reveal whether he thought he was on the cusp of making a great discovery, or whether he feared it was beyond him. This day was no different: he recorded the changing clouds in great detail — that it was altostratus and altocumulus with little streaks of cirrostratus — and that the temperature was mild and the winds were light. Although there were crevasses, Mawson noted that they were "only on the seaward side," where the plateau was creeping inexorably toward the coast and breaking off into icebergs. The "booming sound" that he reported hearing that day may well have been the formation of such an iceberg, or simply the creation of yet another crevasse.[19] Whatever the cause, there was little sense of foreboding in Mawson's observation.

On December 14, they awoke to a morning that began with little wind and the sun shining brightly. Mertz noted that young Ninnis was "happy and cheerful." The lancing of his finger had finally allowed him to sleep for the first time in four days. After boiling up breakfast, feeding the dogs, and packing the sledges, the trio resumed their journey. Mertz slipped his boots into his skis and took his usual place at the head of their procession, providing a guide for the weaker dogs hauling Mawson's fuel sledge. Behind came Ninnis and the heavier sledge, with most of the food, pulled by the strongest dogs. Mertz's role was not only to provide a guide for the dogs, but also to seek out the best route for the sledges and look for the telltale sign of a crevasse, which was usually indicated by a slight indentation in the snow cover. The sunlight that day allowed Mertz to see such indentations in plenty of time to shout a warning to his companions. If it seemed safe, he would then ski across the snow bridge at right angles.[20]

Being on skis, Mertz was applying much less pressure on the snow bridge than if he had been walking. Even the heavy, dog-drawn sledges could safely cross most crevasses, since their runners acted like skis in spreading the weight of the sledges over a relatively large surface area. The safest place for Mawson and Ninnis when crossing a crevasse was to be riding on their respective sledges, so that they, too, would be spreading their weight and applying less pressure on the snow bridge. But it does not seem that Mawson impressed this simple precaution upon his companions, nor did he think to test the weight-bearing capacity of a snow bridge before crossing it. Perhaps he had crossed so many crevasses that he had become blasé about the risks, or he may have been so keen to cover as much distance as possible during these final days of the outward journey that he ignored the danger. Certainly, several crevasses had been crossed in this way without incident before Mawson stopped at noon to calculate their location and take meteorological and other observations.[21]

Soon after they got going again, Mertz detected yet another snow bridge. It was "like hundreds we have crossed in the last weeks," wrote Mertz, who shouted the usual warning over his shoulder to Mawson. According to Mawson's official account, it was not a shouted warning but the sight of Mertz, who was "well in advance of us," holding up his ski-stick that alerted him to "something unusual" ahead. It seems that Mawson was walking alongside his sledge at the time, and, when he reached the place where Mertz had signaled, could see "no sign of any irregularity." According to Mawson, "crevasses were not expected, since we were on a smooth surface of névé well to the southward of the broken coastal slopes." Not seeing anything, Mawson jumped onto his sledge and began working on his calculations to determine their position. "A moment after," wrote Mawson, he "noticed the faint indication of a crevasse," just as his sledge was crossing it obliquely, which was a dangerous way to be doing so. Although it was like "one of many hundred similar ones we had crossed and had no specially dangerous appearance," he "turned quickly round, called out a warning word to Ninnis and then dismissed it from [his] thoughts." In the backward glance that he made at the time, Mawson claimed that he saw Ninnis react by turning the leading dogs so that the sledge would cross the crevasse at right angles.[22]

Neither Mawson nor Mertz saw what happened next. Reconstructing the most likely scenario from the diaries of both of them, it seems that Ninnis was walking alongside his sledge as he turned the lead dogs to cross the nearly four-meter-wide crevasse at right angles. Rather than jumping on the sledge as it crossed, he continued to walk alongside it, and thereby exerted an inordinate amount of pressure on the snow bridge. Whether the bridge was already weakened by Mawson's sledge crossing it obliquely, or whether it was just the weight of Ninnis that made the critical difference, cannot be known. What is clear is that the lead dogs had reached the other side before the bridge gave way and the falling sledge pulled them back, leaving their desperate claw marks on the far edge of the abyss. For Ninnis, there was no time to react. He was so far from the sheer sides of the wide crevasse that he had no chance of scrambling to safety, as he had done when falling into a crevasse on November 21. This time, he couldn't even call out in terror as he fell hundreds of feet into his icy grave.[23]

CHAPTER ELEVEN

A Cascade of Calamities

It was just after lunch on December 14, 1912, when the journey ended for Belgrave Ninnis. Mawson didn't immediately realize that something might be amiss. He'd gone almost a quarter of a mile past the lethal crevasse, laboriously doing his computations atop the sledge, before he looked up and noticed that Mertz had come to a halt and was looking back quizzically in his direction. Following Mertz's gaze, Mawson turned and saw a vast nothingness behind him, with just the tracks of his sledge in the snow and no sign of Ninnis. There was just a chance that Ninnis might have been hidden by a hollow in the landscape, but when Mawson dismounted and rushed back, he saw the terrible truth. The snow bridge had collapsed, and Ninnis had fallen so deeply that he could not be seen. Only a whimpering and badly injured dog and the remains of the heavily loaded sledge were visible on a ledge about 50 meters below.[1] The journey was not only over for Ninnis; it was also over for Mawson. He would later say that he had been planning the following day to depot most of his food and equipment, and make a final dash to the east to maximize the extent of his journey and reach the coast discovered by Scott's *Terra Nova* in February 1911.[2] Now that plan was in tatters.

At first, Mawson and Mertz concentrated on devising a way of rescuing their missing companion. The distraught Mertz thought of placing the remaining sledge across the crevasse and lowering

154 FLAWS IN THE ICE

one of them by rope, even if it was only to bring up the food. But the crevasse was much too wide for the sledge to be placed across it, and anyway their alpine rope could not reach that far down. It was only by using a fishing line that they were able to ascertain the depth of the ledge on which the sledge had fallen. Lying on the edge of the crevasse, they peered past the ledge into the farthest depths of the icy crevasse and could see only an enveloping darkness. Repeatedly they called Ninnis's name, but received no response. "My poor friend had to be dead or unconscious," wrote Mertz. After about an hour, when the dog stopped its whimpering and died, the two men finally gave up any hope they might have of seeing Ninnis alive. If the fall had not killed him instantly, the extreme cold would have done so by then. Nevertheless, they "called and sounded for three hours," not being able to tear themselves away from the site of the tragedy.[3]

Then they did a curious thing. Instead of beginning the return journey, Mawson and Mertz left the sledge and dogs behind, and made a five-mile rush to the east. In his diary, Mertz says simply that they "went about 5 miles more east; it meant the end of the sledging expedition." What was the purpose of this last, desperate dash, when they were so short of food, and every hour counted for their survival? Mawson's diary explains that they "went on a few miles to a hill and took position observations." But he had already taken position observations at noon, and was working out their location at the time that Ninnis fell down the crevasse, judging it to be 68° 53'53" S and 151° 30'46" E. Why do it again? In the official account of the expedition, Mawson provided yet another explanation. This time, he claimed, they "went ahead to a higher point to obtain a better view of our surroundings" and used the opportunity to take "a complete observation for position."[4] Again, the question remains, why did he do it again so close to where he had already done position observations?

Partly, it was to act as a check on his earlier observations. The fact that he felt the need to make such a check provides farther confirmation that, as Madigan and Webb had alleged, Mawson was not very good at calculating his location, and didn't trust his abilities in this regard. Going that much farther east also gave him a much greater chance of exceeding the distance traveled by Madigan and Bage, which is what he had been determined to do. Even though the faulty sledge-meter forced him to guesstimate the distance he had traveled, he claimed after this additional short journey to have exceeded the 300-mile mark. Indeed, his official account claims that he traveled precisely "three hundred and fifteen and three-quarter miles eastward from the Hut," with no indication that this figure was just a very rough approximation of the actual distance that he traveled. The dash was also a last throw of the dice in his efforts to reach the coast discovered by the *Terra Nova* in 1911 and supposedly seen by Wilkes in 1840. Mawson would no longer be able to reach it, but climbing to a greater height might allow him at least to see it in the distance and to comment on the validity of Wilkes's claim to have seen the coastline to the north of Mawson's present position. This is what he did in *The Home of the Blizzard*, claiming that his 2,400-foot vantage point allowed him to see water in the "far distance," and that he couldn't see "anything which could correspond with the land marked by Wilkes as existing so much farther to the north."[5]

As Mawson also noted, climbing to a greater height allowed him "to obtain a better view of our surroundings," which provided both him and Mertz with better evidence as to which course they should now take. They had a difficult choice to make. Mawson had decided some days before to return on a more inland route, in the hope of avoiding the massive glaciers and hidden crevasses that had caused them so much trouble on the outward journey. That would make the return journey even longer, at least in terms of distance. There were two alternatives to the inland route: they could return the way they had come and accept the consequent risks; or they could head for the coast, descend to the sea ice, and make their way back to the hut by that route. There would be food on the sea ice in the form of penguins and birds and their eggs, along with seals and fish that could be caught through cracks in the ice. They might even encounter Madigan's party. Once they were on the sea ice, they could also make themselves visible to the *Aurora* if Davis came looking for them. However, Mawson argued that the compelling advantages of taking such a course were offset by the likely difficulties of the crevasses that lay between them and the ice.

The view from the hilltop seems to have been crucial in dissuading them from trying to return by way of the sea ice. Although Mawson could see that the ocean was "frozen out to the horizon," he claimed in *The Home of the Blizzard* that the "coastal slopes were fearfully broken and scaured [scarred] in their descent to the sea."[6] As he later explained to a meeting of the Royal Geographical Society, "a descent to the frozen sea would be dangerous on account of heavy crevassing in that direction and would undoubtedly cause delay." In other words, it might take longer and they might not get to the hut before the *Aurora* left to pick up Wild's party from the western base. He also argued that "the surface of the sea-ice along that coast was entirely unknown, and it was extremely likely that it would be breaking up."

I find this difficult to countenance, when Mawson had just seen that it was frozen to the horizon, and Madigan was journeying along that same sea ice. Yet, in Mawson's view, these factors were sufficient to outweigh any advantage that would be gained by the "chance of obtaining seals for food."[7] Mawson had shown during his short sledge journey with Madigan how cautious he was about descending a crevassed slope to the sea. Ninnis's terrible fate would have confirmed his fears. Moreover, even if they could successfully reach the sea ice, it would mean that they would be following in the footsteps of Madigan's party, and there would be no glory to be gained there. Mawson had already derided Scott for doing that in relation to Shackleton and the South Pole. It is likely that this is what really made him decide to take the inland route. After all, his trek had failed, and nothing could emphasize that failure more than having to follow Madigan home.

So Mawson kept to his original intention to return to the

hut by a longer route that would take them farther inland. First, though, he and Mertz returned to their sledge and the dreadful crevasse, where they spent another hour or so calling in vain to Ninnis. The men had much to ponder as they grieved for their companion, and perhaps wondered whether others would soon be grieving for them. They had lost all their dog food and all but one and a half weeks of the human food, part of which was made up of "perks," such as chocolate and raisins. Although Mawson would never admit it, his earlier division of the food and fuel between the two sledges was the cause of the dire predicament that now confronted them. The two men would have to make ten days' food last the thirty-five days or more that it would take them to return. They could eke out their food by killing the remaining dogs one by one, and sharing the meat between man and beast, but the dogs were already weak and scrawny, and they would not last long. Mawson had always planned to kill most of them on the return journey, and had already killed three. Now, without any other food to give them, Mertz and he would have to begin killing the remaining six.

Mawson could not count on getting any additional food until he reached Aladdin's Cave. This was a grim thought that offered little hope of them making it back alive. Their tent and tent poles had also been lost in the crevasse, along with Mertz's Burberry over-trousers and Burberry helmet, their pick and shovel, and the sledge mast and sail. They had a spare tent cover, but if they could not improvise some poles, they would be doomed. Mertz also would suffer in a blizzard without his protective Burberry clothing; he had to make do with "an extra pair of woollen under trousers." As they lingered at the lip of the crevasse, while Mawson read a burial service from his prayer book, the full enormity of their situation, and of what they had lost, slowly became apparent. "May God Help us," Mawson beseeched. Mertz had a slightly different take on their predicament. He emphasized how they would "have to stick close together, Mawson and I, and do our best with the few things remaining to us to find the winter quarters."[8]

It is interesting that Mertz wrote in terms of them *finding* the hut rather than simply *reaching* it, which suggested a justifiable concern on his part about Mawson's ability with the theodolite to determine their location and the direction they should take.

Mawson's predicament was beyond anything in his experience. On the Shackleton expedition, he and David and Mackay had been short of food and time to reach the coast so they could be rescued by the *Nimrod*. On that occasion, Mawson had drawn on the local wildlife to supplement their rations, taking penguin and seal meat on the outward journey, and being confident that more seals and penguins would be waiting for him when he returned to the coast. He had also established food depots along the coast in case they were forced to walk all the way back to Shackleton's hut. The fresh meat had been their salvation, providing much better sustenance than the expedition's processed food and, unknown to Mawson, supplying them with sufficient vitamin C to protect them against scurvy. Unfortunately, he did not learn from that experience, and therefore did not impress it upon the members of his expedition. Although Mertz had spent days cooking seal meat before their departure from the hut, it was intended as food for the dogs rather than the men. And now it, too, had been lost down the crevasse.

Having formally buried Ninnis, they embarked on their return journey with a sudden sense of urgency as they raced to reach their previous night's camp, where the third sledge had been abandoned. Leaving the crevasse at 9:00 p.m. on December 14, and still blessed with light winds, they finally reached their old campsite at 2:30 a.m. Despite the nine hours' delay caused by the death of Ninnis, Mawson claimed they traveled 24 miles that day, which was much more than they had ever done before. He faced a difficult balancing act — to cover as much distance as possible each day while eking out their food supply so that it lasted until they reached Aladdin's Cave. He began by killing the weakest of the six dogs, feeding most of it to the other dogs, and frying some of the meat for their own breakfast. Their remaining food supplies were divided up into smaller ration packs to last the weeks that it would take to get back. The dog meat was "voted good though it had a strong, musty taste and was so stringy that it could not be properly chewed." With no food left to feed the remaining dogs, they were not likely to taste any better when it came their turn to die. A makeshift and very small tent was made from the spare tent cover, while poles were improvised from skis and the legs of the theodolite. Even spoons had to be fashioned from wood to replace the ones that had been lost. Mawson also belatedly raised the flag and claimed the place for Britain, after being reminded by Mertz that he had failed to do so the previous day. By the time they were all set to go, the temperature was barely below freezing, and the snow was too soft for sledging. So they waited for the colder nighttime temperatures, and traveled through the night of December 15 — not stopping till 5:00 a.m., by which time they had covered 18½ miles.[9]

The second day of the return journey was also done at night, and their prospects didn't look good. They barely covered half the distance of the previous day, and three of the remaining dogs were almost done in. Mawson had wanted to travel 15 miles, but they only managed nine and a half. There was no stopping to cook lunch, as it would have taken too long to erect their makeshift tent. So they went without liquids, other than snatches of snow, which left them terribly thirsty. Mawson had hardly slept because of "bad conjunctivitis in both eyes," one of which had to be bandaged. With that and the overcast sky, it was difficult to see sastrugi hidden by the whiteout conditions. Even worse, he was uncertain of their direction. The cloud-covered sky made it impossible to take a sighting from the sun, which made them dependent on the compass. However, because of the proximity of the magnetic pole, Mawson complained that the compass was "very dead." As a result, he feared that they were following "rather a zig zag course" and might have "got too far to [the] south." With that and his bandaged eye, no wonder it was "rather a mournful procession," with Mertz out in front on his skis as he pulled the sledge with a towrope while Mawson hauled in harness alongside the worn-out dogs.[10]

One of the dogs was so exhausted that it had to be carried on the sledge for much of the following evening before being killed and skinned by Mertz when they stopped to camp at 5:45 a.m. on December 18. And, of the remaining dogs, only one was sufficiently strong to help haul the sledge. Although Mawson found the "dog meat very stringy," it was still "very welcome." Mertz thought it was "better than nothing, though it's not recommendable." After three days, Mawson estimated they had averaged 15 miles a day. In the unlikely event that they could maintain this rate, it would take about three weeks for them to get back to the hut. However, they could not count upon the conditions remaining relatively favorable, with light winds and little snow. The main impediment to their progress those first few days was the overcast sky, which left Mawson uncertain of the exact course they were following. He was trying to head due west, but conceded that they might be heading either south or north of west. It was "a wretched game," complained Mawson, "plodding along trying to make a straight course with overcast sky." And it only got worse, with Mawson and Mertz stumbling and falling into large sastrugi that could not be seen in the overcast conditions. It was so bad that they were forced to set up camp after doing little more than six miles. Mawson was still uncertain of their course, which he admitted could "be only approximate."[11]

It was not until December 19 that they saw the sun, enabling Mawson to take a sighting with the theodolite and find out that they had been heading on a southwesterly course rather than due west. In fact, there was so much sun that Mawson complained of it being "too hot." The sun was melting the snow, which made them stay in camp until the temperature cooled sufficiently to harden the surface. It meant more traveling at night. Although the sun allowed Mawson to judge his course, it didn't necessarily mean that he could maintain it when areas of sastrugi and dangerous crevasses appeared in their path. And he remained confused about their position, not being able to recognize any familiar features to their north that they had passed on their outward journey. There were just mirages, which left Mawson unsure whether or not they really were following a course to the south of their outward journey. In the midst of this continuing confusion, one of the dogs fell into a deep crevasse and was saved by its harness, only to become so exhausted by the heavy going that it had to be carried on the sledge for the rest of the day. Perhaps because they already had so much dog meat, it was given a reprieve when they camped that night. But when the dog again had to ride on the sledge, on December 21, it was shot and butchered at their next camp, leaving just two dogs.[12]

Each time a dog was killed, the parts that were deemed unsuitable for the men to eat, such as the intestines and skin, were fed to the surviving dogs. It was sufficient to stop the dogs starving to death, which was now the most crucial consideration. They were no longer capable of hauling, and had to be carried on the sledge or allowed to walk alongside. "The dogs pull no more," wrote Mertz on December 21, noting that they "just make sure that they don't collapse, to have food during the whole return trip." Because of the relatively high temperatures, the edible organs were usually consumed soon after the dogs were killed, while the meat was cooked in their cramped tent for consumption on subsequent days. The consequent condensation in the tent was a great problem. Their clothes and bedding were often wet, and it was usually impossible to dry them. When snowdrift caused the inside of the tent to ice up, and then they began cooking, it became particularly uncomfortable. "Everything has been wretchedly wet from drift and cooking [dog meat] in low tent caked with ice," complained Mawson.[13] Without his Burberry over-trousers and helmet, Mertz was more liable than Mawson to be badly affected by the wet conditions. However, the effects on Mertz were mitigated during the first week or so, when the winds were mostly light and there was little snowdrift.

It is impossible to know precisely how much food Mawson and Mertz were forcing themselves to survive on, but it would have been perhaps a third of the daily calorie intake they required for hard physical labor in conditions of extreme cold. As a result, they were slowly starving, and their only hope of survival lay in stretching their rations until they reached Aladdin's Cave. However, given the vagaries of the weather and the difficult landscape they had to cross, they had no way of knowing how long the journey would take. It was a conundrum of the worst sort. If they severely limited their rations, they might have food to spare but nonetheless die from the effects of the strict rationing before reaching their goal. If they were too liberal with the rations, they might run out of food and die of starvation. Faced with this terrible choice, Mawson appears to have opted for a regime of strict rationing. It was a regime that had, after all, served him well on the Shackleton expedition, when he had coped much better than David or Mackay. Of course, there was another alternative: if one of them died early enough, it was likely to leave sufficient food for the other to survive the remaining distance.

There was, however, a crucial difference between Mawson's experience on the Shackleton expedition and his present predicament. Back then, he had survived on a relatively balanced but limited ration of pemmican and plasmon, supplemented with seal and penguin meat. His present ration scale was very unbalanced — indeed, dangerously so. One problem was caused by he and Mertz eating the livers of the dogs, which have high vitamin A content. Indeed, the amount of vitamin A in the livers of Husky dogs is so high that it can be fatal, which is why the Inuit people of the Arctic avoided eating them. However, Mawson's dogs were so emaciated that their livers would have been smaller than normal, and the vitamin A content that much less. It also appears from a reading of the diaries of Mawson and Mertz that Mawson ate more of the livers than Mertz did.[14] So he should have suffered more than Mertz from vitamin A toxicity.

Both men would also have suffered from a lack of vitamin C, which causes scurvy. Although they had consumed enough of the vitamin while they were living in the hut, partly because of Mawson's requirement for them to eat fresh seal and penguin meat, the beneficial effect would have slowly worn away on their extended trek, when vitamin C was notably absent from their food. It could have taken up to two months or more for the symptoms to appear, but it was likely to take much less time in their straitened circumstances and the harsh weather conditions. They might have absorbed some vitamin C once they began eating the dog meat, but there wouldn't have been much in the animals' emaciated bodies. In any case, Mawson and Mertz so overcooked the dog meat, in a vain attempt to make it tender, that any vitamin C would have been boiled away. So, even though they were unaware of it, scurvy was a real danger for them if their journey turned out to be too prolonged. But there was another, more insidious danger — one that other writers have missed.

Among the food that had fallen to the bottom of the crevasse was most of the pemmican, that vital mixture of dried beef and sixty percent fat, which provided the traditional basis of any sledging diet. Instead of drawing on the small quantity of pemmican on the surviving sledge, Mawson decided first to eat the dog meat. This seemed to make sense: the pemmican would not spoil, and fresh dog meat should have served just as well as the seal and penguin meat had on the Shackleton expedition. However, these were not oil-rich seals and penguins, but starving dogs that were being fed on scraps of leather and the skin and bones of their fellow starving dogs. As Mawson and Mertz complained, the flesh of the dogs was very stringy and almost impossible to eat unless boiled in a soup or stew. This was because it contained little or no fat — and fat was essential to keep them alive. Although Mawson was unaware of it, their starvation ration of lean meat left them dangerously exposed to the threat of dying from protein poisoning. This rare condition is caused by the consumption of too much protein, combined with too little fat and too little carbohydrates. Any fat on the dogs would have been confined largely to their organs, such as the liver and brain. So, although it has been suggested that Mertz died from an excess of vitamin A, and therefore must have eaten *more* of the livers than Mawson, it is likely that he died partly because he ate *less* of the dog livers, and therefore consumed less fat.

Interestingly, the Arctic explorer Vilhjalmur Stefansson was about to publish a book about his experiences in the Arctic, where he lived for a month "without oil or fat of any kind," eating caribou meat that contained no discernible fat. Although he and his companions stuffed themselves with the lean meat, they "felt continually hungry" and began to exhibit symptoms of serious illness, including diarrhea. Stefansson's dogs were on the same diet, and were soon "nothing but skin and bones." He was warned by the Inuit that living just on lean meat could kill him.[15] Mawson and Mertz had no way of knowing this, and would never realize that it was the principal reason for their increasing debility. The diaries of Mertz and Mawson provide support for this theory, with mentions of them suffering from exhaustion and almost constant hunger, even after eating a meal, during the first ten days or so of the return journey. Those feelings of hunger after eating a meal are a symptom of protein poisoning, as was the diarrhea that would finally afflict Mertz.

As Mawson and Mertz became weaker from their starvation diet, the sledge was proving harder to haul. And it became even more so when the daytime temperatures softened the snow and made it sticky. To alleviate the extra pressure this was causing, Mawson began discarding anything that was considered extraneous to their current needs. On December 21, he threw into the snow "a few socks, rope, rifle, etc," but it was not enough to make much difference to their increasingly desperate struggle across the snow. The following day, they had to haul uphill, which Mawson noted was "very heavy going," and "made us ill."[16] They still retained their alpine rope, since another fall down even a relatively small crevasse could prove fatal to the victim if there was no rope with which to haul him out. More reductions to the weight of the sledge were made on December 23. It was a "bad state of affairs," wrote Mawson, "as now must abandon camera, hypsometer, etc." The second-last dog was also killed, as heavy snow kept them from continuing their journey. While they waited for it to abate, they spent their time cooking all the dog meat, and made a stew from the dog's legs. Mertz noted in his diary how the cooking made the meat "nearly soft," although Mawson complained that it had not satisfied his hunger. They abandoned more gear the following day, and cooked another dog stew, which was judged by Mawson to be the "best yet." Mertz agreed, noting that he "slept well after having eaten the cooked legs."[17] Only one dog now remained alive.

The diet continued to take its toll on the men. Mawson complained of being tired when they had to haul the sledge up-hill, and on December 23 of being so hungry that he couldn't sleep. When he did sleep on Christmas Eve, the aching hunger prompted him to dream "of a huge fancy cake ... amidst weird surroundings." Their real surroundings were certainly weird enough on Christmas Day, with a strengthening wind creating a low snowdrift as the two men struggled their way back across the massive glacier that would later bear the name of Ninnis. While Madigan's party was camped on the same glacier about 75 miles to the north, and was enjoying a dinner of fried emperor penguin breast and an improvised plum pudding and whisky, Mawson's and Mertz's feast consisted of just "two bits of biscuit" that Mawson had found in his bag. As they nibbled at the biscuit, they wished each other "Merry Christmasses in the future." Along with a dinner of dog stew, this was the extent of their merriment that day. Anything more would have to await their return to the hut, which Mawson calculated was 158 miles away as the crow flew.[18] But they weren't crows, and the distance they would have to cover would be closer to 200 miles.

Mawson and Mertz could do the math. They would have realized that the survival of both of them was unlikely on the food that was available. When they first reached the Ninnis Glacier on December 23, Mertz was concerned that the "obstacles could take us far backwards, and the provisions wouldn't be enough." He was worried that the glacier would force them to zigzag or even backtrack, adding to the distance they would have to cover. It is clear that Mertz was starting to suffer from both the starvation diet and the protein poisoning. "We both realize that hard work and little food don't go well together," wrote Mertz. Yet they needed to travel fast, so that the food didn't have to last so many days. It was the same conundrum they'd been facing all along: if they restricted their food intake, they couldn't travel as fast across the snow; but if they increased their food intake, there might not be sufficient food to last the distance. Mertz was well aware of their predicament. "We have to travel fast," he wrote on December 24, "so that the food provisions would be enough."[19]

What Mawson didn't mention in his diary entry for Christmas Day was how much of the return journey they had completed. After three days, he had been satisfied with the 45 miles they had traveled at an average rate of 15 miles a day. Now, twelve days later, he would have been painfully aware that they had slowed down considerably. Although Mawson was not confident about the reliability of his daily figures, they showed that the pair had only covered 111 miles during the eleven days since the death of Ninnis. Instead of maintaining an average distance of 15 miles a day, they were only doing ten miles a day. Yet even this diminished result had been achieved in mostly good sledging weather. At this rate, it would be at least another three weeks before they reached the hut. A slower pace meant they would have to reduce their daily rations even more to ensure that their food lasted the distance. Already they were on less than half the normal sledging ration, and they were becoming as emaciated as the one remaining dog.

It was on Christmas Day that Mawson made the calculations that would determine whether one or both of them would live or die. It makes for awful reading, revealing the strictness of his rationing. Of the one and a half weeks' food left on the surviving sledge when Ninnis died on December 14, the bag containing one week's food had not been touched. Mawson had eked out the scant provisions in the opened bag for eleven days, even though it contained rations that were originally meant to last for only three or four days. And there was still more left in it at the end of the eleven days. Counting up the vital tins of pemmican on Christmas Day, he found that there were five left in the partially eaten bag, along with twenty plasmon biscuits, sufficient butter for five days, and a good quantity of cocoa, Glaxo, chocolate sticks, raisins, and almonds. By restricting their rations even more, Mawson calculated that they could make the opened bag last until December 31 and still have ten biscuits left over, along with a small quantity of Glaxo, a "fair amount" of cocoa, fifty-two sticks of chocolate, two pounds of raisins, and a few almonds. He thought that this, along with the remaining dog, would be sufficient to last them a farther five days "of not over arduous work." This would leave them with the unopened bag, containing a week's rations. To get back safely across the 160 or so miles remaining, they would need to average at least ten miles a day, wrote Mawson.[20]

As they began suffering more of the ill effects of their unbalanced and restrictive ration, the weather started to batter their tired bodies and take a farther toll on their food intake. The winds in late December made it impossible to stop for lunch and do a boil-up. Not that there was sufficient food for three meals a day. The wind also caused them to take longer to pitch their makeshift tent at the end of a night's sledging, with Mawson complaining on December 26 that it took four hours from the time they stopped sledging to the time they were able to get into their sleeping bags. Getting started each day took a similarly long time, while the eight to ten hours spent hauling the sledge was proving to be "a great strain," which would be "entirely avoided" if they could pitch the tent and make even a hot drink from a triple-used tea bag midway during their daily haul. Mawson found that this couldn't be done in the increasingly adverse weather conditions, although he and Mertz eased some of the strain on their starving bodies by using their tent as a sail, so that at least some advantage could be taken from the wind.[21]

Having successfully crossed the Ninnis Glacier, they began a slow climb toward the second glacier. The even surface would have provided a good testing ground for their sail, had the snow not been so soft from the sun that every step saw them sink their feet deeply into it. If Mertz didn't have to haul the sledge with Mawson, he would have found it easy going on his skis. Indeed, had he been without the impediment of Mawson, Mertz might have been able to use his survival skills from the Swiss Alps to ski all the way back to the hut. But he'd decided to "stick close together" with Mawson, come what may, even though he was no longer well equipped for an extended journey. The warm sun revealed one of his handicaps when it melted any snow that fell on their clothes. "Without wearing mountain pants [Burberries]," complained Mertz on December 27, "the snow can penetrate into my underpants." And when they were in the tent, the sun and the cooker combined to cause the tent to drip constantly onto the men and their bedding.

Without his Burberry over-trousers, Mertz was affected worse than Mawson. He described how he would lie at night in his wet sleeping bag and feel each layer of clothing slowly thaw, one after the other. Being colder and wetter than Mawson, he needed more food to survive. But their rations were strictly divided and only rarely supplemented, as they were on December 27 when they had the "great luxury" of having three-quarters of an ounce of butter and half a plasmon biscuit after their main course of dog meat. The one remaining dog, named Ginger, was kept alive as long as possible. On December 28, when Ginger couldn't go on, it was shot and its meat cooked. The cooking went on for most of the day, causing everything to become "wretchedly wet from drip from drift and cooking Ginger in low tent caked with ice." The following day, Mawson reported that he had a "great breakfast" of Ginger's "thyroids and brain." It is not clear whether Mertz shared in this feast, which would have been relatively rich in fat. Mertz's diary doesn't mention that he ate those organs — just that he got up early to cook more of the dog meat in the hope that it would make it tender. Without the cooking, wrote Mertz, it "wouldn't be edible."[22]

The food was never sufficient, and the increasing wind and

cold was adding to the toll being taken on Mertz's health. With the wind blowing at 30 to 40 miles an hour, the sail helped to take part of the load off the two men. But the wind, and the low drift that it caused, was keeping the relatively unprotected Mertz cold and wet. Mawson made little mention of the effect this was having on his companion until December 30, when he noted in his diary that Mertz was "off colour." Mertz noted only that he was "tired," and wrote just three brief sentences for the day: "15 miles to the N.W. on a good surface. Since 11 pm, first light wind, then increasing wind. As I am tired, I write no more." There is little clue as to what Mawson meant by describing his companion as "off colour." Perhaps it was because they had pushed themselves too hard that day, after encountering a surface of hard snow that was ideal for sledging. Indeed, according to Mawson, they had traveled at a cracking pace, and covered 15 miles before calling a halt. While Mawson proceeded to cook more dog meat for three hours, the ailing Mertz got into his wet sleeping bag, which got even wetter from the cooking. "All his things [were] very wet," wrote Mawson, "chiefly on account of no burberry pants." But he also noted that the tent "dripped terribly [because it was] all caked with ice." On other days, they had been able to dry out their gear, but the constant snowdrift made this impossible. Mawson reported, after a breakfast of dog meat and a little pemmican, that Mertz was "somewhat better."[23] The fat in the pemmican might have produced a slight improvement in Mertz's condition, but he would have had to consume a lot more pemmican to enjoy a full recovery. And Mawson's tight rein on the rations ensured that this would not happen.

On December 31, Mawson reported that both of them were now off color. His failure to specify what symptoms they were exhibiting has made it difficult for historians and biographers to decide conclusively what they were suffering from. Their feeling of being unwell may have been an early symptom of scurvy, which certainly could have started to appear after six weeks of trekking without fresh food. Their ill health also might have been a result of hypothermia, due to the extreme cold and the constant dampness of their clothes and bedding — particularly Mertz's inadequate clothing. It has to be said that hypothermia would have been less of a problem if Mawson had used a three-man sleeping bag rather than single-man bags, and had sometimes shared his Burberry over-trousers and helmet with Mertz, as Mackay had done with David on the Shackleton expedition. Then again, feeling "off colour" might have been due to malnutrition, brought on by the starvation rations that Mawson was imposing on them. Or it might have been due to the vitamin A from dog livers, or the consumption of a diet composed almost totally of lean meat. Most likely, the deterioration in their condition was caused by a combination of all these factors.

With neither Mawson nor Mertz having medical experience, they blamed their ill health on the dog meat, and decided on December 31 to refrain from eating it for a day or so. Their instincts were right. Their bodies were craving fat. In place of the lean meat, they had biscuit, butter, and tea for breakfast before setting off. When poor visibility forced them to camp later that day, they ate a small quantity of pemmican, washed down with cocoa. It provided some fat, but it was nowhere near enough. After waiting in the tent for the weather to clear, they had what Mawson described as a "small meal" before setting off again late that night. Mawson reported that they covered a total distance of seven and a half miles on that trek. As we have seen, this was much less than they needed to do each day.[24] Their situation was getting grimmer, and it would not improve for Mawson as long as Mertz was alive. For the next week, they hardly moved at all, stopped firstly by the weather and then by the deterioration in Mertz's condition.

Mawson had decided to reduce their rations whenever they were forced to spend a day in the tent. He measured out their rations according to the distance they traveled and the energy used, rather than according to the time elapsed. According to his strict regimen, when they stopped for a day or more, they ate hardly anything in order to have sufficient food to last the distance to the hut. This might have been appropriate if they were in good physical health, and sheltering in warm and dry conditions. However, they were starving, and living in bitterly cold and constantly wet conditions, with the drastic reduction of their rations having the entirely predictable effect of making them less able to go on. Mertz, in particular, needed to eat pemmican, and lots of it, if he was to survive. But moderate winds and snowdrift kept them confined to their cramped tent for the first three days of the New Year, which meant that Mawson cut back their rations farther. Mertz was doomed. The last entry in his diary was on New Year's Day:

> 5 o'clock in the afternoon. After 5 miles, already in the sleeping-bags. It's not good weather to travel. Incredibly bad light, cloudy sky, therefore we didn't go far. We wait for better weather. The dog meat looks indigestible for me, because yesterday I felt a little weak.[25]

There would be no respite for Mertz from Mawson's strict rationing regime.

Mawson recorded in his diary that they each ate just 2½ ounces of chocolate on January 1. The next day, they had a "*small* pem[mican] & cocoa & ¾ biscuit." Early on January 3, they each ate two ounces of chocolate. Later that day, "Mertz boiled a small cocoa and had biscuit," while Mawson had some dog liver and cocoa. The dog liver would have given Mawson the fat that they both desperately needed. When the weather cleared sufficiently for them to travel that evening, they had more cocoa, and managed to cover five miles before Mertz's frostbitten fingers forced them to stop. It was only now that Mawson provided some description of Mertz's terrible state. Apart from the frostbite, wrote Mawson, "he is generally in a very bad condition. Skin coming off legs, etc."[26]

Losing his skin was possibly the least of Mertz's problems. It was most likely caused, not by an excess of vitamin A, as some writers have suggested, but by the constant dampness of his clothes and bedding. Had there been any days of sunshine, they would have had a chance to dry out on the sledge. Mertz's problems were more than skin deep. On the one hand, Mawson's strict rationing regime was starving him to death. On the other hand, Mawson's failure to have learned from his experience on the Shackleton expedition, by including fresh seal and penguin meat as part of their sledging rations, was making them vulnerable to both scurvy and protein poisoning. It is almost certain that the latter condition was principally responsible for Mertz's steady decline. It also explains why Mawson was not so badly afflicted, since their diary entries suggest that Mawson consumed more animal fat — whether it was from dog liver, butter, or pemmican — than Mertz during the three and a half weeks that had elapsed after the loss of the food sledge on December 14.

On January 4, Mertz was so unwell that Mawson decided to remain in the tent. He opened a new bag of rations, and fed Mertz "milk, etc." Mawson thought they might move out on the following day, when weather conditions were relatively good for traveling. But Mertz "practically refused, saying it was suicide and that it [was] much better for him to have the day in [the sleeping] bag and dry it and get better, then do more on sun-shining day." Because of Mawson's strict rationing, they had only one meal that day, "a half tin [of] hoosh and cocoa and ½ biscuit." Although there would have been too little food, and much too little fat, in that meal to cause Mertz's recovery, Mawson thought it was "a rattling good meal and I now feel comparatively satisfied as if I just came out of one of [the] best London restaurants." He tried to get Mertz to move, but he remained adamant that he wouldn't move until the following day. Mawson could feel his own life-chances slipping away the longer they stayed there. "All will depend on providence now," wrote Mawson, "it is an even race to the Hut."[27]

Mertz did get out of his sleeping bag on January 6, but he was too weak to help dismantle the tent and pack the sledge. Mawson also was "weak from want of food," but it was Mertz who insisted on stopping after traveling barely two miles. Mawson tried to put Mertz on the sledge and use the sail to help propel it along, but the dying Mertz refused to cooperate. There was nothing to do but stop. Mawson thought Mertz had "a fever [and] he does not assimilate his food." It was an invidious position for Mawson. If Mertz didn't recover within a day or two, and regain enough strength to travel eight or ten miles a day, they would be "doomed." Mawson noted that he could reach the hut himself "with the provisions at hand, but I cannot leave him. His heart seems to have gone. It is very hard for me — to be within 100 m[iles] of the Hut and in such a position is awful." He concluded correctly that Mertz was dying, but he couldn't leave him, even though it meant that "both our chances are going now."

Fortunately for Mawson, he didn't have long to wait. The following day, Mertz was delirious and suffering from diarrhea. There was little Mawson could do, other than clean him up and put him back in the sleeping bag. "This is terrible," wrote Mawson. He claimed that he wasn't concerned for himself, but "for Paquita and for all others connected with the expedition." It was for them he felt "so deeply and sinfully," and "I pray to God to help us." There was no help for Mertz, who died early on the morning of January 8.[28] Mertz's death could signal Mawson's salvation.

CHAPTER TWELVE

Racing Home

As Mawson's far-eastern journey suffered its second death, the journeys led by Madigan, Bage, and Bickerton were having narrow escapes of their own. The southern party of Bage, Hurley, and Webb had been blessed with good weather during the final days of their southward journey, which allowed them to reach 301 miles. It was much less than the 400 miles that Bage had wanted to cover, and it left him frustratingly short of the South Magnetic Pole. But there was no choice: Mawson had instructed all parties to be back at the hut by January 15, 1913.

It had taken Bage's group six weeks to cover 300 miles, and they had only three and a half weeks left for the return journey. Although they'd be going downhill with the prevailing wind at their back, there was barely sufficient food on the sledge, and in the two depots they had left along the trail, to see them safely home. Any delay caused by blizzards, or a failure to locate one or more of the depots, could mean their deaths. Hurley was "half glad, half regretful" at the thought of turning back, noting that the "vacant places seemed to beckon irresistibly." But Lieutenant Bage kept obediently to their schedule. Rather than making a final dash for the South Magnetic Pole, which Webb estimated was just 45 miles away, they turned their sledge around on December 21 and headed north.[1] Events would show that this was a wise decision.

Their return journey would be much quicker. "No more shall we face the blizzard," wrote Hurley, "nor toil up steep ice slopes." The wind would allow them to make use of a canvas sail to help push them along. Indeed, the 49-square-foot sail was so effective on the first full day of the return journey that Hurley and Webb had to be roped up behind the sledge to slow it down as it "glided majestically … like a tiny barque over a frozen sea." Bage remained in harness at the front to maintain the correct direction, while Hurley and Webb struggled to keep the sledge in check and prevent it crashing into Bage or toppling over on the sometimes rough surface. Eventually, they reduced the sail and resumed their familiar positions at the front. With the help of the reefed sail, there was little need for great exertion by the men, who covered 18½ miles that day. And they had no trouble returning the way they had come, with their earlier tracks still fairly clear on the dusting of snow.[2]

It wasn't always that easy. On some days, the wind shifted more to the west, which "skidded the sledge along sideways," while the surface also became more difficult at times, changing to "the dread pie-crust snow which tired us greatly lifting our feet from the deep foot holes." When the sledge-meter became wrecked beyond repair, they used the mounds of snow that they had created on the outward journey as a check on the homeward journey's distance and confirmation of their direction. Christmas Day came and went without a celebratory feast, with the men deciding to wait until they reached the 200-mile depot, where Hurley planned to "surprise my chums by my culinary knowledge." It was a decision forced upon them by necessity. Christmas Day was spent "toiling against diminishing rations on the great plateau," while lunch on the following day was described by a "very hungry" Hurley as a "frugal repast." They were reducing their rations in case they could not find the depot or were forced by bad weather to remain in their tent. Fortunately, the weather held and there was no trouble finding the depot, which they reached at lunchtime on December 27. They immediately erected their tent alongside

Left: A studio photograph of a young Paquita Delprat. *(Mawson Collection, South Australian Museum)*

Above: The young Douglas Mawson. *(State Library of South Australia)*

Mawson being taken down Adelaide's North Terrace by jubilant students after his journey to the area of the South Magnetic Pole in 1908–09. *(Mawson Collection, South Australian Museum)*

Above: In rough seas aboard the *Aurora* en route to Australia. Mertz far left, and Ninnis far right. *(State Library of New South Wales – ON 144/Q72)*

Left: Frank Wild makes history dressed as Sir Walter Raleigh. *(State Library of New South Wales – ON 144/P45)*

Opposite: A spectacular photograph by Frank Hurley of the *Aurora* next to the tongue of the Mertz glacier. *(State Library of New South Wales – ON 144/W147)*

An albatross on its way to becoming a museum piece. From left: Stillwell, Harrisson, and Hunter. *(State Library of New South Wales – ON 144/H50)*

Opposite: Xavier Mertz on skis, with the sheer drop of the ice barrier in the background.
(State Library of New South Wales – ON 144/C121)

Above: Taking advantage of a calm day to complete the building of the hut.
(State Library of New South Wales – ON 144/H555)

Below: Frank Hurley's famous photograph of men battling against the wind as it tears at the hut.
(State Library of New South Wales – ON 144/W5)

Left: With snow and ice up to the eaves of the hut, Xavier Mertz emerges from the skylight. *(State Library of New South Wales – ON 144/H479)*

Above: Preparing food in the hut's kitchen, with the open doorway revealing the adjacent workshop. *(State Library of New South Wales – PXB 1698/1)*

Below: A discussion in "Hyde Park Corner," next to the thin wall of Mawson's cubicle. From left: Stillwell, Madigan, Mertz, Hodgeman, Hunter, Ninnis, and Murphy. Correll is probably the man with his back to the camera. *(State Library of New South Wales – ON 144/W65)*

Above left: Mawson photographs Laseron and Hunter dredging for marine life through a hole in the sea ice. *(State Library of New South Wales – PXE 725/1393)*

Above right: Mertz, Ninnis, and Hunter with a box of frozen Adélie penguins. *(State Library of New South Wales – ON 144/Q594)*

Below: Testing the air tractor. *(State Library of New South Wales – ON 144/Q569)*

Opposite: The height of the ice barrier is emphasized by Hurley's dramatic photograph of the diminutive figures at its base. *(State Library of New South Wales – ON 144/W90)*

Above: Mawson takes the lead hauling a sledge of supplies on the treacherous blue ice of the slope leading up to Aladdin's Cave. *(State Library of New South Wales – ON 144/Q791)*

Below: Mertz deposits bags of food and other supplies in Aladdin's Cave. *(State Library of New South Wales – ON 144/H5521)*

Opposite: Mertz uses his camera to capture Mawson leaning against the sledge in a pensive mood, while Ninnis kneels in the background. *(State Library of New South Wales – ON 144/C20)*

Above: Bage's support party pose by their sledge, with a cairn of snow marking a food depot. From left: Hunter, Murphy, and Laseron. *(State Library of New South Wales – ON 144/Q788)*

Below: Too distant to show their disappointment, Bage and Webb pose for Hurley at the southern limit of their journey. *(State Library of New South Wales – ON 144/Q673)*

McLean photographs Madigan and Correll struggling with the sledge across pressure ridges on the sea ice. *(State Library of New South Wales – ON 144/Q721)*

The sail makes it easier for Madigan and Correll on the snow-covered surface.
(State Library of New South Wales – ON 144/Q639)

Madigan ascends the massive cliff face discovered on his eastern coastal journey.
(State Library of New South Wales – ON 144/Q711)

Madigan and Correll pose with a penguin, which was fortunate to be regarded as a photo opportunity rather than a food opportunity. *(State Library of New South Wales – ON 144/Q650)*

Opposite: The cross erected to commemorate Ninnis and Mertz, whose deaths were made more meaningful by suggesting they occurred in the "cause of science." *(State Library of New South Wales – ON 144/H679)*

Above: Mawson (fifth from right) poses on the *Aurora* with his rescue party and the men from Macquarie Island, while Madigan stands at the back (ninth from right). *(State Library of New South Wales – PXE 725/1045)*

Left: Mawson eagerly prepares to jump ashore in Adelaide, while a relieved Madigan waits to follow the leader he had come to loathe. *(State Library of New South Wales – PXE 725/1281)*

Douglas Mawson

Above: With the battle of the Somme raging across the channel, and wife, Paquita, far away in Adelaide, Mawson poses on the beach with Kathleen Scott and her son, Peter. The photograph was stuck in her diary with part of it cut out, for reasons unknown. *(Kennet diary, Cambridge University Library)*

Left: The hero is honored. Mawson in court dress after being knighted by the King. *(Mawson Collection, South Australian Museum)*

the pillar of snow that marked the depot, while Hurley set about preparing their belated Christmas feast.³

There was no penguin or seal meat to provide the main course. The feast was made from double their normal rations, and composed solely of food that had been brought south by the *Aurora*. For an hors d'oeuvre, Hurley served up "Angels on gliders," which was "a raisin on top of a bar of chocolate, previously fried." Entrée was a biscuit fried in suet, while the Christmas roast was "frizzled pemmican on fried biscuit." For plum pudding, Hurley mixed three grated biscuits with butter, cocoa compound, butterscotch, Glaxo, sugar, seven raisins, a dollop of snow, and three drops of methylated spirit for flavoring. It was then shoved into an old food bag and boiled for five minutes, to the "great satisfaction" of them all. They finished with toasts to the King and their fellow expeditioners, the drink being made by boiling five raisins in methylated spirit, and "drunk in gulps by holding the nose and breath." The feast finished with cigars. It buoyed them up so much that the following day they sledged most of the day and all through the night until they had covered 41½ miles, establishing a new day's record for a man-hauled sledge. It was a mad feat, because it was followed by the exhausted men having to spend seventeen hours of fitful slumber in their sleeping bags, and making just 12 miles the following day.⁴

Nevertheless, since they hadn't reached the South Magnetic Pole, the mad dash could count as an achievement of some sort for the southern journey. More important were the magnetic observations that Webb continued to make on the return journey, often undertaken in the bitter cold and wind as they sat in the lee of a specially constructed wall of snow blocks. On December 24, when they reached the old camp they had created 249 miles from the hut, Webb took a full set of magnetic observations over several hours, while Hurley did the recording. Stricken by snow blindness, Bage was unable to assist, and also unable to maintain the entries in his diary. Another set of observations was taken on December 30. Even though Webb had wanted to complete five full sets of observations, they had to suffice with two. A combination of bad weather and the urgent need to reach the next food depot caused Bage to limit the number of prolonged stops, which thereby reduced the scientific value of their journey.[5]

By New Year's Day, they were just over 130 miles from the hut, which they expected to reach by January 10, well before the deadline of January 15. Although Bage was suffering severely from snow blindness and had to be carried for a day on the sledge in conditions of heavy snow, they continued to cover the required distance each day. But they were fast running out of food. Their next food depot was at the 67-mile mark, where Murphy's support party had left the last of their stores before heading back to the hut. On January 5, with little more than a day's rations left on the sledge, the depot should have been within sight, but the overcast conditions made the ground and sky a uniform color, and the depot impossible for the famished men to see. Without a shadow, wrote Webb, "one could neither see the landscape, nor the surface at one's feet." As a precaution, they cut their rations in half and retreated to their sleeping bags to conserve energy and wait for the light to improve. "There is nought to do but await and see what the morrow will bring forth," wrote Hurley.[6]

The next day was no better. The sky remained overcast, and snow began to fall when they attempted to move after lunch. Once again, they retreated to their sleeping bags and pondered their increasingly precarious predicament. For twelve hours they each made do with one-third of a biscuit "and a tiny stick of chocolate, also ⅓ of an ounce of butter and a cup of tea made with a spoonful of used tea leaves to 3 cups." It was a most frustrating situation, knowing that the depot was within several miles, but having no way of locating it. To keep his companions amused, Hurley composed a long doggerel about the making of their Christmas feast, hoping they might replicate the feast when the sky cleared and the depot appeared. However, the sky was no better on January 7, when they had only one day's rations remaining. After staying all day in their bags, they ate a small amount of hoosh and set off in the direction where they calculated the depot might lie. But there was nothing to be seen, "beyond a slatey expanse of snow and sky." If they waited for the weather to clear, argued Hurley, "we are as good as dead." So they decided, in the event of farther bad weather on the morrow, to make a desperate dash for the hut. What had been exciting to Hurley was now a life-or-death struggle. They had 70 miles of a sometimes difficult surface to cover, and about a day's food to do it on.[7]

After a sleepless night and a close examination of their remaining food, Bage and Webb concluded that it would be impossible to cover such a distance with so little food. Although Hurley claimed that he wanted to press on regardless, he "finally consented, much against my wish, to their ideas." So they would stay and wait for fine weather to reveal the food depot. However, when it appeared that they were going to be continually beset by fog and snow, there was a change of heart again, and they all agreed "to make the grand attempt to save our lives." The ration was divided into minuscule portions to last five days, and all non-essential equipment was left behind. Bage later admitted that he had "surreptitiously decided to make the rations last six days instead of five," just in case. They supplemented the meager ration with a cup of warm water, into which was mixed "a spoonful of glaxo-and-sugar and one of absolute alcohol," which was meant for lighting the primus. To reach the hut, the men had to travel 20 miles each day, regardless of the conditions they encountered. At least, any blizzards would be coming from behind rather than head-on, and they could always roughly judge their direction by the wind — so long as the prevailing southerly was at their back, they knew they should be heading in the desired northerly direction.[8]

For two days, they "marched in a river of snow," somehow covering the required 20 miles or more each day. At times, the snow was so thick that they "could not see a yard ahead." However, on the evening of the second day, the sky cleared sufficiently for them to see the ocean in the distance. "Although in pitiful plight," wrote Hurley, "I could not but admire the wonderful vista unfolded before us." The still sea and the plentiful icebergs left them "gazing on this profound sight spellbound," although they had no idea whether their salvation, the hut, lay to the east or the west of them. All their eyes were badly affected by snow blindness, with Bage worst of them all, and they had lost a lot of weight — indeed, Webb's weight had plummeted from 89 to just 57 kilograms. Knowing that the direction they chose to go in would determine whether they lived or died, they opted to go west, hoping that once they got closer to the coast they would be able to see familiar landmarks. They guessed right. Although encountering an area of hidden crevasses, which threatened to swallow the half-starved men, the cliffs of Commonwealth Bay eventually came into view and, soon after, Aladdin's Cave. With sunburnt and frostbitten faces, the exhausted men scrambled into the icy cavern and ate the most accessible food, which happened to be dog biscuits, before boiling up a meal of hoosh, and sleeping "sounder and happier than we had done for many months."[9]

It was a lucky escape. Bage was so snow blind that he was unable to write of his experiences at the time. On January 10, during the final five miles down the slope to the hut, he was carried on the sledge with his eyes bandaged. This was just as well, because it meant he was unable to see how close he came to being pitched into one of the several crevasses they encountered on the final stretch. The men in the hut were just finishing their dinner when Bage's party loomed into view. They were barely recognizable. They had each lost about 23 kilograms, and were exhibiting early symptoms of scurvy. On being greeted, they were immediately asked how far they had got, with Webb claiming that they had got within 50 to 100 miles of the South Magnetic Pole. "They have thus done," wrote Hunter in his diary, "as fine a journey as possibly could be done & if the other parties are equally successful then our expedition will be a great success." Webb was just happy to be back alive. "When I think of those two blank, dark, dark days, when we fell or scrambled along to we know not what end, it seems incredible that it's really over," he wrote. The following day, Bage celebrated his salvation by eating a lunch of "4 eggs & a tin & a half of salmon not to mention scones etc."[10]

But what did Bage really have to celebrate, apart from their lucky escape? He hadn't reached the South Magnetic Pole, and had only covered 301 miles, rather than 400. It must have occurred to him, and been a source of frustration, that he might have reached the pole if he'd stayed out a few days longer and had more food depots upon which he could rely for the return journey. Moreover, if he'd had dogs to haul the sledges, it's almost certain that he would have reached the pole with sufficient time to take the laborious observations that would have proved its location beyond doubt. As the expedition magnetician, it would have been particularly frustrating for Webb, who had to return home knowing that the South Magnetic Pole had been within his grasp and still hadn't been reached by anyone. Yet Hurley maintained nonetheless that the party's records "will comprise some of the most valuable scientific assets of the Expedition."[11] Of course, at the time he knew nothing about the records of the other parties, who were yet to return.

There was much more excitement in the hut when the *Aurora* arrived on January 13, bringing with it fresh food, news from home, and twenty-one dogs that had been donated to the expedition by Amundsen when he reached Hobart after having conquered the South Pole. "The saints could never be more happy," wrote Stillwell about the arrival of the ship.[12] Hunter described how the men in the hut "rushed out jumping and shouting with joy" as they sighted Captain Davis and the *Aurora*'s chief officer stepping ashore from the motorboat. While the men scrambled to get their hands on letters and news from home, and gorged on oranges, pineapples, and strawberries, Davis struggled to get their attention. There was no time to lose. He wanted all the gear and supplies loaded on the ship so they could get away without delay to pick up the men of the western base before the sea ice made it impossible to do so. Hunter didn't mind. He put aside his unread letters, and helped dispatch three boatloads of gear to the *Aurora*.[13] There was much more to be packed and sent aboard. And there were still parties out in the snow.

According to Mawson's timetable, everyone was due back by January 15, when they were all expected to leave for home. But the day came and went, with no sign of anyone else. It wasn't until the late afternoon of January 16 that Madigan's party made it back, just as Hurley was setting up the scene of a sledging camp for his cinematograph. As the three distant figures appeared on the slope above the hut, Stillwell and Hannam quickly donned their gear and hurried to see who it was. With a brisk wind blowing, they found Madigan, McLean, and Correll coming down the blue ice in fine condition after more than two months on the trail. Madigan was quick to tell the story of his journey and what he had accomplished. Although he had been forced to turn back after 270 miles, he told the men in the hut that there was "another 30 miles which they were able to sight so that altogether they mapped in 300 miles." Madigan had been determined to match, and hopefully exceed, the distance that Mawson intended to cover. Although he didn't reach 300 miles, he thought that mapping 300 miles might still put him on the same pedestal that he anticipated Mawson would occupy.[14] In fact, Madigan hadn't mapped all of the 300 miles of coastline between the hut and the point at which he turned back. The coastline closest to Commonwealth Bay was explored and mapped by Stillwell's party after they left Mawson and Madigan.

Apart from the map of the coastline, Madigan returned with a quantity of scientific treasure that he hoped would add luster to his journey. That was why he called a halt on December 18 to his eastward journey on the sea ice. Instead of pushing on, his party headed for a huge rocky cliff that Madigan had seen on the coast. "We should like to have done 300 miles," wrote a wistful McLean in his sledge diary, "but consider ourselves lucky to have come so far in such good weather." Now they could concentrate on enhancing the scientific results of the journey by collecting as many specimens as possible. They had already begun on December 15 by killing an emperor penguin and taking samples from its stomach of fish, pebbles, and tapeworms. And they continued their collection on the first day of their return journey. Before packing up the tent, Madigan used it to shelter from the snow as he took a full set of magnetic observations, with Correll recording the figures. McLean went off fishing in a break in the ice, using penguin meat for bait, but with no result. Then he found himself lost in the snowstorm, "and wandered for miles, spending about three hours looking for the tent," which he only found by chance in the poor visibility.[15]

Madigan was right to call a halt to their outward trek, since the rocky cliff that had attracted his attention, and which he had estimated to be about 100 meters high, turned out to be a most spectacular bluff rising more than 300 meters above the surface of the sea ice. The first 100 meters was rocky debris from the cliffs, which then rose vertically for the next 200 meters. The sheer cliff, which he named Dreadnought Bluff, stretched for several miles and was composed of "a series of magnificent organ pipes; hexagonal columns the whole height of the face and weathered bright red." Madigan thought they "must be the finest organ pipes in the world."[16] It was an exciting discovery, and would surely exceed anything that the other parties might find, since their journeys took them inland across a mostly snow-covered landscape.

After spending part of December 20 climbing to the base of the sheer cliff to collect specimens of the rock, Madigan's party camped there most of the following day. And what a day it was: with the sun shining for the first time in a week, it was perfect for their purposes. It was their "most interesting day" so far, wrote McLean, while Madigan thought it was just "magnificent." Correll used the theodolite to measure the height of the cliff, as Madigan and McLean "had a splendid ramble up among the rocks on the side of the bluff," where they filled a rucksack with different rocks. Earlier, they had collected specimens of "lichen," along with "glacial mud, clay, sand, birds' bones, fungus, moss and algae." They also spent time taking photographs. Some were of the rocks and the cliff, including narrow seams of coal, which would be of interest only to geologists. Other photographs were of the spectacular scenery, with hundreds of snow petrels hovering in the air near their cliff-top nests, which would interest readers of newspapers and later purchasers of the published account of the expedition. But the first photograph that was taken was the most important and had multiple purposes. As soon as they arose on December 21, the camera was set up on the theodolite legs and the lead to the shutter release arranged so that a photograph could be taken of all three of them "in front of the tent under the bluff, with flags flying." It was a photograph that captured the scenery and their place in it. The photograph announced their discovery to the world, and celebrated their empire's consequent possession of the place. As well, it would surely outdo anything that Mawson, Bage, or Bickerton would do on their journeys. They marked the occasion by boiling up a pound of raisins and dried apple, which was followed by a cup of Mexican chocolate.[17]

With Christmas Day imminent, Madigan was now focused on getting home. "To think we are on the way *Home* is a great feeling," he wrote, with "no more delay — one big bustle; Hooray." To hasten the day, he used the sail to speed their progress across the sea ice, even though the drifting snow was so thick at times that "it was impossible to see a yard in front" and there was a danger of falling through a hidden crack in the ice into the sea. This is what happened to Madigan on December 22. He described how he "sank to the waist before I could call to the others to pull me back, and [the] temperature being about 10° below freezing, I had a pretty thin time." He doesn't mention in his diary that the same thing happened to McLean that day. But the experience could not dull their sense of joyful anticipation as they steadily reduced their distance to the hut. It saw them celebrate Christmas in style, with McLean preparing a dinner of sliced breast of emperor penguin fried in butter and served on plasmon biscuit. It was "our first meat in seven weeks," wrote Madigan, and "was *excellent*." Like Bage's party, they also had a plum pudding of sorts, using ground biscuit, dried apples and raisins, sugar, Glaxo, and "a touch of whisky from the medical supplies." McLean also had secreted some bacon on the sledge, which was now brought out, along with cigarettes and more whisky to toast the King and their companions.[18]

They still had more than 200 miles to go, with their progress being dependent on the weather and the sea ice not breaking up. Fortunately for Madigan, the weather did stay favorable, with the wind often allowing the use of the sail to slide the sledge across the relatively smooth surface of the sea ice. The men were elated by their progress. After doing a record run of 18¼ miles on December 27, they had another celebration: young Percy Correll acted as cook, frying up more of the penguin and boiling up a "raisin pudding." It left them all "quite prostrated," wrote McLean. Their next food depot was 80 miles away, but they had sufficient food to last eleven days. Madigan was so confident of their position that he planned to divert from their course and spend two days investigating a ten-mile line of sheer granite cliffs at a place he dubbed Penguin Point. In fact, he stayed more than three days, waiting for the weather to clear so they could take photographs. When two Adélie penguins went past on the way to their nests, McLean described how they "immediately seized one for eating & cut off the breasts." For taking back to the hut, they collected more rocks, specimens of Adélie penguins, petrels, and skuas, along with other scientific samples, including birds' eggs, several types of insects, fungus, and moss. McLean thought the insects were particularly exciting, along with "a white topped plant with whitish thread like radicles [roots]." The men also did a full set of magnetic observations, and celebrated New Year's Day with more of their plum pudding and fried Adélie penguin, which they thought "tasted better than the Emperor."[19]

Every rock, and every dead bird or other specimen that they collected added to Madigan's claim to be leading the most scientifically significant trek. But they also added weight to the sledge. This probably explains why Madigan didn't avail himself of the penguins, their eggs, or even the occasional seal to add to their depleted food supply. It would have added even more weight to the sledge at a time when Madigan was confident of their existing food being able to last until the next food depot. On January 2, when they were just 44 miles from the depot and had six days' provisions remaining, they were forced to stay in their tent until a blizzard cleared. Madigan was happy to do so. The tent was "very cosy," everything was dry, and he was confident that the food would last. But the blizzard kept them camped all the next day, and a huge glacial tongue with dangerous crevasses lay ahead. Again, Madigan was sanguine about crossing the glacier, which they began to do on January 4. He had learned not to clamber up icy slopes to the ridges on top of glaciers, since crevasses were invariably encountered on the other side. Instead, they kept "rigidly to the hollows and lowest places in crevassed country," finding in this case that they had only crossed four crevasses in the 14½ miles they traveled that day. By the end of the day, they could see Mt. Outlook in the distance, where the food depot was located with ten days' rations and "extra chocolate and biscuit." It was a "fine sight," wrote Madigan.[20]

With four days' provisions on the sledge and just 30 miles to the depot, there seemed to be an ample margin for risk. However, they were still crossing the crevasse-ridden glacier, and light snow on January 5 made it too dangerous for them to move. So they stayed where they were, with McLean breaking the monotony by reading *Vanity Fair* while Madigan filled the time with "yarns on all sorts of subjects, and intermittent naps." The light was better the following day, and they managed to do 12½ miles before being forced to stop once again. It was difficult going, with the surface covered with eight inches of soft snow; despite Madigan's confidence about crevasses, they found themselves frequently falling up to their thighs. Although there was only about 300 meters of the dangerous ground left to cross, Madigan waited more than thirty hours before attempting it. Only when the sun appeared near midnight on January 7 did they quickly pack up and use the fading light to make their way safely past the remaining open crevasses. With the sun barely above the horizon, McLean described how the light was "touching all the ridge tops," making the sea ice appear like "white marble stretching north to a wonderful steel blue water-sky." While they could avoid the open crevasses, they fell into some of the shallow ones that were hidden by the thick layer of recent snow.[21]

There was now a new danger that had to be surmounted: on January 8, the soft snow became much deeper. It was a "very tough day," wrote McLean, with the men sinking to their knees as they struggled onward with a sledge that was almost devoid of food but laden with heavy rocks and other specimens. "We could scarcely move the sledge," reported Madigan, "it sinks in so far that the bow scrapes in the snow and the decking reaches the surface." That evening, they decided to leave all their nonessential equipment, along with a bag of specimens, in a clearly marked depot in the vain hope that it might be retrieved. Even then, despite deploying the sail, they could still "scarcely move" the sledge on the soft snow. By 10:00 p.m., a combination of exhaustion and the snowdrift forced them to camp.

The situation was now becoming serious. They'd eaten all their rations, and had only a small piece of penguin meat left. Most of this was eaten the following morning, in the expectation that they could reach the food depot that day. But the snow became denser, and they were forced to camp once again. They waited in their sleeping bags through the night and most of the next day, January 10, refraining from eating the last eight ounces of penguin meat until the weather cleared sufficiently for them to see the depot. When the weather improved in the late afternoon, Madigan quickly cut the remaining penguin meat into small slices and shredded it. The meat was then boiled up, with the empty pepper-and-salt bag being dipped into the watery stew to add flavor. The very hungry McLean reported that it produced a "savoury result." Thus fortified, Madigan set off to fetch food from the depot, while McLean and Correll watched anxiously as he "floundered away sinking over the knees in the soft snow."[22]

It was a four-mile walk up a 400-meter-high hill, and Madigan barely made it. In fact, he was lucky to see the depot at all. Heavy falls of snow had almost completely covered the mound of snow in which the food had been deposited several weeks before, leaving little more than a flag sticking a meter above the snow. Had the flag been blown away, as they often were, they would probably have perished. Madigan was forced to tunnel down through the snow to the food, some of which he ate before he was able to return to the tent. The whole journey took nearly twelve hours — so long that his two companions were about to go in search of him when he finally reappeared. Reunited, they quickly did a boil-up of hoosh and cocoa in celebration of their "sudden affluence."

The provisions at the depot were sufficient for about two weeks, so food was no longer the problem. However, a new problem loomed. The days they had spent collecting specimens, and then being confined to their tent by the snow, caused Madigan to fear that they would be late back to the hut, which meant that they might be left behind by the *Aurora*. Desperate to catch the ship, and worried how they could travel through the deep snow, Madigan decided they "*must* travel with the *absolute minimum* of weight." So they left behind their crampons, most of their clothing, some of the rocks, three of the birds, and most of their equipment. Survival, rather than science, was now their motivation. With the sledge as light as they dared make it, the three men left the camp at 10:00 p.m. on January 11 to climb their way up the slope to the depot, taking more than five hours to complete the journey through deep snow.[23]

There they remained for the next two days, confined to their tent by heavy snow. Even with all their provisions, Madigan admitted to feeling "rather anxious." When they finally set out on January 14, they cut back farther on their weight by leaving behind yet more rock specimens. The scientific value of the journey was being eroded just as the surface was starting to improve and their progress across the snow was accelerating. It went largely without incident as they passed familiar landmarks and began trekking down the slippery crevassed slope toward Aladdin's Cave, which they had to do without the crampons they had thrown away to save weight. It was "very ticklish and difficult at times," wrote McLean, but they succeeded in reaching the cavern by noon on January 16. Madigan and McLean "made a rush for the opening" and slid "down into the blue depths," where they were delighted to see oranges and pineapples laid out on top of a food bag. "We knew in an instant," wrote McLean, "that the good ship *Aurora* had reached Adelie Land." There was also the dramatic news that Amundsen had reached the South Pole and that the *Terra Nova* had returned without Scott. News of their fellow expeditioners had also been left in the cavern. Madigan learned that Bage had gone 301 miles, but had fallen short of the South Magnetic Pole; that Bickerton had taken the air tractor westward and "all [was] going well"; and that Stillwell and Laseron "had had an interesting time along about 40 miles of coast to the eastward." McLean noted that they were "very 'bucked' with news which meant so much to the success of the expedition."[24]

After a "sumptuous lunch" in Aladdin's Cave, it was a fast slide down the slope of blue ice to the hut. Madigan would later claim that they went down the difficult slope without the help of crampons. That is true, but he did make something approximating crampons. McLean's diary describes how "Madigan screwed some ice-nails into [his] boots" and was able to act as a brake to slow the sledge on the otherwise dangerous slope. As they descended, the familiar landmarks came into view one by one — the islands offshore, the huts and the wireless mast, and "the dear old ship." By 4:00 p.m. on January 16 they were safely home. "Joy, letters, friends, the dear old ship in the Harbour," wrote an exultant Madigan in his diary.[25] Surrounded by the hut's few inhabitants, Madigan described how he had mapped 300 miles of the coastline, and then regaled them with details of the scientific specimens that he had brought back on his sledge. There was no talk of the great amount he had left behind.[26] Happy as they all were by the return of Madigan's party, there was mounting concern about the non-appearance of both Bickerton and Mawson.

Captain Davis had warned that he would have to leave by January 20 to pick up Wild's party at the western base. If Mawson or Bickerton did not return by then, some of the men would have to spend another year at Commonwealth Bay to await their return or to go in search of them. Madigan was appalled at the idea of remaining another year. On January 17, the day after his return to the hut, he went aboard the *Aurora* with Bage, and convinced Davis to delay his departure until January 25 in the hope that the other two parties would return by then. That very night, the men in the hut were woken by the return of Bickerton's western party.[27] There was relief all round. The men in the hut had been concerned about the fate of Bickerton, Hodgeman, and Whetter, since they knew that the party's rations were only meant to last until about January 10. With their return, it left just Mawson's party to be accounted for.

As for Bickerton, he reported that his party had only managed to trek for 160 miles. The air tractor was meant to give them an advantage, and a practice run had gone well enough, taking just an hour to take three men and 400 pounds of supplies up the slope to Aladdin's Cave. All manner of articles, from boots to hammers, had been hung from the air tractor's steel framework when they finally left the hut on December 3. Some of the men remaining behind acted the wag by also hanging carrots and lumps of coal from it. With the engine roaring, the machine struggled up the steepest parts of the slope, and struggled even more when Bickerton set out from Aladdin's Cave pulling a much heavier load, with three men on board and a line of four sledges carrying more than 1,000 pounds of food, oil, fuel, and equipment. The added load proved too much for the engine, which broke down after traveling just 11 miles. After that, Bickerton, Hodgeman, and Whetter were forced to man-haul their sledge for the remainder of the journey.[28]

It was slow and laborious, with a heavy snowdrift often keeping them in their tent or slowing down their progress. Rather than taking to the sea ice, as Madigan did, Bickerton journeyed west on the plateau, often seeing the pack ice in the distance. After twenty-six days, they had traveled just 158 miles, although the distance had to be estimated because the sledge-meter had broken down soon after their departure. Much of the time, they had to stay in their tent because of blizzards, and their progress was also slowed by Whetter, who suffered from painful hemorrhoids. Bickerton's troubles increased when he was struck by dysentery in late December, which convinced him to turn back. He could not afford the risk of going any farther. Just getting home would be a struggle if they had to face the fierce weather that had assailed them on the outward journey. Fortunately, the return journey was blessed with milder weather and no return of Bickerton's dysentery. But his hopes of making history had been dashed. He had little of note to report from his journey, other than the discovery of a small rock that he took to be a meteorite. As for the depot that Madigan had established with great effort in the spring, they failed to find it.[29]

Bickerton's return gave hope to the men in the hut, as they had been much more concerned about his party's fate than Mawson's. If Bickerton's party could make it back in time to catch the *Aurora*, surely so, too, could Mawson and his men. And yet it was Mawson who had instructed all the parties to return by January 15 at the latest. If his well-equipped party, with its dogs and physically fit men, hadn't made the deadline, it suggested that some disaster must have befallen them. Nobody wanted to remain behind to wait through the darkness of another winter, or to mount a search when there was no certainty about where Mawson's party might be. And it was not immediately clear what they should do, since Mawson had left no detailed instructions to cover the possibility of his own non-return. As a result, wrote Hunter, "things are in rather a muddled position" and "are all topsy turvy."[30]

It was left to Davis to take command of the expedition from Murphy, who had been left in charge of the hut by Mawson. Ever mindful of the safety of his ship, and the lives of the men at the western base, the *Aurora* captain had initially declared that he would leave on January 20, and had then agreed to extend his deadline to January 25. This meant they would have to load the ship with some gear and supplies, while unloading other supplies to prepare for the eventuality of one or more parties not returning, and men being left to search for them. While some of the men busied themselves with these activities, Hurley was busy taking more film with his cinematograph. Madigan, McLean, Bickerton, and Stillwell went up on the plateau to find the "air tractor" and push it back to the hill above the hut so that Hurley could film it the following day, "running down to the landing place." Although it was ten miles away, they left at lunchtime and were back by 10:30 p.m. They took just over an hour to cover the final five miles from Aladdin's Cave, which was a great contrast to their experience during the winter. It was "a nice little pleasure jaunt," wrote Stillwell. The following day, he and five others were filmed by Hurley in yet another stage-managed piece for cinema audiences, coming "down the hill on the bus for the sake of the 'cinny.'"[31]

When Mawson still didn't appear, Davis set a new deadline of January 30. In the meantime, he acted on the assumption that "there was now no likelihood of [Mawson's] party returning," and that the priority was therefore "to make things comfortable for those who are to remain." They erected an aerial for the wireless mast so they could maintain contact with the outside world; they covered the windward side of the hut with an old sail from the ship; they stacked a year's supply of food outside; they brought additional coal from the ship to ensure there was sufficient fuel for the hut; they brought ashore "a good supply of fresh literature, wines, whisky etc" to last them through the depths of the coming winter; and they collected thousands of Adélie penguin eggs, and killed a dozen seals and more than three hundred penguins so they would have sufficient fresh meat. Everyone was forced by Davis to work to that end, including Hunter, who had instructions from Mawson to continue the collection of biological specimens, and wanted to trawl in the sea while they waited. Much to Hunter's disappointment, he had to stop his scientific work, and was told by Davis that, because of damage to some equipment, there would be no trawling done in the Southern Ocean during the return voyage. "The oceanographical part of the expedition's programme is thus a complete failure," wrote Hunter in an overly dramatic outburst.[32]

While preparing for the worst, Davis made last-minute bids to search for Mawson, even though it would farther delay his own departure and possibly imperil the relief of Wild's party. On January 24, Stillwell, Hodgeman, and Correll climbed the icy slope to Aladdin's Cave before heading off to the southeast. After about five miles, fog and snowdrift made visibility so poor that they decided to return.[33] A more organized effort was made on January 25, when McLean, Hurley, and Hodgeman set out with a sledge to Aladdin's Cave, from where they also headed off in the direction from where Mawson was expected to return. They were instructed to establish a food depot as far east as they could manage, and to be back by January 30. The three of them went off in the face of a strong blizzard that caused them to pass by Aladdin's Cave without seeing it. Once it was eventually located, the snowdrift had become so thick and the wind so strong that they were forced to wait until the next day for clearer conditions. However, the calmer weather did not last long. McLean and his companions only managed to cover five miles before the drift and strong winds again forced them to camp and to spend thirty-six hours huddled in their wet sleeping bags. On January 28, the final day of their outward journey, they were 26 miles from the hut, and built a mound of snow, on top of which they left a black flag and a bag of biscuits, sugar, chocolate, and three oranges. Then, with the blizzard at their back, they raced for the hut.[34]

Davis had provisionally selected six men to remain behind once the *Aurora* left. There were few volunteers for this task. While they wanted to rescue Mertz and Ninnis, none were keen to spend another winter in the hut with Mawson. But they were men with a sense of duty, and all complied with Davis's instructions. Madigan was put in charge, while the other five were Bage, Bickerton, Hodgeman, McLean, and a wireless operator who had come on the *Aurora*, Sidney Jeffryes. Hurley talked of staying, presumably to record the rescue of Mawson, but thought better of it and took his leave. The six staying behind were instructed to organize a monthlong search for Mawson's party before the summer ended, and to mount a more extensive search during the following summer, when they would be relieved by the return of the *Aurora*. There were varied reactions to being asked to remain for another year. McLean agreed because it was his "duty to the Expedition and to Dr Mawson." Madigan was conscious of "losing much by staying here another year," but told his family that he felt compelled to stay because "I am a member of the expedition, and I cannot desert it when it needs me." In his diary, though, Madigan wrote with a mixture of disappointment and bitterness. He had been looking forward for so long to leaving on the *Aurora*, and now he had to endure another year of privation and dangers, and perhaps lose his Rhodes scholarship and even the woman he wanted to marry. Bickerton, too, was torn between resignation and despair, telling his sister that it was "a rotten game & a rotten place but nevertheless has to be done by someone."[35]

Even those who had been "most optimistic" about Mawson's return, such as Stillwell, were "beginning to have fears not easily calmed."[36] In another attempt to find Mawson's party, Davis took the *Aurora* 50 miles along the coast to the tongue of the Ninnis Glacier. Leaving Commonwealth Bay early on January 29, Davis kept the ship as close to the edge of the ice as he dared, while he and his men scanned the coast in the hope of seeing some sign of them. Davis hoped they might have headed to the coast, and would be waiting to be rescued there, in the same way that Mawson had done on the Shackleton expedition when Davis had fortuitously found them on the Ross Sea coast. However, despite firing signal rockets into the sky and flying a large kite to a height of 500 feet, there was no response from the ice-bound continent. Neither did it seem possible to Davis for Mawson to have descended the sheer ice cliffs to the sea. With Mawson now more than two weeks overdue, Davis was sure that "there must be something seriously amiss."[37]

Davis had never intended to wait as long as he had. He had only extended the departure deadline in the hope that the missing men might appear. With no sign of Mawson, the *Aurora* was readied to leave. Everything had been done to make Madigan and his five companions as comfortable as possible for the coming year. All Davis had to do was send the launch into the boat harbor to fetch the ten expedition members who were going home: John Close, Leslie Whetter, Frank Stillwell, John Hunter, Percy Correll, Walter Hannam, Frank Hurley, Charles Laseron, Herbert Murphy, and Eric Webb. On January 31, the ten enjoyed a farewell dinner in the hut, expecting that they would leave the following morning, only to have Commonwealth Bay reinforce its reputation as the windiest place in the world. Such an intense gale blew down from the plateau that Davis was compelled to raise anchor and shelter in the relatively calmer seas near the sheer cliff of the continental barrier.[38] Days passed with no letup in the storm. The ten men stranded at the hut began to fear that they might be abandoned there, along with Madigan and his five companions, while Davis feared that he might lose his ship to the wind-whipped seas. None of them knew that the man with the departure ticket for all of them — Mawson — was holed up in Aladdin's Cave, just a few miles away.

CHAPTER THIRTEEN

Stumbling into History

Mertz had died a grisly death. In his last hours he had been delirious and raving, and soiling his sodden pants, thrashing about alongside Mawson in the tiny tent. After Mertz broke one of their makeshift tent poles, Mawson was forced to restrain him to prevent farther damage. Without a tent, Mawson would be dead, so he used his bulk to hold Mertz down. Eventually, he slipped into a coma (from which he would never wake). Then Mawson placed the unconscious Mertz back in his sleeping bag, where he died "peacefully at about 2 am on morning of 8th." Mawson blamed his companion's death on "weather exposure & want of food."[1] Mawson couldn't have known it at the time, but it wasn't the *lack* of food that killed Mertz so quickly. Rather, it was the *type* of food they both were eating — particularly the scrawny dog meat with its almost total absence of fat, which caused them to suffer protein poisoning. Their condition was made worse by scurvy, by a possible excess of vitamin A, by starvation, and by exposure to the cold and wet.[2]

There are three important questions that need to be asked at this point. To what extent was Mawson responsible for their plight? Had Mawson come to the terrible conclusion that there was only sufficient food for one of them to get back to the hut alive? Did Mawson's experience on the Shackleton expedition give him confidence that he could endure starvation rations much better than Mertz? If so, is that why Mawson put them both on what he called "extremely low rations," in the hope that Mertz would die before he did and that Mawson might then survive on the remaining rations? For that is how the events played out. There may never be definitive answers to these questions. Once Mertz stopped writing in his diary, with the last entry being written just a week before his death, Mawson was the only witness to Mertz's tragic decline and ultimate demise.

Whatever the answers, Mawson's chances of survival had now increased. Food that had been shared out sparingly between the two of them would now be Mawson's alone. Not that there was much of it remaining. It's difficult to know exactly how much food was still on the sledge at the time of Mertz's death. All the dogs had been killed, and their bodies butchered, and most of the meat consumed. Yet there could have been sufficient food at this point for one person to get back to the hut, even though there wasn't sufficient for two. On January 6, Mawson calculated that he "could pull through by myself with the provisions at hand." Two days later, following the death of Mertz, he still made no mention in his diary of being fearful about his food supply. Mawson simply expressed concern that the days spent in the tent might have "cooked [his] chances altogether, even of a single attempt either to the coast or to the Hut." He was particularly concerned that "lying in the damp bag for a week on extremely low rations has reduced my condition seriously." Although Mawson's diary makes little mention of his own health until this point, he now claimed that he was in the "same condition" as Mertz, and that he had similarly "lost all skin of legs & private parts" and had sores on his finger that wouldn't heal, which was a possible sign of scurvy.[3] He might have had a better chance of getting back alive now that Mertz was dead, but his survival was certainly not assured.

Despite this, Mawson was determined to push on, estimating that he was about 100 miles from the hut. He took Mertz outside to bury him, and spent a day making adjustments to his gear. He cut the sledge in half to save weight, sewed a sail from materials, which presumably included parts of Mertz's clothing, and did two boil-ups. He also ate "a little more food than usual," expecting that he would set off the following day. However, the wind remained too strong. Mawson would have been able to haul the sledge, but it would have been impossible for him to pitch the tent by himself. So he stayed another day, increasing his rations in the "hope that it will give me strength for the future."[4] This gives credence to the theory that Mawson had put himself and Mertz on starvation rations in the hope that Mertz would succumb before he did. Now that Mertz was dead, Mawson did the opposite of what he had done when Mertz was alive. Instead of drastically reducing his rations whenever he was confined to the tent for a day, Mawson now increased his rations while he was in the tent so he would have the stamina to go on.

Yet another day was spent in the tent on January 10. Even though the wind dropped by late afternoon, Mawson spent time repairing a broken shovel that had been discarded, and patching his Burberrys. He also described how he "boiled all the rest of [the] dog meat." What dog meat was he referring to? It had been a fortnight since the last dog, Ginger, had been killed by Mertz on December 28, with Mawson spending several hours cooking some of its meat. Mertz had taken over and cooked more of its meat for an hour and a half. Even more meat was cooked the following day, and Mawson spent three hours cooking yet more of the meat on December 30. It was another week before Mawson mentioned in his diary on January 6: "I cook up dog meat," although he may have been just heating up dog meat that had already been cooked. So it is surprising that on January 10 he reported cooking the last meat from Ginger, the dog that had been dead for two weeks.[5] Might it have been something else that he was cooking?

It has long been rumored that it might not have been just dog meat that Mawson was boiling — that he might have taken the opportunity to boil some of Mertz's flesh so that he would have a greater chance of making it back alive. After all, they had been killing their dogs and eating them. Why not make use of his dead companion's body to ensure his own survival? Some credence was given to these rumors when an American journalist later claimed that Mawson had admitted to having considered such a course for the two days he spent beside Mertz's body. Indeed, it would have been incredible for him not to have considered it, given the shortage of food. According to the journalist, Mawson said that he decided against it, noting that "if I did get back to civilization it would always leave a bad taste in my mouth, so I buried him and went on." When this was published in New York, Mawson strenuously denied having ever said it.[6] His denial is not surprising. There is no heroism to be had in cannibalism. His vigorous denial has been accepted by historians, who argue that it would have contravened Mawson's values and that, anyway, he had no need to do it, once Mertz was dead and all his intended rations were available for Mawson's consumption.[7]

Whether or not there was sufficient food to assure Mawson of getting back alive remains a matter of some doubt. When Ninnis died and the food sledge was lost in the crevasse on December 14, the food on the other sledge was only sufficient for one-and-a-half weeks, calculated at the normal ration scale. Those bags of food and the flesh of the six emaciated dogs had already been drawn upon by both men during the three and a half weeks leading up to the death of Mertz. It would have been impossible for both men to reach the hut alive on the little food they had available on December 14. Although Mawson thought on January 6, a day before Mertz's death, that he could reach the hut by himself, he considered on January 9 that there was "little chance of my reaching human aid alive." His concern now was more to do with his physical condition than the quantity of food remaining. He described how his feet were in "a deplorable condition," with huge blisters having burst, his "frost-bitten fingertips festering, mucous membrane of nose gone, saliva glands of mouth refusing duty, skin coming off whole body." Indeed, his "whole body," wrote Mawson, "was apparently rotting from want of proper nourishment."[8] If eating some of Mertz's flesh could help him recover his strength, heal his sloughing skin and weeping wounds, and increase his chances of reaching the hut, it should not be surprising if he decided to do so. And it is hardly appropriate for us to quibble with his decision. If Mawson did cannibalize Mertz's body, it would have been because he believed it was going to provide the "proper nourishment" that his body demanded. In fact, though, Mertz's body was as scrawny as the dogs, and eating his flesh would not have produced a speedy revival in Mawson's health.

It wasn't until January 11 that Mawson finally dismantled the camp, hitched himself to the cut-down sledge, and began the onward journey slowly and painfully on blistered feet. Scoffing down a "liberal allowance of chocolate," he aimed at covering ten miles that first day, but was forced to stop after doing little more than six. Although it was a calm and sunny day, and he was on a downward slope with a good surface and using a sail, Mawson found he was so "nerve-worn with feet" and generally exhausted that he had to stop. He was in such a bad state that he was hardly able to erect the tent. Yet the sunshine was so energizing and restorative that he became optimistic about his chances. If he had twenty days of such weather, and his feet healed quickly, Mawson thought he must be able to reach the hut. But the next morning began with a snowstorm that kept him in the tent for most of the day. At least it would give his feet more chance to heal, he thought.

When the sun did come out in the afternoon, it melted the ice on the roof of the tent, and sent him outside to sort out the remaining food so he could "get an exact idea of it." It's hard to believe that he hadn't done this calculation when camped for days beside Mertz's body. Yet there is no mention in his diary of how much food was remaining, or the amount of his daily ration, once Mertz was not alive to share it. All he noted was that he wished his food supply was "twice as much" and that, in his desperation, he was "continually picking fragments from the different bags."[9] In fact, it is clear from his other notes that he was now much more liberal with his rations. For instance, instead of his previous regime of sharing one tin of pemmican each day with Mertz, there was sufficient pemmican remaining for him to have one tin each day for himself. Instead of one plasmon biscuit a day, he could now have two, along with a normal daily ration of Glaxo and cocoa, and five ounces of chocolate, and one and a half ounces of butter.[10]

On January 15, the day when all the parties were meant to be back at the hut, Mawson reported he was "keeping food and mileage list at end of book now as checks on each other." They were essential calculations to make, and a difficult balancing act for Mawson to do. If he ate too much without covering the required distance, he risked running out of food and starving to death before he reached the hut. On the other hand, if he ate too little food, he risked being too weak to haul the sledge the distance that was required to reach the hut. On the previous two days, he had managed to cover about five miles each day; but on January 15, when he still had more than 80 miles to go, he was stopped by poor visibility and a strong headwind.

Mawson was in dangerous territory again, crossing the Mertz Glacier with its multitude of crevasses and steep slopes. As a result, he struggled with the effort of hauling the sledge, particularly when the snow became soft and wet. He also continued to be uncertain of his distance and direction, with the sledge-meter practically useless, and the theodolite without its legs. He also forgot one day to wind his watch, which never gave accurate time thereafter. This increased the difficulty of determining his location and the direction he should take. His daily diet now included meat at most meals, along with portions of pemmican and biscuit. The lean meat was probably more dangerous than nutritious, but the large percentage of fat in the pemmican would have compensated for the lack of fat in the meat. Despite the bigger rations, Mawson was still half-starved and weak, and his feet remained in a poor condition. He was wearing up to five pairs of socks to cushion his red, raw feet, and was spending "quite a while" dressing them each day.[11] But at least he was alive.

Whatever the precision of Mawson's calculations about his

food consumption and distance traveled, he could not predict the weather or the snow surface, which could throw out all his scribbled calculations. This is what occurred on January 17, when the overcast sky made it almost impossible for him to see where he was going. Rather than stopping to camp until the weather cleared, Mawson "blundered blindly on." The day was relatively warm, and Mawson had "taken off most [of his] clothing and left [the] rest very open." The previous day, he had barely stopped himself and the sledge within a meter of a "great yawning crevasse." Much worse was about to befall him. He described how he "escaped several large open crevasses by Providence, not seeing them till past them." Yet he continued to push on, until suddenly finding himself falling down a crevasse until he was dangling at the end of his harness. Fortunately for Mawson, the sledge held fast at the edge of the crevasse, and didn't tumble down on top of him. But he was in a desperate position. He was "weak," his clothes were filled with fallen snow, his "finger ends [were] all damaged" and "fast chilling," and, of course, his feet remained in a terrible state. How was he to escape from this dire situation? Mawson described in his diary how he "thought of the food left uneaten in the sledge" and, with the conviction "that Providence was helping me ... made a great struggle, half getting out, then slipping back again several times, but at last just did it."[12] This incident came to be portrayed as the great, courageous climax of Mawson's journey.

Although his diary entry described "dangling on end of rope in crevasse," Mawson provided no indication about the length of the rope and therefore how deep he fell down the crevasse. However, he later made up for this omission in *The Home of the Blizzard*, where he specified that he was "dangling fourteen feet below on end of rope in crevasse." Interestingly, this description in his book is part of a paragraph that purported to be a direct quotation from his diary. But it is no such thing. When the paragraph is compared with the diary, it is clear that it is a heavily embellished account, deliberately designed to heighten the drama of his fall and his subsequent emergence from the crevasse. Moreover, Mawson created a problem for himself in later claiming to have fallen 14 feet, because his diary indicated that he had slipped back "several times" until finally managing to get out. Given his poor physical state, it was beyond the bounds of credibility for Mawson to claim that he had climbed up a 14-foot rope only to fall back "several times" before successfully emerging. He got around this problem in *The Home of the Blizzard* by changing the number of times he fell back. Instead of "several times," it became just two.[13]

If Mawson didn't fall 14 feet down the crevasse, how far did he fall? A good clue was given by Mawson himself when providing an account of the episode to London's *Daily Mail*, which had helped raise funds for the expedition and had an exclusive contract to publish news of it in the United Kingdom. As Mawson told that newspaper: "Several times I fell into crevasses to the length of my sledge pole and was scarcely able to crawl out." A more recent Australian explorer has argued that there was no such thing as a "sledge pole." In fact, there were two things that Mawson might have described that way: one was the pole on the sledge that was used to attach the sail; the other was the pole that Mawson mentioned using to test the snow bridges. Indeed, they may have been one and the same pole. Madigan wrote of having a bamboo mast on his sledge that was seven feet high, while Bage wrote in his diary of having a mast that was seven and a half feet high. In other words, they were about half the length of the sledge rope, which means that he fell little more than his own height. Some additional credence is given to this by his mention in the newspaper article of "crawling" out of the crevasse, rather than "climbing" out. That said, it was still a mighty effort, with a very fortuitous outcome, for a person in Mawson's wasted condition to be able to haul himself out of the crevasse, even from a depth of just seven feet.[14]

In his diary, Mawson suggested that the food on the sledge inspired him to make a supreme effort to extricate himself from the terrible predicament he was in. The thought of the strict rationing he had endured, only to die dangling in a crevasse with all the self-imposed privation having been for nothing, was what impelled Mawson to choose life over the quick death that could so easily have been his. But that's a rather prosaic rationale for a budding polar hero trying to excite the imagination of a mass audience. So the account in *The Home of the Blizzard* made much more of the moment when he was supposedly dangling at the end of the rope. Rather than just scrambling out of the crevasse to get at the rations, Mawson now claimed that he experienced an epiphany of sorts as he hung in the chasm, caught between life and death. He could so easily have released himself from the harness, and "all the pain and toil would be over." Calling it a "rare temptation ... to pass from the petty exploration of a planet to the contemplation of vaster worlds beyond," Mawson described how he rejected the temptation, and chose life. While his diary noted how he felt that Providence was helping him, *The Home of the Blizzard* went much farther, creating an episode of suspenseful drama in which Mawson's version of a deity came to his rescue:

> My strength was ebbing fast; in a few minutes it would be too late. It was the occasion for a supreme attempt. New power seemed to come as I addressed myself to one last tremendous effort. The struggle occupied some time, but by a miracle I rose slowly to the surface.[15]

This was a story crafted to appeal to a wide audience. And because his diary would be kept under wraps until long after his death, Mawson could be confident that no one would notice the inconsistencies between his diary entries and his account in *The Home of the Blizzard*. But back on January 17, 1913, it remained doubtful whether Mawson, let alone his diary, would ever make it back, even after he had crawled from the crevasse.

Being "wet and cold and overcome," and with visibility still poor, Mawson decided to stop for the day in the "hope that something will happen to change the state of the weather." He was so badly shaken by the crevasse experience that he was unable to sleep, and had "a rotten time." Death seemed to be stalking his journey, taking his companions one by one, and now coming for him. On the Shackleton expedition, he had taken control of the situation from David and ensured that their trek to the region of the South Magnetic Pole was completed without serious mishap. That experience had given him the standing and the confidence to lead an expedition of his own, only to land in the windiest place on earth. All his plans had to be redrawn, with his far-eastern trek meant to be the new crowning glory of the expedition. Now it was collapsing around him. The only way to retrieve the position was to return with a story of great danger and hardship, which he had managed to surmount by dint of courage and perseverance. But he couldn't be sure of making it back alive. Rather than dying because of lack of food or illness, Mawson feared that the weather was going to kill him by not allowing him to cover the distance he needed to do each day. Yet, for all his fears, Mawson trusted in "Providence" to get him safely home, noting that it "has so many times already helped me."[16]

Mawson was now several days overdue, and he had no way of knowing how long the *Aurora* would wait for him or whether any search parties would come in search of him. He could only press on across the massive Mertz Glacier, taking advantage of any suitable weather that presented itself, and watching out for crevasses. Concerned by his slow progress, Mawson reduced his ration only to see "several festerings [had] broken out again." On January 19, he was troubled by a boil on his leg, and "took off all [his] clothes" and burst it. He was determined to go on and not be brought down by his physical failings. These days really tested Mawson's stamina, courage, and self-belief. He was "quite faint" after pulling the sledge half a mile up a steep hill on January 18, the day after his ordeal in the crevasse, and admitted that he couldn't "stand much heavy work." But it wasn't just the physical effort that tested him. There was also the psychological trauma of being caught on the glacier in poor light among "a maze of huge crevasses." There was nothing for it but to take his chances and hope, as he found with several crevasses, that "they were well choked with snow." Perhaps concluding that this description downplayed the drama of his situation, Mawson went on to paint a somewhat bleaker picture:

> I stopped awhile and considered the question. Everything seemed hopeless — the serac seemed to be endless, the glacier cracked and boomed below. It seemed impossible for me, alone, to cross it, for any moment I expected to go down. I determined at last to stick to the course as much as possible, push on, and rely on Providence.

It was slow going. From January 18 to 20, he barely made three miles a day. But he had succeeded in crossing the glacier, and was now on the lookout for landmarks that he had passed on the outward journey.[17]

Everything was directed toward getting to the hut as quickly as possible. He discarded more gear to save weight, polished and tarred the sledge runners to improve their passage across the snow, and set off on days when the overcast sky might have otherwise convinced him to remain in the tent. Progress continued to be slow, and Mawson kept hoping for "a good day tomorrow." Even when he got a good day, as he did on January 21, he struggled to make the best of it. Although the weather was clear and calm, and there were no crevasses to be tackled, Mawson was confronted with a succession of very steep slopes that left him exhausted and his supply of "perks" greatly depleted. To lighten his load even more, he discarded his crampons, the alpine rope, and the stick he used for testing the depth of snow bridges over crevasses. These were hardly nonessential items, but Mawson's plight was sufficiently desperate for him to conclude that his chances of reaching the hut were better without them. If he didn't reach the hut, the lighter sledge would allow him to get closer to it in the hope that his body and his story might be found by rescuers. The lighter load certainly helped him on January 22 to cover the greatest distance he'd done for some time — five and a half miles — which took him high onto the polar plateau.[18]

After that day's success, Mawson was confident of being able to reach the hut. He just had to cover that same distance each day, which was much less than the 15 miles he had been used to doing when all three of his party had set out the previous November with the dogs. However, even five and a half miles left him feeling weak at the end of the day, convincing him of the need to recalibrate his remaining rations to make sure he ate enough to give him the strength he would need. So he had what he called a "grand pem" for dinner on January 22, using a lot of meat. For breakfast the following day, he had "fine real pem, good half tin dry, a whole biscuit and decent tea and butter," which left him feeling "very full." These meals would have been a good antidote to the protein poisoning from which he had been suffering. But the quantity of food was never sufficient to bring about a full recovery, since Mawson remained on short rations, noting on January 23 that he planned to "finish rest of first half food in 5 days provided I keep up average of 5 m[iles] per day, which appears reasonable."[19]

Mawson reconsidered his decision when snow began falling on January 23. Although he kept on regardless, with his goggles filling with snow and the sledge being blown over frequently, he eventually was compelled to camp after completing a "little over three miles." The poor visibility made it impossible for him to follow his course, and left him uncertain as to his location at the end of the day. His optimism of the previous day turned to pessimism. "Shall have to come back on food now," he noted in his diary, only to become optimistic again the following day, when he managed to cover five miles despite strong snowdrift. For part of the time, he rode on the sledge and allowed the wind in the sail to push it across the soft snow. Having covered his desired distance, Mawson decided to stick to his liberal ration scale, "notwithstanding the bad outlook in weather." He hoped it would improve his condition, with both his hands having "shed the skin in large sheets," making them "very tender."[20]

The weather turned out as he feared, with a "violent blizzard" keeping him in his tent on January 25. This gave Mawson another chance to assess his position. He was particularly concerned about the condition of his feet, which he blamed on having too little food, the tenderness of the new skin, and the lack of activity. To protect his feet against the cold during the day of enforced idleness, Mawson wore his Burberrys in his sleeping bag. With the snow pressing heavily on the roof, the tent assumed a coffin-like shape to Mawson as he lay there thinking of food, of different ways to cook it, and of how to save on his use of oil. He had watched Mertz's slow demise, and was determined not to go that way. After all, he was a Britisher and a young Australian. Although the coffin-like shape made him "shudder," he hastened to assure anyone who might read the diary that it was only "for the moment" and that, like a good Britisher, he was "full of hope and reliance in the great Providence, which has pulled me through so far."[21] Having crossed the glacier, he had some reason for confidence. But he was now ten days overdue at the hut, and there was no telling what might await him when he arrived. Would the other parties have returned, and what state would they be in? Would they have encountered similar weather, and suffered tragedies of their own? And would the ship still be there to take him home? Only rarely did Mawson give any hint in his diary of these concerns, but they would have preoccupied him as leader of a heavily indebted expedition that was now marked by tragedy and disarray.

The tone and content of his diary had gradually changed since the death of Ninnis, and even more so after the death of Mertz. Instead of copious notes written for his fellow scientists about the clouds, the wind speed, the snow surface, and their own location and direction, his diary entries became more self-consciously those of an explorer writing, albeit in a rather forced manner, for a general audience about his heroic struggle to get through against the odds. On January 26, he described how he awoke to a "continuance of [the] blizzard, [with] heavy pelting pellets of radial snow." In earlier days, these conditions would have kept Mawson in his tent. Now, though, he professed to be undaunted, telling the reader that he

got off after noon in dense falling snow & drift and went with the
wind. This was a great experiment as I had no idea whether I could
put up tent in it. However all went well except that I got into an
awful mess — everything saturated with snow, and perspiration, in
gear also. It was midnight before I was ready to cook dinner — took
a time to put up tent and get snow out of things.

That day's effort had seen him cover nearly eight miles. But it had
come at a cost. All his clothes, his sleeping bag, and his gear were
wet from the blizzard and the business of setting up the tent and
boiling his dinner. So his caution reasserted itself, with Mawson
deciding not to repeat the experience the following day when the
blizzard was still blowing. He also would have been deterred by
the warning signs from his body, which was shedding handfuls of
hair from his head and clumps from his beard.[22]

Although his mind was set on reaching the hut, the closest food
and safe refuge was on the plateau at Aladdin's Cave. As he sat out
the blizzard on January 27, Mawson estimated that he was just
42½ miles away from the cave. Moreover, the intervening ground
was familiar to him from the outward journey, and he knew
it wouldn't be too difficult to traverse. So it was with a certain
confidence that Mawson set out on January 28, after digging out
the tent and the sledge from nearly a meter of wind-driven snow.
His confidence was heightened when the sun appeared and the
"sky cleared [to a] really fine afternoon." It allowed him to gauge
his location and the direction he needed to take, and to dry out
his sodden clothing and bedding. "What a change it makes in one,"
wrote Mawson. Even better, he covered more than ten miles that
day, and he thought he could discern the distinctive features of
Commonwealth Bay in the distance.[23] Salvation was close.

It was closer than he thought. On January 29, as a moderate
wind whipped the snow across the landscape, Mawson came across
an unexpected sight. To the right of his course was a snow mound
topped with a black cloth. If Mawson continued to harbor any
fears about his food running out, those fears were now at an end.

He found a note that had been left there that very morning by McLean, who had gone out with Hurley and Hodgeman, looking for him and his companions. The mound was the farthest limit of their search, where they had left a cache of food in the hope he would chance across it. The note told him the direction and distance of Aladdin's Cave, and the location of two other food caches. McLean's note also informed him that the *Aurora* had arrived, that all the other parties had returned safely, and that the wireless was working. His survival was now ensured. But would his expedition be regarded as a success or an ignominious failure?

CHAPTER FOURTEEN

Home at Last

The information in McLean's note gave Mawson much to think about. He had been worried that one or more of the other parties might have met with tragedy, which would add to the pall that would be cast over the expedition by the deaths of Ninnis and Mertz. Now he could set his mind at rest on that score. He would also have been reassured by the news that Bickerton's party had only gone 160 miles west, that Bage hadn't reached the South Magnetic Pole, and that Madigan had fallen short of going 300 miles to the east. This left his journey as the longest. Other information from McLean was less reassuring. Mawson learned that Amundsen had reached the South Pole in December 1911, and that Scott's fate was unknown. Their stories were likely to overshadow the story of Mawson's expedition and his standing as a polar hero, which would affect what he was likely to earn from publishing deals and lecture tours.[1]

Mawson's immediate struggle might have ended that day. Had he arrived there just a few hours earlier, he could have been carried back to the hut on McLean's sledge. Instead, he was forced to push on alone to Aladdin's Cave, which he learned from McLean's note was closer than he thought — rather than 26 miles, it was just 21 miles away. But the drama had not ended for Mawson. Instead of the mostly soft snow over which he had been traveling, he was on ice, and had no crampons to provide a secure footing. As Madigan had done, he had thrown away his crampons to reduce the weight on the sledge, even though he knew he would need them for the dangerous descent to the hut. So he was forced to fashion some new crampons on the morning of January 30 before setting off for Aladdin's Cave.[2] It was lucky that he took the time to do so.

Although McLean had left directions to Aladdin's Cave, Mawson was confused about what course to follow. First going one way and then the other, he soon found he had gone too far north and was in an area of "slippery ice overlooking [the] sea," where his crampons were particularly useful. It was not only slippery. The area was heavily crevassed, with the "sledge breaking through dangerously in several places." It was Mawson's worst nightmare, and caused him to stop and camp for the day, even though he thought he could see Aladdin's Cave some miles away. His makeshift crampons had also broken, which made it awkward and possibly dangerous to continue on the ice. So he spent the next day and a half making "new and better crampons," using screws and nails from the theodolite box, the sledge-meter, and wherever else he could find them. As a result, it was not until the late afternoon of February 1 that Mawson reached Aladdin's Cave, discovering that it had been only two and a half miles from his previous day's campsite. At last, salvation was his. He could get out of the wind and snow, and eat fresh food for the first time in more than two months, starting with the fruit brought on the *Aurora*. "Great joy and thanksgiving," wrote Mawson.[3]

Having just missed McLean by a few hours on January 29, Mawson could assume that the *Aurora* was still in the vicinity. However, he could not be sure how long the ship would wait. After all, he was already two weeks late, and McLean would have reported that there was no sign of Mawson's party, which might have convinced Captain Davis to raise anchor and set off west to pick up Wild's party before the spreading sea ice made their rescue impossible. Yet Mawson made no move to complete the last five and a half miles separating him from the hut. The hours were slipping by, the hut was almost within sight, but Mawson seemed intent on staying put. Rather than heading down the slope while the good weather held, Mawson decided he "must camp for the night." He complained that his makeshift crampons needed "improving as one is quite unsatisfactory and has strained my right leg."[4] Even today, with the benefit of one hundred years' hindsight, this seems an extraordinary decision. Mawson knew the ship might not be there if he delayed any longer, and he knew how suddenly a blizzard could blow up and force him to remain in the cavern. Unsurprisingly, this is precisely what happened. While he dallied, a blizzard began to blow. And it would keep blowing for the next seven days.

Of course, Mawson couldn't know what was going to happen for the next week. But he should have known enough to seize the chance of good weather when it presented itself. Instead, after staying there for one night, he settled down in the cavern, securely shut off from a world that he didn't seem anxious to face. Doubtless he had been traumatized by his experience. However, that trauma, and the drive for life that had impelled his lone journey, should have impelled him to complete the few miles separating him from salvation. Or so one would think. What was holding him back? Was it the fear of the crevasses and the ice cliffs, or simply his frail condition? Was Mawson in a dilemma about how to explain the deaths to men who he knew held Mertz and Ninnis in much higher regard than him? Or was he deliberately missing the ship so that his return would not be overshadowed by the world's continuing obsession with the stories of Scott and Amundsen? Did he think that being effectively trapped in the Antarctic for another year would draw attention away from them, and see him return in triumph in 1914? One or more of these considerations must have weighed on his mind, holding him back from taking that final step to the hut.

On February 2, although the wind moderated and the snowdrift largely abated, Mawson remained ensconced in the eerie light of the cavern, patiently putting together a new crampon for his right foot, made from the wood of fuel boxes, food bags, and a dog harness. Concerned at being caught in the open by a blizzard, he had decided to take his loaded sledge down the slope with him so that he could retreat into the tent if necessary. This made the crampons more important, as he would have to use them to slow the speed of the sledge on the downward slope. This was the same Mawson who had thought nothing of glissading five thousand feet down the side of Mt. Erebus on Shackleton's expedition, using an ice axe as a brake. Now it took all that day to make just one crampon. Even then he wasn't satisfied. He spent part of the next day, as he waited for the thick snowdrift to abate, partly completing a crampon for his left foot, before running out of materials. The weather was "most exasperating," wrote Mawson, who was becoming concerned that "scurvy or something of the kind were upon me." It is not surprising, given the two and a half months he had spent without fresh food, that he was beginning to exhibit the classic signs of scurvy — his joints were sore, and he was bleeding from the nose and his fingers. Oblivious to the cause of scurvy, Mawson blamed it on the staleness of the food in Aladdin's Cave. He couldn't know that the fresh fruit he was eating was already starting to cure him.[5]

The weather failed to improve on February 4, with strong winds continuing to create an impenetrable wall of snow, which also blocked the opening to the cavern. So Mawson spent the day in his sleeping bag, listening for the wind to drop. But it didn't slacken. It was only now that Mawson wondered anxiously in his diary: "Will the ship wait?" Yet he failed to make a move the following day, even though "the velocity of wind and amount of drift subsided considerably." If he had "good crampons," wrote Mawson, "it would be a pleasure to walk down to the Hut"; but the makeshift ones he had, and the need to take the sledge on which to carry the tent in case of a blizzard, made it "a toss-up." He wasn't prepared to risk it. He went outside to fetch bags of food and other things that had been scattered by the wind, finding wood that could be used to make another crampon to complete his second pair. Even with this additional insurance, Mawson stayed put throughout

February 6 and 7, concerned that the wind remained too strong for his crampons to cope. He also worked on the sledge, fitting it with what he called "a patent anti-crevasse bar" to enable him to sail down the slope "in [a] blizzard if necessary."[6] But he made no attempt to try it out during the days of blizzards that he endured.

It was only on February 8 that Mawson made a move. Although he could hear from inside the snow-blocked cavern that the wind was decreasing "rapidly" from 8:00 a.m., and could see through the ice that the sun had appeared, Mawson waited until 1:00 p.m. before digging himself out. It was only then that he prepared to leave, confident that he would not be caught in a blizzard and possibly plummet over the sheer cliffs at either side of Commonwealth Bay. That had been his great fear on his earlier journey with Madigan back in August 1912, when Madigan had written derisively of Mawson having been reluctant to leave his sleeping bag to face the challenges of the snowdrift. Now Mawson had different concerns as the sledge slid down the slope with him roped up behind, acting as a brake to slow its progress:

(1) Had the ship gone?
(2) If so, had they left a party at the hut?
(3) Or had they abandoned us altogether?

These were questions that he should not have had to ask if he had fulfilled his role as expedition leader and had left clear instructions to cover the possibility of his party being late to return. As for the answers to the questions, they gradually became clear as he descended the slope and "saw enough of the anchorage to be fairly certain that the ship at least was not there." Farther down, as "the boat harbor burst into view," Mawson "saw 3 men working ... on one side of it." His frantic waves brought them running.[7] It was a meeting fraught with emotion on both sides.

Mawson later provided several different versions of his stay at Aladdin's Cave and his descent to the hut. In a talk to the Royal Geographical Society in June 1914, he said simply that, after reaching Aladdin's Cave, "a strong blizzard reaching a velocity of 80 miles per hour caused farther delay" until it calmed on February 8 and allowed him to get to the hut. He didn't mention that he'd been there for a week and that his delayed departure had been caused, apart from the blizzard, by him spending so much time improving his crampons. Mawson provided more detail in *The Home of the Blizzard*, describing how he'd reached Aladdin's Cave to find three oranges and a pineapple, and that he "waited to mend one of the crampons and then started off for the hut; but a blizzard had commenced." So he "camped in the comfortable cave and hoped for better weather next day." But the strong winds and dense drift continued "for a whole week," with Mawson spending "the long hours making crampons of a new pattern, eating and sleeping." As the days passed, he said he "became so anxious that I used to sit outside the cave for long spells, watching for a lull in the wind."[8]

This official account made several important changes to the details he recorded at the time in his diary. The changes had the effect of absolving him from responsibility for missing the departure of the *Aurora*, for causing Madigan and the others to spend another year at Commonwealth Bay, and for forcing another relief voyage to be made. In fact, he needed to accept responsibility for those consequences, for his diary suggested that Mawson could have made his way to the hut late on February 1, taking advantage of the relatively good weather and taking a chance with his makeshift crampons. Even if he had delayed for a day, his diary reported that there were six hours or so of relatively light wind and drift that could have permitted him to complete his journey on February 2. Instead, he spent time making a completely new crampon from materials found in and about the cave, while the wind and drift became stronger. His claim that he spent "long spells" sitting outside the cave waiting for good weather is ludicrous — it would have killed him. Moreover, there was no mention of this in his diary, and no indication that he was eager to get away. Indeed, even though the wind had dropped to a "gentle breeze" by 9:00 a.m. on February 8, and the sun had appeared, Mawson's diary revealed, as we have seen, that he did not begin to break out of the snow-blocked cave until 1:00 p.m. By the time that Mawson was pushing the snow aside, Davis was just taking the *Aurora* out of Commonwealth Bay.[9]

In his diary, Mawson described looking for the ship as he neared the hut, and being fairly sure that it was no longer there. He made no mention of seeing any sign of it, either in the anchorage or on the horizon. What he did say was that he "still hoped she might be searching for us along the coast to the E[ast] and returning before going west." But the ship had left for the west several hours before. There was obvious dramatic potential if Mawson could claim to have sighted it disappearing over the horizon, which is exactly what he did claim in his talk to the Royal Geographical Society. It was as he was coming down the slope to the hut, said Mawson, that he "saw the *Aurora* on the horizon, outward bound." What a dramatic moment, to have fought against the odds and made his way back to the hut, only to witness the means of his salvation sailing away. Mawson was still finishing off *The Home of the Blizzard* when he gave his talk in London, and he made the story even more dramatic for the book, which was published in early 1915. Again, he wrote of not seeing the ship in the anchorage, and hoping that it might be "hidden by the ice-cliffs" or going in search for him "along the coast to the east." It was then, as he "gazed about seeking for a clue," that "a speck on the horizon caught my eye and my hopes went down. It looked like a distant ship; it might well have been the *Aurora*." What had not occurred to him at the time, but had become a certainty in June 1914, had now become just a possibility. Perhaps someone had advised Mawson that there was no way he could have seen the *Aurora* nearly five hours after it steamed out of Commonwealth Bay at full speed.[10]

The gales that kept Mawson confined in the secure comfort of Aladdin's Cave caused an anxious time for the men in the hut, as well as for those on the *Aurora*. Of the sixteen men in the hut, ten were meant to leave aboard the *Aurora*. But there was no way of getting them safely to the ship. The dense snowdrift enveloping the hut was driven by winds that averaged 60 miles an hour, and gusted to 80 miles an hour. Such was their fury that they forced Davis to take the *Aurora* into the relative lee of the Barrier, as he struggled to keep the ship away from the wild waves of the open sea. For a week, Davis was rarely able to leave the bridge, as the engine strained in vain to keep the *Aurora* in place during the frequent squalls. Whenever it was swept out from the Barrier, "the rising waves broke on board and rendered steering more perplexing," wrote Davis. The handling of the ship was made even more difficult by the wind sweeping the struggling vessel with a "blinding spray" that "froze solidly on board." By February 7, the ship was sheathed in ice, with nearly a foot of it having accumulated on the forecastle.[11]

The ten men who were due to leave on the *Aurora* spent a worrisome week trying to catch sight of the pitching vessel through the dense mist created by the windswept waves. "Every time that we could see her," wrote Hunter, "we were glad to find her still there." If the ship was swept out to sea by the storm, they feared that Davis could well decide to head off to pick up Wild's party and not return to Commonwealth Bay until the following summer.[12] During their enforced week ashore, some of the men occupied themselves by killing penguins and seals for the six men who had to remain there. "We have literally been wallowing in blood and meat," wrote Stillwell, who estimated that "about 250 penguins ... have been killed and the breasts cut out and brought in," along with a dozen-or-more seals. Some of the men had fun at the expense of the usually lazy Close, telling him that "there was every chance of the ship leaving without us," which gave "great impetus to his fever for killing seals and penguins," since he thought he would have to subsist on them for a year. Close was right to be concerned, since Davis had decided that he would have to leave by the afternoon of February 8, whether or not he was able to take off the ten men.[13]

Fortunately, as Mawson discovered, the wind had calmed sufficiently by the morning of February 8 for the men to be retrieved. Davis hoisted a flag on the *Aurora* at 7:45 a.m. as a signal for them to come aboard. When there was no response from the apparently sleeping men, a rocket was fired, which had the desired effect. The departing men made their hurried goodbyes before heaving all their remaining gear into the boat and making their way through the still-treacherous seas to the ice-covered *Aurora*. Madigan, Bickerton, McLean, and Jeffryes went with them for a final discussion with Davis, "before they were hurried back into the motor boat." A fireman on the *Aurora*, Stanley Taylor, described how they "had to force them off the ship" and into the ship's boat for the trip ashore. Davis was keen to sail as soon as possible.[14]

At 11:20 a.m., the ship headed off. Taylor described how "everybody had a smile on their face" as Davis "opened the engines out to full speed."[15] Their joy was not shared by those ashore. The departure of the *Aurora* was "a melancholy business," wrote McLean. From the top of a rocky ridge overlooking Commonwealth Bay, Madigan watched as the ship "ran up the Blue Ensign and dipped to us," while the men on shore "answered with a [Union] Jack on a bamboo pole." As the ship steamed away, we "watched her go and smiled," wrote Madigan, who reflected bitterly on how he "had dreamt for months of leaving here ... in January" and now had to stay for another year.[16] According to the instructions left by Davis, their first task was to mount an immediate search for Mawson and his party. As it happened, they didn't have far to look.

Just after lunch that same day, Madigan was helping Bickerton and Jeffryes to fix a steel cable for the wireless when Madigan "looked up towards the plateau, and stared amazed: a man was coming down!" As he and Bickerton rushed up to discover which of the three missing men it was, Jeffryes sped into the hut to tell the others. McLean was preparing a shoulder of mutton for the oven when Jeffryes exclaimed: "there's someone coming down the hill!" Leaving the meat, McLean scrambled up the slope to find Madigan and Bickerton coming down with the ragged and emaciated figure of Mawson. "It was an awful tale he had to tell," wrote McLean, "a series of tragic events which had meant the lives of Ninnis and Mertz and a desperate fight for life by himself." Madigan and Bickerton were particularly distraught on hearing about the two deaths. They had been close friends of both Mertz and Ninnis, with all their bunks being in "Hyde Park Corner." Now they knew their friends would never return. At the same time, the return of Mawson meant they mightn't have to spend another year at Commonwealth Bay after all.[17]

For Mawson, there was a natural sense of great relief. Writing up his diary entry for February 8, which he did some days afterward, he made his successful return appear more miraculous than it had seemed to him during the journey. Several times in his diary he had been relatively optimistic about getting back, but now claimed that his return to civilization had "appeared utterly impossible." Indeed, Mawson wrote, rather than expecting to return, he had been focused simply upon "reaching a point where my remains would be likely to be found by a relief expedition," although he "had always hoped against hope for more." Now that he had achieved the unexpected, he was "overcome with a soft and smooth feeling of thanksgiving."[18]

Mawson was mentally and physically exhausted beyond measure. Despite having rested and fed himself for a week in Aladdin's Cave, he had lost much of his body weight. It was now more than three weeks past the deadline he had given for the different trekking parties to return, and he would have been surprised to learn that the *Aurora* had only been gone from Commonwealth Bay for about five hours. Hannam was in charge of the wireless on the ship, and had told Jeffryes to send any messages on the hour from 8:00 p.m. onward, since the reception was better at night. So Jeffryes waited the obligatory few hours before beginning to transmit the news of Mawson's return and asking Davis to turn around and pick them all up. Had the ship been much farther away, it probably would have been beyond the reach of the wireless signal, which was very limited during the summer. Even so, only two words of the initial signal could be understood, with "Mawson" and "safely" being scribbled down by Hannam and greeted with relief and excitement by those on board. Only when it was repeated did the full and terrible import of Mawson's message become apparent. "Oh God what a message to receive," wrote Hunter, "to think that our two staunch, happy & true comrades … have crossed the great divide." Not knowing whether his message was being received, Jeffryes kept repeating it for five hours, leaving "poor Hannam … terribly cut up at having to listen to it."[19]

Davis was in a quandary. He was already more than three weeks overdue, and was worried about being caught by the ice when he was trying to pick up Wild's party. He not only had the survival of Wild's party to worry about, but also the lives of the men on board, who risked having to face a winter trapped in the ice. The exhausted Davis turned back anyway, only to find he was heading into winds of 50 miles or more an hour. And when the *Aurora* reached Commonwealth Bay the next morning, on February 9, it was all for nothing — the sea was too rough to launch the motorboat. From the shore, with their belongings packed once again, Madigan "watched anxiously" as he waited "to see the motor boat go over the side, watched all day, but no boat appeared." If only they had their own boat, bemoaned Madigan, "we could have got off, I swear it." With the wind showing no sign of abating, Davis had yet another difficult decision to make. He didn't want to make that decision alone, so he gathered all the expedition members in the wardroom to get their support. Davis explained how they could not afford to wait any longer without risking their own lives and those of the western party. Much as they might regret it, the ten expedition members agreed unanimously that the ship had to depart without farther delay.[20]

Nobody on shore noticed the *Aurora* steaming away at 6:30 p.m. that same day — either because they were having dinner, or because the snowdrift was obscuring their view of the bay. Worried that Davis might not wait for the weather to clear, Mawson sent an appeal to him that evening. "Anxious to get off," Jeffryes tapped out in Morse code, "hope Capt Davis could wait a few days longer."

Mawson was conscious of the terrible position that Davis was in, and refrained from explicitly instructing him to remain. In the event, the ship had already left by the time Mawson's message was sent, and Hannam didn't hear any sound from his wireless set on the *Aurora*. "We listened for messages during the night," noted Hunter, "but none came." It wasn't until the following morning that the men on shore noticed, to their dismay, that the ship had gone. They had been "overjoyed at the prospect of getting off," wrote McLean, and now discovered that they had been abandoned for another year. Mawson noted that it was particularly frustrating, because the "wind calmed off in [the] afternoon, so that we could have got off if [the] ship [had been] there."[21]

Although Mawson and his six companions continued to hope that the *Aurora* might return for them once Wild's party had been picked up, there was little realistic chance of that occurring. They would have to reconcile themselves to their situation, and live in one of the world's most isolated and forbidding places for another year. It was particularly hard for the six men who had agreed to remain behind to search for Mawson's party. Led by Madigan, they had agreed to stay for a noble purpose, which disappeared as soon as Mawson was sighted, waving from the slope behind the hut. Their attitude toward Mawson would be sorely tested over the following year as he recovered his strength and began to craft an image of himself as a courageous and resourceful polar explorer. The British Empire needed heroes, and Mawson was determined to provide it with one. His own future, and the success of the expedition, depended on him turning the needless tragedy into a triumph of exploration and masculine endeavor.

CHAPTER FIFTEEN

The Final Year

For several weeks, Mawson and his six companions were in limbo. Although Mawson had been informed by Davis that the shortage of coal would prevent the *Aurora* from returning until the following summer, he didn't tell the six men.[1] So long as they thought there was a chance of them not having to spend another year at Commonwealth Bay, there seemed little point in resuming a full program of scientific activities. Some of their gear remained packed to go, just in case there was a hurried departure. They didn't even bother having a night watchman to guard against the risk of fire or other calamity — fire being a particular danger in Antarctica, where there is no water to extinguish it. With Mawson too traumatized and ill to take charge, everyone did what they liked. "We do what we feel inclined to these days," wrote Madigan on February 16.[2] Prior to Mawson's return, Madigan had been put in charge of the hut by Davis and might have asserted some authority, but he had lost interest in the expedition. He was frustrated that Mawson had arrived a few hours too late for them to get away on the *Aurora*, and that Davis, when he came back, had not waited for calm weather before peremptorily leaving again to pick up Wild. His frustration turned to anger as he slowly learned the details of Mawson's ill-fated journey.

As for Mawson, the exultation and relief that he had felt on reaching the hut soon left him. He needed food and rest. Had he been taken off on the *Aurora*, he might well have died from the strain of the voyage, as he was prone to seasickness. "A great tiredness overcame me," wrote Mawson soon after his return. He complained that his "internals [were] overthrown, legs swollen, etc." Rather than improving quickly, Mawson's legs only got worse. After three days in the hut, he noted they were "now swollen very much." And it wasn't only his legs that worried him. On February 12, he wrote of being "shaken to pieces somewhat," and thought it would "take some time to pull me up to anything like I was physically before that awful journey home."[3] Yet there was no sign of any physical debility in the confident, handwritten wireless messages that Mawson hurriedly wrote on February 10, just two days after his return to the hut. And neither Madigan nor McLean wrote any description in their diaries of Mawson's physical condition. Indeed, they didn't write anything for the first five days after his return, while Bage seems never to have resumed his diary at all. If Mawson was in as poor condition as he claimed to have been, it's difficult to know why none of his companions ever provided an independent description of their leader's state. Was it because of their resentment about the deaths of Mertz and Ninnis, or was it because Mawson's relatively good health after the ordeal raised questions in their minds about the possibility of cannibalism? Unfortunately, we shall never know, as the diaries offer no clues.

Handing his messages to the new wireless operator, Sidney Jeffryes, who had come down on the *Aurora*, Mawson hoped that the ship would still be close enough to receive them. He wanted the messages to be sent on to two organizers of the expedition, Edgeworth David and Professor Orme Masson, once the *Aurora* reached Australia. There was also one for Paquita. Although the messages were not, as it turned out, heard by the *Aurora*, they provide interesting insights into Mawson's state of mind and immediate priorities. Without mentioning Mertz or Ninnis, he apologized to David for the "accident which has changed the tide of affairs and delayed my return for a year." He asked David and Masson to raise funds to cover the extra expenses of £10,000 that the expedition had incurred because of him staying another year and the *Aurora* having to be sent back down to fetch him. Mawson was confident of being able to maintain wireless contact with the world by way of Macquarie Island during the coming winter, when there would be less atmospheric interference. This would help to raise funds from the sale of articles to the world's press, although he warned the expedition's press agent, Conrad Eitel, not to "squeeze the press too hard for cash." In fact, Mawson was confident that the extra funds would be forthcoming from the Australian state and federal governments, and from New Zealand.[4]

Mawson was more interested in having his story widely publicized than in getting the maximum revenue for it. He wanted to craft a story that would transform his bumbling and tragic journey into a heroic epic. And he wanted himself, rather than his two dead companions, at its center. In the first account that he wrote for newspapers, Mawson provided a brief outline of his journey, noting how Ninnis "fell into an unfathomable crevasse" and Mertz later died from "ulcerative colitis," which McLean speculated might have been the cause of Mertz's demise. It was left to Mawson "to reach the hut alone after one month's privations across crevassed country in thick weather." Much to the annoyance of the other men in the hut, there was no mention in these initial messages of their more important and scientifically productive journeys. The creation of Mawson the hero had begun. As for his physical health after the ordeal, Mawson brushed away any concern that Paquita might have had, assuring her that he was "in perfect health after strenuous journey and will return safely about middle of February next." In a message to Paquita's father, Mawson described himself as being "quite sound and well but anxious to return."[5] In fact, it would take him months to recover fully. But he wouldn't sit and mope. Mawson had to retrieve the reputation of the expedition.

Although he was confined at Commonwealth Bay, Mawson would use his control of the wireless, and his writing of the expedition's official account, to transform the story of the sorry tragedy, with his role highlighted above all others. The contract with his men prevented them from publishing their stories until two years after the end of the expedition, and Mawson told Eitel to ensure that none of the men returning to Australia lectured about their experiences.[6] He didn't have to worry about the leaders of the two most important journeys, Bage and Madigan, who were confined with him at Commonwealth Bay and couldn't send messages without his permission. Mawson made no mention of their considerable achievements in his messages, and Bage and Madigan could only sit and fume as they looked over Jeffryes's shoulder at the messages he was tapping out with his Morse code key.[7] Mawson's messages had the desired effect. After receiving his first brief account, David assured him that "All thrilled with admiration at your heroic conduct and thank God your life was spared. More sympathy than ever with you in most sad tragedy."[8]

While Mawson could keep Madigan and Bage in the shadows, Frank Wild was different. Having almost reached the South Pole with Shackleton, and having been the leader of the western base, he was sure to be eagerly questioned by reporters as soon as the *Aurora* landed him in Hobart. Mawson had no way of knowing what Wild's party had achieved and what Wild might say when he reached Hobart or went home to London, where he would be pressured to tell his story and give an account of the expedition to the Royal Geographical Society. Mawson would have been mindful of how Shackleton had arrived back in London a year before Scott, following their "farthest south," and was consequently hailed a hero. In an attempt to silence Wild during the coming year, Mawson instructed Davis to employ him as a supernumerary ship's officer until after Mawson and his companions had been relieved by the *Aurora* next summer. He asked Eitel to confirm that Wild had signed a contract "regarding non-publication." If put into effect, these instructions would keep Wild silent and away from London.[9]

The failure of the *Aurora* to receive these wireless messages meant that Mawson's instructions were never implemented. In any case, Wild wasn't interested in cooling his heels in Hobart. When Mawson later learned that Wild was planning a lecture tour of Australia with lantern slides, he grudgingly agreed, provided that the capital cities were reserved for himself.[10] Such a restriction ensured that Wild's proposed lecture tour would be financially unviable, so Wild left Australia to try his hand in England. Mawson didn't want him lecturing in England either, even though David strongly recommended that he be allowed to do so, provided that the lectures were only illustrated by lantern slides rather than by film. David couldn't understand how Mawson could object, since the lectures would increase public interest in the expedition and lead to greater newspaper and book revenues. But Mawson explained to David that he had already arranged to give a lecture to the Royal Geographical Society, followed by about thirty public lectures around England. He didn't want Wild stealing his thunder, and was only prepared to let Wild "deliver subsidiary public lectures." When Davis urged that Wild be allowed to "lecture without limitation," Mawson conceded that he could give a lecture to the Royal Geographical Society on condition that it was "a small lecture … on the western parties work," while he would give "the big lecture" when he returned. Mawson made it clear that he expected "Wild and Davis to be present" in the audience at his "big lecture."[11]

As it turned out, Mawson's fears about Wild were unfounded. Wild didn't have the ambition or charisma of Shackleton, and although Wild certainly told his story to the press after he arrived in Hobart on February 23, it was not sufficiently gripping to overshadow the story that Mawson would tell. As he later admitted to Mawson, "We did not do so well at my base as I should have liked."[12] Yet Mawson didn't know this in February 1913, as he lay in his bunk worrying about how the world would greet his own return. The six men in the hut had little sympathy for him. During his first five days in the hut, wrote McLean, they were "listening to Doctor Mawson's terrible experiences piecemeal."[13] Yet, as we have seen, neither McLean nor Madigan wrote anything in their diaries until February 13. Their silence was eloquent, with no description in either diary of Mawson's physical or mental condition. The six men blamed him for the deaths of Ninnis and Mertz and for their own enforced stay at Commonwealth Bay. He was supposed to be the leader, and yet he had left behind two dead companions. It wasn't Mawson who had been heroic, they felt, but Mertz, the cross-country skier who could have made his way back to the hut if he hadn't been harnessed to the sledge with Mawson. Any sympathy that the men might have felt dissipated as Mawson disclosed the details of his return journey and the time he had spent creating makeshift crampons, which might otherwise have seen him return to the hut in time for them all to have left aboard the *Aurora*.

This litany of lost opportunities particularly angered Madigan. He complained in his diary about Mawson's "chapter of calamities" that might otherwise "have saved us." And he became more frustrated and angry after the final departure of the *Aurora*, when calmer weather over the subsequent three days would have allowed them to leave. It seemed that Madigan's self-sacrifice had all been for nothing. While he was relieved that he didn't have to search for the missing men, he wrote bitterly in his diary of having "sacrificed a year of the best time of my life, and perhaps of Wyn's [his future wife's] life; I have prolonged the fear and worry of my Mother, for nothing! I did what I thought my duty to the Expedition and my lost comrades, and this is my reward." He faced a year of "just wait, wait, wait." He didn't know whether Oxford would allow him to delay his studies for a second year, and he didn't know whether Wyn would wait for him. The others would have been similarly frustrated by their predicament, although the direct evidence for this is scant.[14]

McLean tried to be positive about their plight, describing how they began to resume some of their scientific duties and were "very happy together." When the weather was suitable, there were always sights to be seen outside. On February 14, McLean went to the boat

harbor with Madigan to try their hand at fishing. The "bracing swell
... reminded us of home," wrote McLean, "except for the floating
ice and an occasional seal who would come swirling to the surface."
Although they didn't manage to catch any fish, they had "a good
sun-bake and yarn" before returning to the hut to tuck into "some
fine savoury omelettes" cooked for them by Mawson. After being
without adequate food for so long, it is not surprising that Mawson
seems to have become obsessed with cooking and eating. But, rather
than sympathizing with him, Mawson's behavior made them more
hostile. While the others did their various duties and chores, albeit
in a rather leisurely manner, McLean noted that Mawson just "reads
letters, cooks and fossicks about." Madigan was blunter, claiming
that Mawson just "eats." He was always at the stove. It was usually
Mawson who cooked breakfast. And it was Mawson who cooked a
fine lamb dinner and plum pudding on February 28.[15]

Both McLean and Madigan hoped the *Aurora* would return
before the end of March. "I really think the ship will be able to
get back," wrote Madigan, "I pray to God she does." With the days
already darkening, he found that the prospect of spending another
winter at Commonwealth Bay was becoming "daily more appalling."
What made it particularly depressing for Madigan, and also for
Bickerton, was the thought of having to spend a year in Hyde
Park Corner, where the two empty bunks of their friends acted as
a constant reminder of their loss. Their old familiar corner now
seemed "desolate" to Madigan, who had "heard Bickerton sobbing
under his blankets." Madigan shared Bickerton's sense of grief:

> Of the four happy members of Hyde Park Corner, the fast friends,
> the comrades of the long winter, of many a midnight talk and smoke
> round the stove, of sledging journeys and hardships shared together,
> of fellow sympathy and confidences only known in the Antarctic; of
> those four friends only two remain.

As for the "terrible end" of Mertz and Ninnis, he couldn't bring
himself to write about it.[16] When he eventually did so, Madigan

made it clear that he regarded Mawson as being largely responsible.

Madigan's mood was not helped by having to destroy eleven of the twenty-one dogs that had been recently landed from the *Aurora*, after having been left behind in Hobart by the triumphant Amundsen. There was little for the dogs to do now, and it would be hard work caring for them through the winter. So the best ten were selected and kept, along with three pups left behind when Mawson had set off on his journey. The eleven doomed dogs were shot by Madigan and Bickerton, and tossed into the sea. With Mertz and Ninnis gone, the care of the remaining dogs became Madigan's responsibility — a duty that provided a valuable break from the monotony of life in the hut. Spending time with the chained-up dogs also lifted his mood, as they greeted him fondly and demanded attention. "I pat one for a while and all the others jump and bark," wrote Madigan, "so I end up going round and having a chat with the lot, which wastes quite a lot of time." He also set up his meteorological instruments again. But none of them had their old passion for their work, and Mawson's authority seems to have been eroded. They were "marking time ... to see whether the *Aurora* will return before we finally make winter preparations," wrote McLean, who described their life as being "like a big picnic," noting how they sometimes didn't have breakfast till 10:00 a.m. or start work till 11:00 a.m. "Everyone does what he likes," wrote Madigan, "which is very often nothing," although the meteorological and magnetic observations were maintained.[17]

When Madigan resumed his diary on February 13, the depth of both his grief and anger was clear. "Calm is settling over me again," wrote Madigan, "I never thought it would come. One must be a philosopher in this world, it is the only way; to take things as they come and harden one's heart." For the next few weeks, he filled his diary with descriptions of his daily work, mainly in relation to the dogs. He also went skiing with Bickerton and McLean, after Mawson shared the unused Norwegian skis between them, and he practiced sledging with Amundsen's dogs. It helped to keep his mind off his dead friends and the frustrations of his situation.

However, his concerns could not be kept at bay, particularly after a "hell of a blizzard" swept down from the plateau in early March, causing Madigan to conclude gloomily that it meant "goodbye to all hopes of the *Aurora*," since it should have arrived by then if it was coming. McLean thought so, too, although on March 6 he took "spy glasses" up the hill and crouched among crowds of molting penguins to scan the horizon for a sighting of the ship. "The ship is a week overdue," wrote Madigan on March 7, adding bitterly that "she won't come." Yet he still went up the hill with McLean and Bickerton on March 11 to again look for the *Aurora*, which Mawson knew wasn't going to come.[18]

As hope of their rescue was gradually relinquished, and Mawson's health recovered, he instituted a regular routine for the hut. Starting on March 3, they began taking turns at cooking and being night watchman, with Mawson being first to take on the latter role.[19] As they resigned themselves to another year's isolation, Madigan was overcome with renewed feelings of anger and depression. "There is a curse on this place," he declared, "I hate it, it is loathsome to me. I feel rotten today and have never had such gloomy thoughts." This was partly a delayed reaction to not receiving letters that he had expected from various friends and relatives. And it also was due to his continuing feelings of grief over the deaths of Mertz and Ninnis. Try as he might to block such thoughts from his mind, Madigan was reminded each night of his missing friends by their empty bunks. He wrote of how he missed Ninnis "in the old corner. Your life object was to get on a Polar expedition, and what an end to all your hopes! I can't restrain the tears now when I think of you." Similarly with Mertz, Madigan reminisced in his diary of the "many drinks" they had been planning to have in the Swiss Alps. Now they would never have the chance. "The world is a grim sort of place," concluded Madigan, while McLean also admitted to feeling "a bit melancholy," but was confident it would "soon wear off."[20]

Their mood might have lifted when they faintly heard the wireless station on Macquarie Island communicating with

Hobart on February 14, and, a week later, began their own fitful communication with the outside world. Although they didn't know it at the time, wireless operator Walter Hannam had successfully sent a message back in September 1912, telling Macquarie Island that all were well, but had not heard any confirmation message from the wireless operator on Macquarie Island. Now the wireless became another bone of contention between Mawson and the others when he reserved it for official expedition news, beginning with messages to the King, the governor-general, and the Tasmanian premier. In his message to the King, Mawson claimed his expedition had been "successful in opening up a large area of new land east and west of Commonwealth Bay and in obtaining magnetic data at a number of stations in close proximity to the magnetic pole." He asked the King's permission "to name a large area of newly discovered land, King George V Land."[21] He was annoyed that Wild had told the press of his own naming of the region around the western base as Queen Mary Land. Mawson was anxious to make clear that his naming of King George V Land "takes precedence over Wild's new land which may eventually be called Queen Mary Land."[22]

What did it all matter? Now that he finally had contact with the world, there was limited interest in his story. Certainly there were newspaper headlines, even in the *New York Times*, about the story of his desperate struggle for survival. But the reports could be measured in column inches rather than pages. It was all because of Scott, whose frozen body had been discovered, along with his two companions, in their snow-covered tent on the Ross Ice Shelf, just 20 miles from a food cache that would have saved their lives. The tragic story was flashed around the world on January 11, 1913, just six weeks before Mawson tried to attract public attention to his own story.

It was not until February 19 that Kathleen Scott learned she was now a widow. She was aboard a liner that was taking her across the Pacific to New Zealand, where she had planned to await her husband's triumphant return. Leaving her young son behind

in England at the beginning of January 1913, she had left on a
meandering journey that took her to New York and then across
the United States, where she rode for four days with cowboys,
before catching her ship in California. It sailed before the news of
Scott's death reached her, and was out of wireless contact until it
approached the Cook Islands. After being told of Scott's death by
the distraught captain on February 19, she responded: "Oh well
never mind I expected that — thanks very much — I'll go and
think about it." She went off to a Spanish lesson and then sat out
on deck to read an account of the recent sinking of the *Titantic*.
She was "determined," she wrote, "to keep my mind off the whole
subject until I was sure that I could control myself." The following
day, when the ship called at the Cook Islands, she described in
her diary how she went ashore in the rain with a young South
American man who "quietly worships me." The pair "watched the
breakers roll in over the reef" before "returning by moonlight
wet to the skin." Once she reached New Zealand, she was able to
read the letters that Scott had left in the tent for her and others.
Kathleen was reassured that his heroic status was unsullied by his
failure. "My Peter has now a great birthright," she wrote, "& we
must be proud & happy, & make our gratitude drown our pain."[23]

By then, Mawson was sending his own messages to the press
and to the fathers of both Mertz and Ninnis. In turn, Mawson
received a message from Kathleen Scott, who was then in Sydney,
sending him "love and sympathy" and telling him to "come
back safe." Mawson told her that the message "touched my heart
and presses the key of the most tender feelings imaginable." He
extended his own sympathy for the death of her husband, and
assured her that Scott's story would ring down the ages. He told
her that he was looking forward to meeting her again, and asked
that she "Please accept my Love."[24] On March 7, he sent a message
to Paquita's father in Adelaide and later that month to Paquita,
describing how he "only just managed [to] reach [the] hut." He
assured her that the effects of his ordeal were "now gone but lost
my hair," which had come out in clumps during the return to

the hut. "You are free to [re]consider your contract" [to marry me], wrote Mawson, "but trust you will not abandon your second hand Douglas." Young Paquita assured him that she regarded the contract as the "same as ever only more so."[25]

On February 28, a reply from King George V, approving the naming of "the newly discovered lands after him," had been received by Macquarie Island, but took days of repeated sending before the entire message was able to be received at Commonwealth Bay. It was a historic occasion, noted McLean, since "it is the first time any Polar Expedition wintering, has been in communication with the outside world." But the others were still living in a world of silence as far as their loved ones were concerned, with Madigan complaining on March 9 that Mawson had sent personal missives to "Adelaide University, Professor David, Mrs. Scott, his brother and various others," while making "no mention of when we can send private messages." It wasn't until March 16, after speaking to Mawson, that Madigan got messages off to his mother and Wyn, receiving a reassuring communication a few days later from his fiancée about his extended stay. But then Mawson informed the men that the expedition would not pay for their private cables.[26] Some sent them anyway, regardless of their relatively high cost.

The flow of official and private messages helped to break down the sense of isolation that had been such a feature of life in the hut in 1912. This was even more so when news messages started to be received. After seven were received on March 8, McLean noted how it was "quite like a morning paper to hear the contents at breakfast time." When the atmospheric conditions in the evening allowed for clear wireless reception, "the real event of the day" became reading the wireless news. "By 10:30 p.m. we are all agog," wrote McLean.[27] The most dramatic news brought confirmation of the death of Scott. The *Aurora* had carried news in January of Amundsen reaching the South Pole and of Scott's party heading in his wake. When confirmation of his death was received at Commonwealth Bay on February 22, 1913, Mawson simply noted in his diary that he knew "what this means as I have been so near it myself recently."[28] While he knew what it must have been like for Scott, he could only guess at what Scott's tragic story would mean for his own chances of capturing public attention. News messages from Australia would gradually allow him to appreciate the extent to which Scott and Amundsen's stories had captivated the world, and the need for him to construct a story that could compete with them. It wouldn't be easy. The London publisher William Heinemann, who was going to publish Mawson's book and tried to sell the newspaper rights to stories of the expedition, had complained in October 1912 that editors were refusing to offer anything for the rights. Now that the pole was conquered, wrote Heinemann, "the only people who care [about the Antarctic] are geographers and scientific people: not the general public."[29]

Mawson couldn't afford to be discouraged by these pessimistic assessments, and worked hard at portraying himself as a hero — much to the disgust of Madigan, who thought with some justification that his own journey and achievements should out-shine those of Mawson. For a brief moment, when he'd been put in charge of the search for Mawson, Madigan might have imagined that he would emerge as the real hero of the expedition. It was not to be. On March 9, after Mawson sent off a swath of messages, Madigan used his diary to vent his anger:

> I am afraid to write down what I think of Mawson now, my opinions have changed greatly … Bickerton and I agree in our opinions. One thing I can say, and am sure I will never go back on; and that is, that in this show it is Mawson and the rest nowhere. I don't know what the public will think of his sledge journey; he has sent messages which make him appear a hero.

Yet Mawson's "journey was a most unexpected failure," wrote Madigan bitterly, with the explorer having contravened "every principle of sledging in this country."[30]

In justifying his damning comments, Madigan pointed out that Mawson had tried to explore the coast, rather than leaving the coastal exploration and mapping to Madigan. In doing so, Madigan claimed that Mawson "made the inexplicable mistake of traveling for 300 miles along the ice falls close to the coast, which everyone knows is the worst crevassed area one can find down here!" It was this apparent decision by Mawson to intrude on Madigan's work that led to the death of Ninnis, which in turn led to the death of Mertz. It was no wonder that Madigan was angry. But he had another reason: he feared that Mawson would rob him of the credit for exploring the coastline, and that Mawson's journey would be portrayed to the world "as the principal journey." Yet Mawson's journey was worthless, declared Madigan:

> He only saw the coast I did, visited no rocks, has no reliable astronomical observations, and in fact, his work is absolutely of no value after mine, which does the whole thing in detail; his merely is an outline of my work![31]

Indeed, Mawson practically admitted as much in his diary, when he confessed on January 9, just after the death of Mertz, that he greatly regretted his "inability to set out the coast line as surveyed for the 300 miles we traveled and [record] the notes on glaciers and ice formations, etc." Mawson conceded that he no longer knew his current position with any certainty, "as the theodolite legs have been out of action for some time, splinted together for tent poles."[32] In fact, Mawson had been uncertain about his position from the beginning of his journey.

It wasn't until March 16 that they received a message that the *Aurora* had arrived in Hobart with Wild's party aboard. Now they knew definitely that they would have to resign themselves to making the best of their extended stay at Commonwealth Bay. McLean confessed to feeling "a bit melancholy," while Madigan resolved to throw himself into his work, since "work is the only thing to keep one's mind at peace." He had the dogs to care for, his daily meteorological observations to do, and all the observations from his sledging journey to write up. Mawson also suggested that he write a record of his journey, which could be included in the book that Mawson was writing for Heinemann. "That sounds all right," wrote Madigan, "I will try to throw off a yarn in the winter." Any spare time would be spent on study, catching up on his knowledge of Greek, and reading his mineralogy books, with Mawson offering to give him "an advanced course in mineralogy." That was "very good of him," noted Madigan, although "my feelings just now towards him are not very charitable." And they were set to worsen. When Madigan was cook on March 14, he "had words" with Mawson when the "Old Man, as usual, came messing around the kitchen ... I am afraid I will fall out with him before the winter is over."[33]

A few days later, Madigan was furious when Mawson pressed him to "do several hours" of mineralogy with him each day. Although Madigan had thought it was good of Mawson to offer, he now regarded it as an imposition, protesting in his diary that he didn't "want to be a slave." Perhaps it was the days of terrible blizzard that had been besetting the hut, or the task of clearing out the belongings of Mertz and Ninnis from Hyde Park Corner, but Madigan was in no mood to placate the "Old Man." Although the study would stand him in good stead when he went to Oxford, he saw everything through the prism of his resentment toward Mawson. "Lately I have had no time to myself, but Mawson seems to think I do nothing," he wrote. Just because Mawson "does absolutely nothing but eat," complained Madigan, "he fancies everyone does the same."[34]

Madigan's lack of sympathy for Mawson was partly due to Mawson's reserved nature, which made him unwilling to unburden himself to his companions. In this, he was much like Madigan, who concealed his depression and put on an appearance of being carefree. It was what men of that time did. There might have been more sympathy on offer if they could have read the entries in Mawson's diary, which told of his concern about his "nerves." Mawson feared that he was insane, although he blamed his breakdown on spending so much time trying to work out the heights of his eastern trek. After starting the complicated calculations on March 22, Mawson resolved the following day to do "more exercise and less study," in the hope it might cause "a beneficial turn" in his mental state.[35] It only got more difficult as the darkness of winter exacerbated the moods of all of them.

CHAPTER SIXTEEN

The End of Exile

The atmosphere in the hut was worsening. At a special dinner to celebrate McLean's 28th birthday, Madigan initially refused to respond when Mawson called for "some 'funny stories' about sledging." "I can't be funny now, at least not on demand," wrote Madigan. "I don't think anyone can. I said some perfect drivel finally." McLean didn't seem to notice Madigan's reticence, noting in his diary that he had a "good evening" and that "everyone was very decent to me."[1] Madigan's relationship with Mawson reached new lows when Mawson sought his assistance in checking the positions that Mawson had calculated during his trek. Madigan was preparing a map of his own journey, and continued to be angry at Mawson for having traveled so close to Madigan's area on the heavily crevassed coast, and losing Mertz and Ninnis because of it. Mawson "has practically no observations or angles," complained Madigan, "and talks about getting 'checks' from me!" Moreover, declared Madigan, "I stayed here at great cost for Ninnis and Mertz, and lastly him, and we have not even received his thanks, *but quite the reverse.*" It was not just Madigan who was annoyed; everyone was "sick to death with everything, and chiefly with Mawson himself."[2]

McLean was more reticent about expressing his feelings, and made no criticism of Mawson at this time. In a relatively rare display of angst, McLean admitted on June 4 to feeling "very lowly to-day. One gets like that at times — we all have attacks occasionally."[3] Madigan, though, was fairly unrelenting in his criticism of Mawson. On April 16, he claimed that Mawson had "lost his temper" over a casual comment that Madigan had made. In the face of Mawson's intemperate outburst, Madigan fought back, noting that Mawson "has annoyed me excessively for months and today he used words to me I won't take from anyone, and I told him so." According to Madigan, Mawson was taken aback and "talked absolute piffle for a long time after that," asking Madigan to go to his room, where he "tried to make out he was very anxious to do all he could for me which is very inconsistent with his behavior; and I don't want any favors from him." Although they ended up shaking hands, Madigan was unrepentant, claiming that "it was entirely his fault."[4]

Again, Madigan was anxious to ensure that the readers of the diary — his family and fiancée — understood that it was not just him: "there is general dissatisfaction, everyone shares my opinion." For good measure, he added what he hadn't mentioned before, "that the way [Mawson] talks of Ninnis and Mertz has disgusted us all from the first," which suggests that Mawson tried to shift the responsibility for the two deaths onto the men themselves — that they had knowingly embarked on a dangerous expedition and been the authors of their own misfortune.[5] If he made such comments to Madigan and the others, it is no wonder that Madigan was angry.

Realizing that his harsh comments about Mawson might be regarded askance by the readers of his diary, Madigan tried to make some amends a couple of days later, when he wondered whether keeping a diary that year was "going to be worth while." After all, he was "very gloomy, and will probably feel ashamed of some of the things I have written."[6] Other than that, though, he let his previous comments stand. Over the following months, he would make more comments that called into question the caliber of Mawson as an expedition leader, and even his character. Sometimes, Madigan's silence could be as eloquent as his criticisms.

When Mawson's birthday was celebrated on May 5, Madigan made no mention of the occasion. While McLean gave a brief report of the birthday dinner, when they had "the usual speeches, wine etc," and Bickerton, Hodgeman, and McLean all contributed something to the occasion, Madigan seems to have contributed nothing. Even McLean made little mention of Mawson's birthday compared with some other occasions. As for Mawson himself, he made the most perfunctory comment, noting only that his birthday was "celebrated by dinner cooked by Dr McLean and Bickerton." Ever since the departure of the *Aurora*, he had rarely written more than a daily line or two in his diary.[7]

Their moods darkened as it got closer to mid-winter. On May 22, as the days shortened dramatically, Madigan railed against wasting "two golden years of the best time of our youth." His mood was made all the worse by "that blighter Mawson in the Hut; I regret greatly that my opinion of him has fallen so. I could not write down what I think of him, what we all think." He complained that Mawson's "daily conversation is disgusting … How an engaged man can talk incessantly as he does I cannot imagine. We pity the woman who has to live with him."[8] Not that Madigan was a complete prude, but Mawson appears to have gone beyond the pale by making frequent derogatory comments about women. When he resumed reading the Sunday Service in late May, the devout Madigan could "scarcely sit and listen to him, he is a perfect hypocrite. I doubt if I will attend again."[9] In fact, he did grimace his way through more services by Mawson.

Then there was Mawson's scientific work, with Madigan alleging that Mawson "has not done *one* scientific thing down here." This was far from true in relation to the expedition as a whole. But Madigan was referring to Mawson's eastern journey, where Mawson had been lost for much of the journey, scorned Madigan, and "spent days, with the help of Bage, trying to find out where he went while sledging, as none of his observations agree with the sledgemeter." Among other things, Mawson was desperate to prove that he had made a longer journey than either Bage or Madigan, and he needed the figures to prove it. As Mawson mapped out his route, using unreliable measurements from the sledge-meter and problematic calculations of his successive locations, it ran fairly parallel and close to Madigan's coastal route. It meant "goodbye to all I might have got from a successful journey," wrote Madigan. Whereas he had "found the heights, studied the geology, [and] accurately fixed the points," Mawson had "lost two men and made six others miserable, and nothing more; not even seen a rock."[10]

The diaries of Madigan and McLean provide the best descriptions of life in the hut during that second year, although Madigan sometimes left gaps of several days when nothing was recorded, usually because he was depressed or angry. When Madigan made consecutive entries in late May, he explained that he was feeling "rather cheerful today, I don't know why, these moods take me about once a month." Then he got depressed again, wishing that he "had not listened to Mawson" and gone on the expedition. He wondered whether he should abandon his Oxford plans, but feared the effect it would have on his reputation and the years it would take "to work up to a marrying salary." All he could do was wait and pray for it all to end. "Impatience and inaction are eating me up," complained Madigan on May 30, "I can't rest. To see time slipping by, and to be getting no nearer my glorious goal, is hard to bear. To think of Wyn waiting and longing drives me mad." And so it went on. It was made worse when the wireless mast was damaged by the wind on June 8, cutting communication with the outside world, as it was to turn out, until early August. "What long dreary months are before us," wrote Madigan on June 10, "I dread to think of them. I seem to be getting old, to be vegetating." And his disgust with Mawson made the waiting that much worse. After having another blazing row with Mawson in mid-June, he resolved to "go on doing my work quietly, and not speak to him unless absolutely necessary, which is when spoken to."[11]

Compared to Madigan's diary, Mawson's continued during this period to be a disappointment for historians. Most of his entries were brief, such as the one for April 17, which was as short as he could make it: "Bage's birthday. McLean cooks." Sometimes the entries covered multiple days, such as the period May 15 to 22, when a whole week was summed up in three matter-of-fact sentences. For the period from May 27 to June 5, he wrote a total of thirty-seven words, all of them about the wind and snow. For three of those days, he wrote: "Continuance of weather — nothing special happens." Once, he just wrote "ditto." Although he had Paquita waiting for him, and his marriage had had to be delayed for a year, Mawson made little or no reference to her, or indeed to anyone outside the hut. When he received a wireless message from Paquita in early April, his reaction in the diary was simply: "Hear from Paquita." [12] Although it was a diary seemingly written only for his eyes, Mawson rarely used it to unburden any of his innermost feelings and concerns.

The rows that Madigan wrote about at length were not mentioned at all in Mawson's diary. The diary of Samuel Pepys, which some of the others used as an exemplar for their own, was ignored by Mawson. When the wireless mast was damaged on June 8, cutting off their vital contact with the world, Mawson recorded the event briefly and unemotionally, ending with the hope that "something can be done." Although he may have felt concern about losing contact with his loved ones, or about whether the sudden lack of contact might cause them unnecessary worry, Mawson made no mention of it. Neither did he make more than an occasional mention of his physical and mental condition, and the rate of his recovery.[13] The ideal for Mawson was not Samuel Pepys, but the Canadian writer Robert Service, with his stirring tales of the Yukon that Mawson would read aloud to the men in the evenings. The stories he most admired were of self-contained, courageous, and resourceful men. They were not men who unburdened themselves in diaries. Anyway, he had little time for diaries. During much of this second year, he was shut away in his cubicle, trying to write his account of the expedition. Mawson was depending on its success, hoping that it would make money and vindicate his leadership.

By mid-June he had finished the second chapter of the book, which would be published as *The Home of the Blizzard*. The title stakes out a claim of its own, establishing for readers the extraordinarily harsh conditions endured by his expedition, far harsher than the conditions endured by any other, whether in the Arctic or Antarctic. Although the two-volume book bears Mawson's name, most of it was written by other members of the expedition, who each wrote accounts of their particular journeys, while Davis wrote about the voyages of the *Aurora*. Mawson concentrated on typing up an account of the months leading up to the summer sledging season and two chapters on his tragic journey, which he intended to be the dramatic highlight of the book.

As he wrote away in his cubicle, the men outside would have been conscious that Mawson was creating his place in history and putting them into subsidiary roles. He was exercising the privilege of the playwright, and it was particularly galling to Madigan. Even McLean seems to have taken some exception to this. In his diary entry for July 25, McLean noted the different activities that day of each man, ending with Mawson: "The Doctor types 'The Book.'" Unfortunately, his drafts of those chapters no longer seem to exist, and Mawson revealed nothing in his diary about the process of writing them, other than to note that too much writing made him "quite down in general health."[14] It was not only that writing was a chore for Mawson; revisiting the events would have taken its toll. But he had to complete it, and do so quickly, in order for it to be published as soon as possible after his return to London. The debts of the expedition, and the additional costs incurred by the second year, were weighing heavily on all of them.

For Madigan and his companions, there was uncertainty as to whether they would be paid for their sacrifice. Mawson made it clear that the extra year caused by his late arrival at the hut would entail a great deal of extra costs, for their salaries and supplies, and another year's use of the *Aurora*. "I will be lucky to get my salary," moaned Madigan, while Mawson's announcement on May 29 that they would have to pay for all their wireless messages caused fresh resentment. "Surely we might have been allowed a few at the expedition's expense," wrote Madigan, especially "the first ones telling our people we were remaining behind." Now he would have to pay for them all. Moreover, Mawson insisted that any private messages had to be approved by him, and he would decide when they were to be sent. He "would deprive us of every pleasure if he could," wrote Madigan bitterly, declaring that Mawson "seems to think he owns our souls."[15]

On the day that Madigan was venting his anger, McLean was writing with delight about learning to toss pancakes, and how it "was splendid out this morning with the sun shining brightly and a gusty wind." Earlier, he had described how one night was "calm and clear with milky moonlight about midnight. The snow was crisp and beautiful and it was like walking in fairyland to tramp over the sastrugi round the house." Five days later, he went for a walk with Hodgeman, and was overwhelmed by the scene: "The sky, the sun, rocks and snow were exquisite — one needs to see them and to breathe in the chill plateau air to realize how wonderful everything is."[16]

Apart from the interest that could be found in the ever-changing environment of Commonwealth Bay, they could also find amusement in the hut. Even Madigan could get his companions laughing, reported McLean, especially when he was cooking and "making all sorts of running remarks about things." "It does not take a great deal to amuse us and the smallest things, childish sometimes, give us a good deal of enjoyment," he wrote.[17] They also entertained themselves, and presumably worked out some of their frustrations, with nightly sparring matches, using a pair of gloves that had been left behind by a member of the *Aurora*'s crew. There was also the diversion to be found by writing for the magazine *Adélie Blizzard* that Mawson had reinstituted under the editorship of McLean. He had started the magazine the previous year, and collected a large number of articles without actually publishing them. Now McLean took charge and produced the first twenty-six-page issue at the end of April, claiming that "everyone is excited about its appearance." The first extracts were read after they finished dinner on April 30, starting with "An Ode to Tobacco" by Bage. The second issue was even bigger, with McLean offering a cigar for the best "verse of two couplets on the month of May." Madigan was the winner, although he was a reluctant contributor after his contributions the previous year had not been used by Mawson.[18]

Although Madigan sometimes accompanied McLean on his walks, he had tired of it all. Whereas the previous year he had written in his diary of the seasonal changes to Commonwealth Bay, "this year ... the surroundings have become commonplace."[19] Madigan still enjoyed the time he spent with the dogs, but he could be merciless when they misbehaved. He believed that Greenland dogs had to be harshly treated to make them obedient sledging dogs. When one of his favorite dogs was set upon by the others and disemboweled, Madigan was furious. After shooting the dying dog, he didn't punish just the dogs he had seen fighting, but described how he "thrashed every dog with an ax handle. They bit and fought but I beat them to a standstill. I was mad. I had to knock [one dog] senseless with a stone before I could catch him." Mawson was shocked. He reported the death of the injured dog on the day it occurred, and two days later described how "Madigan gave all the dogs a severe hiding; no discrimination — those that did not participate were to regard their gruelling as deserved for not assisting [the injured dog]." Only much later did Madigan concede with some remorse that most of the dogs had been innocent of any involvement.[20]

Madigan's brutal treatment of the dogs might also be read as a symptom of the mental state of the men. A leader such as Shackleton would have found ways to lift their morale, but Mawson didn't have Shackleton's qualities. The previous year, Murphy might have lightened the mood with stories or jokes, or the men might have combined to put on a musical or organize a celebratory dinner. But there seemed little to celebrate during this year of involuntary exile. As mid-winter approached, Madigan's feelings toward Mawson became darker still, writing of the "unpleasant truth as to Mawson's character ... and his inexplicable treatment of us." Although he could "never respect Mawson," he decided that his best course was to keep as quiet as possible.[21] In the claustrophobic circumstances of the hut in winter, where reading was the main recreation, and the most minor thing could start a blazing argument, it was a wise decision for Madigan to make. He would, however, have trouble sticking to it.

Mid-winter day had provided a cause for celebration in 1912, going long into the night and leaving some with hangovers. This year, the dinner was much more subdued. Because it was a Sunday, it began with what Madigan called "one of those dreadful mockeries [of a Service] by Mawson." Then Madigan gave the dogs a treat by feeding them thawed seal meat, rather than frozen. McLean was the cook, and reported that the evening "was a success and though there was little of the rollicking merriment of last year we enjoyed it in a quiet way." It was quiet indeed. McLean brought out the last of his cigars to share around, while Mawson let the occasion pass without any of the usual toasts that he made on such occasions. So Madigan and McLean raised their glasses of Australian claret to toast the woman who had given McLean the cigars.[22] They were each in their own little worlds, and wishing that they were somewhere else.

One of them was in a particular world of his own that none could enter. Wireless operator Sid Jeffryes was the newcomer among the seven, the outsider who had not shared the vicissitudes of the previous year and was now their intermediary with the outside world. Each night, Jeffryes would be lying in his bunk, listening among the background crackle of the wireless for the familiar sound of the Morse code messages from Macquarie Island. To the increasing concern of his companions, Jeffryes's comments and behavior were becoming more and more odd. On July 7, he started a fight with Madigan and began "hitting wildly" at him before Madigan was able to restrain him. Jeffryes later claimed, after being locked up in a Victorian mental asylum, that he only attacked after Madigan "made a scurrilous insinuation against Mawson, with regards to Mertz." McLean was convinced that their wireless operator was showing "undoubted signs of delusive insanity," which McLean naively hoped would "pass off."[23] But the madness deepened, as Jeffryes flung around all manner of accusations about his companions. Mawson tried to reason with him, before threatening to sack him from the expedition and stop his pay. They were so concerned after he talked of shooting and asked for poison that the guns were shut away out of his reach. Mawson wanted to keep him from cooking, but was persuaded by McLean to let Jeffryes do it on his own birthday, with Jeffryes producing a pudding that Mawson described as "a revelation in rotten egg and grease."[24]

Although this new situation saw them combine to meet the common threat, it also increased the tensions within the hut and made them more eager than ever to leave, especially as the darkness of winter dragged on. By August, McLean was "tired of reading" and tired of his six companions. He couldn't even console himself with the thought that they were undergoing great privations for the empire. Far from it, wrote McLean, they were "once more in wireless communication with the world," and they were enjoying "splendid food, a comfortable hut and almost everything we need." It was so different from the "awful privations and heroic patience of the old Arctic explorers, [that] it makes one feel ashamed."[25] And there was little to lift their spirits or test their mettle as men, although Madigan was mightily amused one cold day in September when Mawson, while kneeling next to him to look at a red crustacean in the water, broke through the ice edge and fell into the sea. It was left to Madigan to drag his soaked leader to safety. As the freezing Mawson ran to the warmth and security of the hut, Madigan had "one of the best laughs I have had this year."[26]

Mawson could have done more to improve their morale. He was aware of the psychological problems caused by wintering in the Antarctic, but he seemed incapable of lifting their mood. He had his own problems. There was the pressure of writing his part of the book, the concern about the expedition's finances, and now the worries about Jeffryes, with Mawson finding it impossible to get him to do his wireless duties properly, let alone any other work. Mawson drew up a contract setting out Jeffryes's duties, which the wireless operator signed but then failed to implement. Apart from constantly hectoring him, Mawson felt that he couldn't compel Jeffryes to do anything, since he needed him to work the wireless, however inadequately. Then he discovered that Jeffryes had sent off a message saying that they were all mad except him. Jeffryes then told Mawson that the others were trying kill him, but that he had been somehow saved by Mawson putting "him under a hypnotic spell." As if this wasn't enough worry, Mawson's health was causing concern. He complained in late July of being in "very poor" health, noting that he had "a mild irritation of the bladder" and "a large deep-seated inflammation over practically the whole right side of my face." Mawson described how it erupted as a boil, although it may have been a tooth abscess, since he also noted that "some teeth want attending to." It wasn't only Madigan who was counting down the days until their departure.[27]

As that day came closer, the atmosphere in the hut became even more fraught with tension. On November 1, Mawson reported having "some words with McLean over nothing," and the following day complained in his diary about Madigan reading all day. It didn't matter to Mawson that it was a Sunday and that Madigan had only begun reading his romantic novel after first feeding the dogs and attending to his meteorological instruments. Mawson gave a talk to them all in an effort to "galvanise them." He announced that he would do a short sledging journey with Hodgeman and Madigan to find the cache of specimens left behind by Madigan when returning from the eastern coastal journey. It was only a round trip of about 100 miles, and seemed like an excuse to do something before the *Aurora* arrived to pick them up in mid-December. Perhaps it was a test by Mawson to see whether his own journey had broken him physically. Madigan didn't mind, noting that there was "a charm about sledging, and practically no risk where we are going, and a pleasant change, which will make the time fly." Although it would get him out of the hut, he would find himself in the even more claustrophobic conditions of a small, blizzard-hit tent with the expedition leader he couldn't abide. McLean could see no sense in it, noting that "nothing of great advantage can be done in such a short time & the risk is not worth the candle."[28] He was right. But Mawson had to bring something positive from his second year at Commonwealth Bay, apart from the daily meteorological and magnetic observations.

They didn't leave until November 24, which was only three weeks before the ship was due. Mawson left behind a letter for Davis, appointing him leader in case of his disappearance or death, and instructing him to publish "a popular account of our adventures the proceeds of which will be primarily devoted to paying off the debts of the expedition."[29] Mawson, Hodgeman, and Madigan took two sledges — one of which had been given to them by Amundsen — and all the dogs. One sledge was loaded with the food and gear, on top of which was loaded the other sledge, which would hold the rocks and other specimens that they hoped to collect from the cache. Embarrassingly, Mawson was no sooner gone than he was back, much to McLean's amusement, after forgetting to take a shovel and a bag of clothes.[30] McLean, Bage, and Bickerton were staying behind to keep a watchful eye on Jeffryes. To guard against accidents, Mawson took a wireless set that Davis had brought on the *Aurora* for carrying on a sledge.

The trek turned out to be a waste of time. The radio didn't work after the first day; Mawson and Madigan brawled about Mawson's handling of the dogs; and there was no sign of the cache, with Madigan concluding that it was "probably many feet under the snow." Then they were caught by a blizzard and forced to spend the next six days confined to the tent, which was "very tedious," wrote Madigan. It was worse than tedious, being confined in such a small space with Mawson. And there was more to come when a second blizzard brought them to a halt on December 9, just 14 miles from the hut. They were running short of dog food, and the blizzard didn't let up. Mawson began sniping at Hodgeman, which prompted Madigan to have "an awful row with Mawson," which Mawson described in his diary as 'having "a rough-up with Madigan re my stopping." Neither man could storm out into the snow. They just had to lie there in their sleeping bags and fume at each other. "I am sick to death of this," groaned Madigan.[31]

For Mawson, it seemed that failure was being piled upon failure. After the tragedy of the previous year and his inability to achieve the great aim of the eastern journey, he had embarked on another journey, albeit a brief one, that had seen him getting confused about his bearings and failing again to achieve even the simple aim of finding the cache. Subject now to the heightened antagonism of his two companions, Mawson wrote down a list of apposite quotes from Macbeth — most having a theme of thwarted ambition. With only several miles separating them from the hut, there was not even the chance of him succumbing to a noble death like Scott's. As the blizzard tore at the tent, Mawson was reduced to the depths of his own depression as he wrote in his diary:

> The dreary outlook, the indefinite surroundings, the neverending seethe, rattle and ping of the drift. The flap of the tent; the uncertainty of clearance, the certainty of protracted abomination. The dwindling of food, the deterioration of tent, dogs, etc. The irksomeness, bone-wearying cramped quarters, the damp of the cold. The anxiety for the future, the disappointment for prospects.

But the blizzard lifted on December 12, and the sun began to shine. It would soon be time to confront the world.[32]

The end came with a rush. When they reached Aladdin's Cave, Madigan treated the dogs to a massive pile of pemmican in his joy that they would finally be going home. Late in the evening on December 12, the three men made their way carefully down the slippery slope toward the hut, with Madigan using dog chains as brakes to slow the sledges on the ice. On the horizon, steaming toward them from the northeast, was the *Aurora*, the focus of their hopes for the last ten months. But there was also another sight, and it wouldn't have brought them any joy. In their absence, Bickerton had used a broken wireless mast to fashion a massive cross, which was erected on a nearby hill to commemorate Ninnis and Mertz. Bickerton's inscription declared that his friends had died "in the cause of science," which was a vain attempt by Bickerton to make sense of their needless deaths.[33] For Mawson, the cross was a grim reminder of the task that lay before him if he was to make his ill-fated expedition seem a success in the public mind.

For the moment, the sight of the distant ship preoccupied their thoughts, and impelled them to hurtle down the slope "at a rattling pace," despite one or other of the overfed dogs stopping to vomit "every hundred yards or so." The ship was still far off when they arrived at the hut, whose occupants were unaware that their long-awaited salvation was almost at hand. McLean was ecstatic: "Our troubles, anxieties, worries are over at last — we should be the happiest fellows on earth." While they busied themselves with lighting a signal fire of welcome on a nearby hill, and flying a flag from the recently erected cross, the sledging party raided the kitchen of all its remaining "dainties" — "lamb's tongues, pickles, gherkins & the like," and Mawson had "a bath and clean-up" for the photographs and films that soon would be taken for posterity by Frank Hurley, who Mawson had enlisted to return for just such a purpose. They all snatched a couple of hours' sleep, or rested impatiently in their bunks, as the ship spent hours seeking a safe anchorage in Commonwealth Bay. It wasn't until early the next morning that Davis and Hurley burst through the door to wake Mawson and his six companions.[34] After nigh on two years, it was time to go home.

CHAPTER SEVENTEEN

Creating a Hero

Mawson had told the world that he was embarking on the greatest scientific expedition ever sent to the Antarctic. The science he had in mind was geography. His expedition would be about territory and uncovering its secrets, and thereby staking a claim to a large part of the continent. It would be a journey of discovery that would chart more than a thousand miles of hitherto-unseen Antarctic coastline. He was not a headline-grabbing adventurer devoid of serious purpose, implying that the expeditions of the pole-hunting Scott and Amundsen were devoid of such purpose. Had Mawson timed his expedition to conclude prior to those of his two rivals, he might have been hailed a hero and carried shoulder-high through the streets of London and New York, much as he had been carried by his students through the streets of Adelaide after the Shackleton expedition. By 1914, though, popular excitement about the Antarctic had come and gone. After being transfixed by the stories of Scott and Amundsen, the world was now focusing on the coming war in Europe. There was little that Mawson could do to compete. However, he was determined to try.

Rather than rushing back to Australia on the *Aurora*, Mawson embarked on a meandering voyage to remind the world of the difference between his expedition and those of his rivals. He wanted to return in as much triumph as he could muster. Davis was instructed to bring deep-sea dredging equipment so that he could do the oceanographic work that he had been unable to do on the previous voyage. Biologist John Hunter returned to take charge of the program, while Frank Hurley brought his cinematograph to capture more of Mawson's feats for future theater audiences. To also help cover his debts, Mawson insisted on taking back anything that might be of value, including the clapped-out engine of the air tractor. Madigan, Bickerton, and McLean couldn't resist poking fun at his frantic search for value among the expedition's detritus in and around the hut. When they took the final load of goods to the *Aurora*, they hung the launch with junk of all descriptions and made a slow, ceremonial circle around the *Aurora*, much to the amusement of its captain and crew. And when it came time to sling a case of seal meat aboard to feed the departing dogs, Bickerton accidently unloaded the contents onto the occupants of the launch before throwing one of the gory pieces onto the deck of the *Aurora*, where it "hit the unsuspecting Mawson."[1]

On the afternoon of December 23, 1913, as the weather deteriorated, Madigan and Bickerton were given the task of going ashore to nail up the doors and windows of the hut, and stuff the chimney with bags to stop the entry of snow. They couldn't know whether an expedition would ever again live within its walls.[2] Piling the remaining dogs on board the launch, together with the odd piece of gear, they carefully threaded their way through the broken ice that had been swept out of the formerly frozen boat harbor into Commonwealth Bay. "Now finished with Winter Quarters," wrote Mawson matter-of-factly in his diary. As the *Aurora*'s anchor was hauled up for the last time, McLean rejoiced at the thought of having finally seen the last of the hut: "and I say 'Thank God!'" Nevertheless, he reflected in his diary that "Going to a new place, unexplored and wholly unsullied will soon I suppose be an impossibility in this world which grows smaller year by year."[3]

Antarctica seemed loath to let them go. It was Christmas Eve before the *Aurora* was ready to leave, only to be beset by one of the vicious storms with which they had become so familiar. The strong winds and heavy seas, combined with poor visibility, left the ship floundering in the bay, where hidden rocks waited for the unwary. The seas were so heavy that the launch was torn from one of its davits and left crashing with each wave against the side of the ship. Two of the officers rushed to cut it away with axes, leaving the wrecked boat in the clutches of the seething sea. Not surprisingly, the men had no appetite for Christmas dinner, or food of any kind, making it "a very miserable Christmas," wrote Mawson. Madigan described how he vomited four times on Christmas Eve but, in an act of bravado, managed to smoke a cigar on Christmas Day. It wasn't "a very propitious beginning to a day we hoped to celebrate very specially," wrote McLean.[4]

Over the next five weeks, Mawson took the *Aurora* westward as far as the coal would allow, seeing for himself the ice shelf where Wild and his party had been based, and then headed for Adelaide. His conflict was now with the cautious Captain Davis, known for good reason as "Gloomy," as Mawson tried to chart as much of the coast as possible and maximize the number of dredgings to buttress his scientific credentials. The second officer on the *Aurora*, Percival Gray, shared Davis's misgivings about Mawson, describing him as being "reckless to idiocy" when he tried to have Davis push the vessel through thick pack ice. Although Mawson and Davis shared a cabin, they regularly refused to speak to each other for days at a time. As the two-month voyage neared its end, Madigan and the others helped to tidy and paint the ship for its arrival in Adelaide. On February 23, 1914, the warmth of Australia was beginning to be felt, and they had a final concert during which Madigan and McLean reprised their roles as Brutus and Cassius, and toasts were drunk to Mawson and Davis. Gray described how the expedition leader and his captain

sat with their backs to each other. Gloomy with his head clasped in his hands, and when it was time for them to make speeches, both said very flattering things about each other! They are a pair of children. Poor old Mawson made a dreadfully lame halting speech. He is about the worst speaker I have ever heard.

Yet it would be Mawson who would be the center of attention as the ship neared the Adelaide wharf and he and Madigan prepared to jump ashore before the ropes were tied.[5]

Mawson had already written a brief version of his expedition's story for the world's press, and it was front-page news in the *New York Times*. It was all about himself and his "almost miraculous escape" on an expedition that was "most successful."[6] There was much more of the same over succeeding weeks, as Mawson toured some of Australia's capitals, filling in more details of his tragic journey in a way that portrayed himself as a hero, blamed his dead companions for him being too late to catch the *Aurora*, and largely neglected to mention the more valuable journeys of Madigan and Bage. The self-crafted image of the hero was completed by his marriage on March 31, 1914, to Paquita. Held in Melbourne, the reception at the Delprat family home was a most lavish affair, with models of the *Aurora* on every table, surrounded by penguins made of icing. The following day, the couple left by ship for London, accompanied by McLean and Davis. Mawson employed McLean to help with the production of the book, which meant trying to inject some life into Mawson's dull prose. They had a big task ahead of them, to complete a book that could captivate a public bored by polar adventures.[7]

The party arrived in London to muted fanfare on May 3. Shackleton and Wild were there at the station to meet them before the newlyweds took adjoining rooms at the Grosvenor Hotel, with "Gloomy" Davis next door and McLean nearby. They couldn't afford such salubrious quarters for long. The expedition's debtors were already on Mawson's trail. Vickers wanted nearly £1,000 for the aircraft it had supplied, while others made demands for a similar amount. Mawson told Vickers he couldn't pay because the expedition remained several thousand pounds in debt. The company would have to wait, he said, until his book was published. The explorer sent the worn and damaged aircraft engine back to Vickers, and asked for a reduction in the debt. His cheeky request was refused.[8] Then there were the men to be paid, with most receiving just a fraction of what was owed to them. Mawson hoped that proceeds from sales of the book and a lecture tour of Britain, Europe, and the United States would raise the required funds. But the publisher, William Heinemann, was only paying an advance of £1,000, and none of that would be handed over until the final draft was completed. That wouldn't happen until September. In the meantime, Kathleen Scott continued to prove herself a good friend to Mawson by giving £1,000 to his cause, after they had dinner on May 21. Although Mawson was suitably grateful, Paquita took a dislike to the exuberant and flirtatious widow who, she thought, seemed to know her husband just a little too well.[9]

Mawson was also pursued by the Mertz family. In a letter he sent Mertz's mother in March 1914, just after he landed in Adelaide, he told her that he couldn't provide her with a full account of her son's death until he arrived in London, and that he didn't expect to be visiting her in Switzerland until late 1914. In the meantime, he sent a farewell letter that Mertz had left for her in case he didn't return from the sledging journey. However, Mawson didn't send her Mertz's sledging diary, assuring her that he would bring it with him to Switzerland. He didn't tell her that he wanted first to draw upon it for his account of the sledging journey, and to check what Mertz had said about the circumstances of Ninnis's death. For the time being, he tried to satisfy her with a brief account, claiming that her son had more rations than Mawson had, and that Mertz believed his "alimentary system was not so well capable of dealing with dog meat." Fearing that she would jump to the natural conclusion that her son's death had effectively saved Mawson's life by ensuring he no longer had to share his rations, Mawson declared that "nothing was more detrimental to my prospects of safe return than Mertz's death, [which] practically eliminated my last hope of reaching the hut."[10] This was stretching the truth. Mertz's illness and ultimate death may have delayed Mawson's return to the hut by several days, but it is also true that food was the essence of Mawson's survival, and that Mertz's death had guaranteed him additional food, particularly the life-giving pemmican, which he had quickly started eating once Mertz was dead.

It was not only Mertz's mother that he had to worry about. Mawson was sent an aggressive letter from Mertz's brother in the United States, apparently demanding that any money owing to Mertz should be paid to the family. Mawson told Mertz's mother that her dead son had not insured his life before their departure from Hobart, so there would be no money forthcoming from that quarter. Moreover, he claimed that Mertz "quite understood that there was considerable risk of loss of life, and I feel sure that he was always prepared for that." As for any outstanding salary, Mawson agreed to pay an unspecified amount of money owing, but there would be nothing else in the way of compensation. He informed her that one of the reasons he appointed Mertz was that the Swiss ski champion "was well-to-do and had no one depending upon him." On the other hand, if the family could prove that they "depended upon him for support," he thought that a public appeal might be started to raise money for them, although Mawson wouldn't organize such an appeal himself.[11]

Once he arrived in London, Mawson wrote to Mertz's father, asking for permission to print a page from Mertz's diary in his forthcoming book, claiming that he had not yet read it but nevertheless expected that Mertz's diary entry would clear him of any responsibility for the death of Ninnis. He also informed Mertz's father that his son's death was due to his difficulty in digesting dog meat, and that he had died "much sooner" than Mawson expected. Indeed, claimed Mawson, "the day before he died I had no intimation that his condition was very much worse than my own." This is at odds with Mawson's New York Times article, in which he claimed that it was clear to him five days before Mertz's death that his condition "was worse than my own." Mawson's diary entries supported his claim in the newspaper article. Mertz's father wouldn't have known of the discrepancy between the two accounts, and readily gave his permission for the page to be photographed and printed in Mawson's book. However, he also asked for more details of his son's death and the payment of any salary that was owed, and let Mawson know that he had been in contact with the Ninnis family, which raised the possibility of both families going public with any concerns they might have had about their sons' deaths. Although the Ninnis family seemed not to have had any such concerns, the letter from Mertz's father placed Mawson in a quandary, since he didn't have the money to pay the outstanding salary. He admitted that other members of the expedition were waiting for the publication of the book to receive their salary.[12]

Over the next six months, it was McLean who was mostly responsible for editing the work of all the contributors and bringing Mawson's dry-as-bones text to life. He was helped by the half-blind Antarctic historian Dr. H. R. Mill, with McLean reading the draft aloud to get feedback from his historical adviser. However, their work was in vain. The world was lurching toward war, and books about Antarctica were no longer wanted. In mid-July 1914, Heinemann told McLean that he thought it advisable to delay the book's publication, which anyway wasn't ready for the printer. If the expected war was over by Christmas, as many people expected, Heinemann planned to publish it in January or February 1915. McLean assured Mawson that the delay would give time for the book to be "vastly improved." It gave McLean more time to embellish the writing and to arrange for photographs and maps, although Hurley had left on an expedition into central Australia and was not forthcoming with many of the spectacular color photographs that Mawson wanted to use, and which would have distinguished the book from those of other Antarctic explorers. Ultimately, there were just 21 color photographs, compared with 373 black-and-white ones, spread across both volumes.[13]

As we have seen, Mawson was relying on sales of the weighty tome to raise funds to meet the remaining debts of the expedition. But he had another purpose in London, which was to address a meeting of the Royal Geographical Society. This would allow him to trumpet the achievements of the expedition to people who mattered to him. When the audience of worthy geographers and scientists met in Queen's Hall on June 9, he began by reminding them that his expedition had been all about science, whereas those of Scott and Amundsen had been following in each other's tracks to a goal that had already been practically reached by Shackleton. He hoped there would not be any more such expeditions "until at least a superficial knowledge of the whole [continent] has been attained." Having dispatched Scott and Amundsen, he went on to detail the activities and achievements of his expedition and the voyages of the *Aurora*. The various journeys were each accorded just a paragraph, while his own journey with Mertz and Ninnis was spread over eight paragraphs. Not surprisingly, Mawson's account was devoid of any missteps or misjudgments by himself, and had everyone doing a splendid job in a "whole-hearted and unselfish way ... with no thought of [personal] gain."[14]

As leader of the expedition, the gain was mostly Mawson's. It was Mawson who called on the King at Buckingham Palace to talk about the expedition and who, at the end of June, was knighted by the King for his expedition's achievement. He was also guest of honor at a special luncheon at the British Empire Club, where the tables were sprinkled with lords and lesser nobles who had come to shower adulation on the explorer. But there was no joy for Mawson from the British government, which refused to annex the huge expanse of Antarctica over which Mawson and his men had taken such trouble to raise the British and Australian flags. That disappointment was balanced by the opportunity that Mawson and Paquita had to enjoy the latest offerings of London's theater, with Mawson also being part of the Australian contingent at a costumed ball at the Royal Albert Hall, which was held to celebrate the centenary of the end of the Anglo-American war. There was also an opportunity to rekindle his relationship with the widowed and independently wealthy Kathleen Scott. They met on at least two occasions, and she wrote asking that he keep her contribution of £1,000 secret. In writing, she used a warm and easy familiarity, referring to Mawson as "dear person," and assuring him that she had no better use for the money than to give it to his expedition.[15]

With Paquita accompanying him, there was limited opportunity for the relationship to develop in ways that he may have liked. Still, there was much more on his mind.

Leaving the loyal McLean to complete the book's preparation, the Mawsons left London for Australia on July 20, going by way of Switzerland to see the grieving Mertz family so that he could hand over the sledging diary and explain in person the circumstances of their son's death. Then it was back to Australia for the newly knighted explorer. He had to preserve his position at Adelaide University, which had been filled by a temporary lecturer for more than two years, and he had to address a conference in Sydney of the British Association for the Advancement of Science, with attending scientists coming from across Britain and Europe. Mawson chaired the section on Antarctica, and gave a talk on the expedition. He also did some paid public lectures, which he illustrated with Hurley's film of the expedition. However, Mawson's story of the Antarctic could not compete with the stories of the European war, which had erupted a few weeks before he began his Australian lecture tour. With his university lectureship secured, and the academic year coming to an end, the couple headed back to England in late October. The prospects for his book and British lecture tour did not look good. The finances of the expedition were so dire that the bank dishonored a check for £60 that he sent to Bickerton.[16]

Mawson had been planning a lecture tour of Europe, but the outbreak of war put paid to that. It also destroyed any chance of the expedition book, or a proposed British lecture tour, attracting much public attention. He could only hope that the war really might be over by Christmas, and that the public might rediscover an interest in Antarctica. It was not to be. Although the war dragged on, the publication of the book went ahead regardless. Heinemann had outlaid so much for its production that it could not be delayed any longer. Anyway, the Americans were not yet at war, and Heinemann hoped that he might sell a decent number on the other side of the Atlantic. In the event, only 3,500 copies were printed for the whole English-speaking world and, even though it was well reviewed, less than two-thirds of them were sold by the end of the war. Australian booksellers were only prepared to order two hundred copies. They might have sold more in Britain had Mawson been there to promote it, but he went off to the United States, where a lucrative lecture tour had been promised by a promoter, while the pregnant Paquita returned to Australia to have their baby. The lucrative American lecture tour turned out to be a chimera, and barely covered its expenses. One of Mawson's English supporters berated him for leaving London to "vanish into the unknown" when he should have stayed and promoted his book in Britain with lectures and films.[17] But stories of the distant Antarctic could not compete with stories of the terrible war on their doorstop.

The war ruined everything for Mawson. What was he to do? Shackleton had gone back to the Antarctic with Wild and Hurley, but there was no prospect of Mawson being able to mount another expedition, even if he was inclined to do so. Neither did he seem keen to stick at his teaching post at Adelaide University. He was still comparatively young and fit, and joining the war was the obvious outlet for his restlessness. But he hung back from enlisting. There was his wife and baby daughter to consider, and he clearly did not relish the prospect of dying in some distant trench. As an officer in the Australian army, Bage had gone to Gallipoli, and very soon had his head blown off by Turkish rifle and machine-gun fire when he was sent in broad daylight to mark out a new position for Australian troops to occupy.[18] In a letter to Webb in August 1915, Mawson noted Bage's death and claimed he had been "itching to get to Gallipoli, but all the time am held up with expedition affairs." He argued that the "immense expenditure of the expedition will be largely lost if the scientific results are not published in full in the best possible way." And he couldn't see how that could be done by anybody but himself. To assuage the guilt that he clearly felt, Mawson told Webb that there were "many who should be at the front before ourselves."[19] As far as expedition members were concerned, Mawson was not leading by example.

Apart from Bage, several of the leading expedition members had been quick to offer themselves for the war. Hodgeman had become a captain in the Royal Leinster Fusileers; Bickerton was serving in France as a machine-gun officer; McLean had joined the medical corps and was working among the trenches in France; and Davis was captain of a British naval vessel. As for Madigan, he had finally made it to Oxford, only to have the war break out. Once again, his studies were interrupted when he immediately enlisted and was made a second lieutenant in the Royal Engineers. "Everyone has to think of the Empire and not himself," Madigan wrote to Mawson in September 1914. By the end of 1915, Madigan had been sent to the trenches and was shot in the thigh during the attack on Loos. Even David joined the Australian army, being appointed a major at the age of fifty-seven in an Australian Tunnelling Corps that was partly set up at his instigation. The corps was intended to tunnel under enemy trenches so that explosives could be set to blow them up, and David was seriously injured during one such operation in the trenches of France in 1916.[20] Mawson, however, had no intention of enlisting. When he left England for the United States in January 1915, he told Ninnis's father that it "may be a long time before I am again in London," although, if the war ended soon, he would be "again in London towards the end of the year on Expedition business."[21]

The pressure on Mawson to enlist had become greater after Gallipoli, as the army appealed for reinforcements, and a public campaign for conscription became more vociferous. Mawson became the leader of this campaign in Adelaide, urging that able-bodied men be compelled to join up, at a time when he was not prepared personally to volunteer.[22] His position was untenable. Mawson finally offered in September 1915 to place himself in "a scientific capacity" at the service of the defense department in Australia. Why he didn't join David and other engineers and geologists in the Tunnelling Corps is not clear. It would have fitted his qualifications, but he wasn't keen to expose himself to the hazards of the trenches. Perhaps sensing this, the Australian Defense Department advised Mawson to offer his services to the British War Office. In November 1915, Mawson tried instead to serve with Australian forces in Rabaul, where the fighting with token German forces had long since ended, but where he could do geological work. Again he was unsuccessful. Finally, in March 1916, the chief of Defense Staff in Melbourne successfully asked Adelaide University to give Mawson leave so that he could offer his services to the War Office in London. Leaving Paquita and his infant daughter behind in Australia, Mawson went by way of the United States to seek a senior military post in Britain.[23]

CHAPTER EIGHTEEN

Mawson's War

Mawson arrived in London on May 10, 1916, just as concern was being raised about the fate of Shackleton's expedition to the Weddell Sea. Nothing had been heard from Shackleton for two years, and there were calls for a rescue expedition to be mounted. Here was something that Mawson could do, using his experience to raise the necessary funds and organize the relief ship. He was quickly appointed to a Shackleton relief committee, which was chaired by Admiral Sir Lewis Beaumont of the Royal Geographical Society. Mawson was back in his element, and could avoid the maws of war a bit longer. Indeed, he thought of going on the relief ship himself, which might keep him out of the war for another year or more. However, the organization of the relief effort had hardly started before the elderly Admiral Beaumont was complaining to Kathleen Scott, for reasons that are not explained, that he wouldn't serve on the committee if Mawson remained on it.

Mawson was saved from this humiliation when word was received from the Falkland Islands on May 30, 1916, that Shackleton was safe. His ship had been caught by the ice in the Weddell Sea and eventually crushed, forcing Shackleton and his men to make a dramatic journey across sea ice to Elephant Island. From there, Shackleton and some of his men had embarked on a voyage by small boat to South Georgia, when they had to cross snow-covered mountains before reaching sanctuary at a whaling station. The feat was made all the more incredible by being done in the cold and darkness of the approaching winter. And the dramatic moments were captured for the public by Hurley's spectacular photographs and films.[1]

Shackleton's feat would come to be regarded as one of the great survival stories of all time and a testament to his leadership skills in not losing one of his men. Yet Mawson was dismissive on first hearing the news of Shackleton's almost-miraculous escape. After being called in to a newspaper office to make sense of Shackleton's rather garbled cable, and going to the Admiralty to see what could be done about sending a vessel to pick up Shackleton's stranded men on Elephant Island, Mawson returned to his room at the Euston Hotel. His first thought was to ring Kathleen Scott with the news, but it was nearly midnight, and he penned a note instead. While acknowledging that Shackleton's party "certainly have had a bad time," he told Kathleen, who despised her dead husband's rival, that he thought Scott's nemesis had over-dramatized the story to make "it all sound as dreadful as possible." There also would be little in the way of scientific results, added Mawson caustically.[2]

The following day, he wrote to Paquita from the Royal Societies Club, conceding that Shackleton's party "had some narrow escapes," but that they had "little scientific results." Moreover, wrote Mawson derisively, any book of the expedition would only "make a good *small* volume." Mawson's mood that day was not helped by him having to sell an unspecified amount of platinum that he had brought from Australia, hoping to make a tidy profit. He found that the British government had set a fixed price for the valuable metal and was forbidding its export, due to the war. He was accordingly forced to make a patriotic sacrifice and sell it at half the price he could have got in the United States. It was yet another of his fortune-making schemes that failed to materialize.[3]

With the Shackleton relief committee coming to an end, Mawson would have to turn his attention to war work, but he would be disappointed there as well. Mawson wanted to be a high-ranking scientific officer. However, the best offer he received from the War Office was the lowly rank of second lieutenant in the Special Brigade Royal Engineers (Chemists), which was involved in gas warfare. Neither the rank nor the job appealed to him. He used all his London contacts to seek a more exalted post.[4]

While Mawson was marking time, he took the opportunity to become reacquainted with Kathleen Scott. He called at her home on May 16, and they talked for a couple of hours about the relief of Shackleton. A bad cold then kept him confined to his room at the Euston Hotel. Once he recovered, wrote Mawson, he promised to call on her again, "for it is really a great pleasure for me to see you and to talk over these things with you."[5] He was among dinner guests on May 25; and then, on June 7, Kathleen recorded in her diary that Mawson took her out to dinner and dancing. When it came time to leave, she noted with some surprise that he kissed her hand. "He's a dear & very clever," wrote Kathleen, "but this will never do." At the time, she was being pursued with considerable ardor by forty-nine-year-old Lord Montagu, who had lost his mistress the previous year when the ship they'd been on had been sunk by a German submarine. Now Montagu "poured out his whole soul to me" and "wanted to love me for ever," wrote Kathleen. She wasn't interested in his proposal. Prime Minister Herbert Asquith, whom Kathleen had sculpted in 1912, was also a frequent visitor to her home. Asquith often visited after cabinet meetings, and discussed secret matters concerning the war. Kathleen loved his attention, as she did that of most of the men who pursued her. As her biographer and granddaughter Louisa Young observed, the "war seemed to send everyone if not sex mad, then love mad, passionate friendship mad, waste-no-time mad." Doubtless, it was life-affirming amid the death and despair of a war that was killing millions, and when German Zeppelins were dropping bombs on London.[6]

As the British and French prepared in June 1916 for the battle of the Somme, Mawson continued his pursuit of Kathleen. On the bank holiday weekend in early June, he spent time with her at a beachside cottage at Sandwich. Kathleen walked into town to collect him from the station, and noted in her diary that he was:

very nice & was a great success. He's brimful of interesting information — chiefly scientific. I enjoyed him very thoroughly indeed — & he did too. Everything was nice — even the rain & the wind & the cold — he enjoyed everything. He's a very real person I think.

There was no more mention of Mawson during that long weekend. Instead, the diary entry for the second day of the weekend simply had a photograph of them on the beach in neck-to-knee bathers, with Mawson holding young Peter on his shoulders. The entry for the third day had a photograph of Mawson in the garden, dressed in trousers, shirt, and tie, and holding a watering can. When the battle for the Somme erupted in early July, it was possible to hear the artillery barrages from faraway England. But there was no sign in the photographs that the war was casting a shadow over Sandwich on that idyllic weekend. Kathleen would later tell Mawson wistfully how a visit to the house in Sandwich "never fails to remind me of you." She recalled the time they had spent in a "little tent on the beach which when the wind blew its canvas used to send you to sleep." One of her friends predicted that Kathleen would discover that Mawson was "'not very nice.' I wonder!!" wrote Kathleen.[7]

She had plenty of opportunities to find out over the next month. On June 15, Kathleen and Mawson went to Golders Green to view a bare-breasted bust of War by Australian sculptor Bertram Mackennal. Although Kathleen liked the sculpture, she thought that Mackennal was "an impossible little snob." With the sun shining, the pair returned "on the top of a very delightful bus!" They went dancing that night, accompanied by Percy Dearmer, the canon at Westminster Abbey, and his twenty-three-year-old son, Geoffrey, whom Kathleen adored. She'd adored his younger brother, Christopher, even more, but he had been killed at Gallipoli. "Geoffrey is not half as beautiful as my lovely Christopher," wrote Kathleen in her diary that night, but was sufficiently similar "in his voice & sensitive mouth to make me feel very lonely & hungry for my Christopher." Mawson was no young Adonis, but he persisted with his pursuit of her, going to Kathleen's for tea on June 19, and the following day taking her to see his film of the expedition. After a visit that evening from Asquith, who "gets more interesting & wonderful every time," she dined with Mawson. On the weekend of June 24–25, she took him back to the cottage at Sandwich, declaring that it was a "signal success from every point of view," with Mawson being "a charming companion" who "fits in delightfully down there."[8]

Mawson was smitten. He wrote to "dear Kathleen" to let her know that he was "still enjoying my trip to Sandwich — I will always be able to enjoy it — certainly when you have forgotten all about it, it will be fresh with me. The pity was that it ended so soon in actuality, but fortunately the aftermath of contemplation lingers on." As it happened, their time for such diversions was coming to an end. Mawson had finally secured a position that would take him away from London, and people were beginning to talk about their relationship. In his efforts to secure a senior military post, Mawson had approached the munitions minister, Lloyd George, and had been offered the rank of acting army captain working on the Liverpool docks, supervising the loading of explosives and artillery destined for the Russian port of Archangel. It was not what he had been hoping for, and he waited until being refused a position by the Admiralty, which might have kept him in London, before finally accepting the Liverpool position. He would be working under the elderly Lord Moulton, a scientist and former Liberal politician who was director-general of the Explosives Supply Department in the Ministry of Munitions. Moulton was also a friend of Kathleen's, and wanted to know where Mawson had spent the weekend. Mawson warned Kathleen that Moulton had been "very inquisitive," with Mawson feeling he had little choice but to tell him that he "had been down to your house at Sandwich for [the] week end." Mawson told Moulton he had spent the time there correcting a manuscript.[9]

The couple were now on notice that their relationship was

becoming a subject for gossip, which may have been why Kathleen remained in London the following weekend. She still saw Mawson on both days. On the Saturday, he was among a small group who had tea at her home, before he went out dining and dancing with her, while on the Sunday he came and told her "some very interesting things about disease" while she worked on a marble sculpture in the garden. After spending a few days inspecting explosives factories, Mawson was back for dinner at Kathleen's on July 5, and two days later took her and Peter to a private showing of war films before going to the Savoy to see an exhibition of caricatures by the Australian cartoonist Will Dyson. That Sunday, as the relentless slaughter on the Somme continued, she went to Kensington Gardens with Peter to collect caterpillars, before spending a "very delightful" time with Mawson in a row boat, and "got home very late." It wasn't warm enough for such activities, wrote Kathleen, but it was "otherwise very delightful." The following Friday, she recorded how she left her sick son at home to dine "with Douglas at Pall Mall & went to the Rivoli." He was back on the afternoon of Sunday, July 16, when she was working in the garden on a marble sculpture, and he called by in the company of others.[10]

Mawson may have dropped by to show off his uniform. It was hardly the senior scientific post he'd envisaged for himself when he left Australia, but at least he was in an officer's uniform, and would be able to say upon his return to Australia that he had played a useful role in the war. He could hardly confess that he'd spent the war years relaxing on the beach and dancing the nights away at London clubs while a million men were being slaughtered on the Somme. Although his new post was not a senior one and would not test his abilities, it was a role of some importance.[11] The explosives being sent to the Russians would help keep them fighting against the Germans on the eastern front, and thereby prevent the German pressure on the western front from becoming overwhelming. But it took him away from Kathleen and the other delights of wartime London.

It was only now that Mawson suggested to Paquita that she might think about joining him in England. Writing on July 25, 1916, from Liverpool's North Western Hotel, where he'd taken up permanent quarters, Mawson told her that she "would be a delight — a help — and a grand companion for me ... If you can arrange to leave the child, then we can go into the matter."[12] Even if Paquita was agreeable, it would be months before she would be able to arrive. In the interim, Mawson continued to rely on the companionship of Kathleen. Just four days after writing to Paquita, he left Liverpool for London. The couple were off to the seaside again. According to Kathleen's diary, it was a "piping hot" Sunday that saw them go for a "*very* long walk from Hastings. Lost our way. Had lunch etc in a quarry." They had tea with friends, and stayed overnight before returning to London.[13] That weekend, however, seems to have been the end of Mawson's summer idyll with Scott's widow. There was nowhere for their relationship to go. With a young wife and baby, it would have been untenable for Mawson to marry Kathleen. And there is little indication that she was prepared to marry Mawson. He may have had a stronger place in her affections if he had paid more attention to her son, Peter.

Although the procession of munitions ships heading for Archangel kept him busy in Liverpool, Mawson still had opportunities to be in London. Little more than four weeks after their hike to Hastings, he was back knocking on Kathleen's door, ostensibly to access some expedition slides that he stored there. It was a night of excitement and some danger, as sixteen Zeppelins floated across the nighttime sky, dropping their bombs on the city. As it happened, Kathleen was out of harm's way, visiting Ireland, as a disappointed Mawson was informed by her maid. "It did not seem the same place without you," wrote Mawson, who told her that he hoped she would "be in town the next time I visit." He was unsatisfied with his life and work in Liverpool, and was uncertain what he would do during the coming winter when Archangel would be frozen in by Arctic ice and the flow of munitions ships would cease. There was a possibility of going to Russia, but he didn't want to do that. He wanted to be "settled in a job," preferably in London. Then he "would get Paquita over as I know she would like it."[14] Perhaps he hoped that Kathleen would use her high-placed political contacts to secure him such a position.

All the while, Mawson was being pestered to settle the expedition's remaining debts of nearly £2,000. About half the money was owed to Vickers for the aircraft, and the company had been pursuing him for more than two years. He now told Vickers that he had no prospect of ever paying the debt because of the war, which had caused "a chapter of disappointments." It would have been more accurate to say "a book of disappointments," given the poor sales of the expedition book. Mawson asked the company to write off the debt and treat it as a donation, which it finally agreed to do.[15] He asked Australian prime minister Billy Hughes for the remaining £970, telling Hughes that the sixteen volumes of scientific results that were being prepared for publication "will be of real value to general science and a unique advertisement for things Australian."[16] Some members of the expedition, including Madigan and McLean, were also chasing him for the rest of their salaries. The loyal Dr. Archie McLean wrote from a military hospital in France in July 1916 asking for money that was owed to him from when he was working on the book in London.[17] In turn, Mawson was using solicitors to pursue the expedition's London secretary for some money that had been taken by him in lieu of salary without Mawson's authority. No wonder Mawson didn't know which way to turn.

Should he stay or go? That was the question for Mawson in late 1916. If he stayed, there was the possibility of his debtors making him bankrupt. His position in Liverpool might not have been senior enough for him, but at least it was far from the fighting and the Zeppelins. However, in October the Zeppelins extended their operations and began to bomb industrial areas near Liverpool as well. Nowhere was safe. Yet he now followed up his earlier letter and cabled Paquita, telling her to leave their baby behind and brave the voyage across the Pacific and Atlantic to join him in

Liverpool. He didn't know whether he was coming or going. At the same time as he told Paquita to come to England, he asked Thomas Cook to provide a quote for a leisurely first-class return journey with Paquita to Australia by way of Russia and China, which would minimize the risk of being sunk by a submarine en route.

Once home, he would be out of the war altogether. A plebiscite in Australia had just rejected a government proposal to introduce conscription for military service, so he wouldn't be dragooned into the tens of thousands of Australian reinforcements being sent to shore up the Allied armies on the Western Front. Mawson could take up his teaching post at Adelaide University and resume his work on preparing the expedition's scientific results for publication. In a letter to the Adelaide University registrar, Mawson justified his proposed departure from England by claiming that there were sufficient men of "high scientific attainments" in England and more than enough officers. It would be inadvisable "from a national point of view," wrote Mawson, for him to serve in any other capacity than a scientific one. He didn't want to get his head blown off like poor Bage or fall down a hole like Edgeworth David, when Australia needed him to train scientists for the future. That was his justification. After all, the government had shown the importance of science by withdrawing young Frank Stillwell from military service to investigate the gold reefs of Bendigo. Anyway, predicted Mawson, the war would soon be over.[18]

For reasons that are not clear, Mawson changed his mind about leaving. Perhaps it was due to the arrival of Paquita, which would have made the English winter more bearable for him. Or perhaps it was because he was given a more interesting post in London, and close to Kathleen, after complaining to his superior officer in December 1916 that his experience and qualifications were being "wasted" in Liverpool. There was "practically no one in the Empire," wrote Mawson, who possessed in such high degree his "combination of laboratory scientific knowledge with field experience," which "surely ... ought to be useful."[19] Although his commanding officer wasn't sympathetic, Mawson went over his head and appealed directly to the politician in charge, Walter Runciman, who set him to work drawing up a report for the Russian government on the "manufacture of certain explosives in this country." This was code for poison gas, with Mawson's report being meant to help the Russians boost their production of such gases. It would entail him inspecting munitions factories and reporting on their manufacturing processes. It meant that he and Paquita could leave Liverpool for London, where their second daughter was born in October 1917.[20]

Mawson's work made him aware of processes being developed in England to convert coal into petroleum, which could be valuable to Australia in view of its large reserves of brown coal. Mawson suggested to Professor Orme Masson, head of Australia's new organization for science and industry, in October 1917 that he be employed in England to report on these technical processes. At the same time, he was seeking an extension of his leave from Adelaide University until mid-1918. Masson took six months to reply, informing Mawson that the organization wasn't interested.[21] He had more luck with the university, which agreed to yet a farther leave of absence. Mawson's position was taking a turn for the better. Although the Russian Revolution in November 1917 had brought an end to Mawson's work on behalf of the Russians, he remained involved with coordinating Allied supplies of explosives, poison gases, and petroleum, and was promoted in January 1918 to head his particular section in London. In March he requested and was given a promotion to the temporary rank of major. It wasn't just a major's uniform that he wanted; Mawson also wanted more money. As soon as he got the promotion, he complained of being on leave from a £700-a-year position in Adelaide, yet only being paid £400 for his war work.[22]

Mawson's time in England came to an end in early 1919, when he and Paquita and their infant daughter boarded the troopship *Euripides* for home. Prior to departure, he attended a luncheon at Kathleen Scott's home, along with Nansen, author J. M. Barrie, and Geoffrey Dearmer. So much love in the one room, Kathleen must have thought, and it was all focused on her. What bliss to be so surrounded, and two of them were polar heroes.[23]

Although Mawson was on the point of leaving, it wasn't the end of his relationship with Kathleen. The pair continued to be close, albeit not in a geographic sense. She wrote to Mawson in April 1920, telling him how Sandwich always reminded her of their time on the beach together. "Goodbye my dear," she wrote, "I wish you were here. Don't get completely lost."[24] As it turned out, Mawson didn't return to London until 1926. Even though Paquita was accompanying him, Kathleen sent Mawson an urgent note, imploring him: "Hurray! Hurry up & come to see me. Come before Saturday because I go away for the week end — I am very free until then." She warned she was now "an old grim grey decrepit hag." She had also remarried, although she advised Mawson that her husband was away. "Come soon," she wrote, signing off, "Ever Kathleen."[25] It is not clear whether Mawson answered her plea. Whatever his response, their relationship would never again be what it had been in that mad summer of 1916.

Just as he had had much to ponder when ensconced for a week in Aladdin's Cave in February 1913, so Mawson had much to think about as he relaxed aboard the *Euripides* on the voyage back to Australia in March 1919. Also on board was David, who was returning with the rank of lieutenant colonel and a more illustrious war record than the much younger Mawson, whose belated enlistment had not brought him the glory he had sought. The war had also ruined his chances of finding fame and fortune through his book, film, and lectures about the Antarctic. The expensive two-volume *Home of the Blizzard* had not been a commercial success, and Mawson had failed in his attempts during the war to publish a single-volume popular version. Nonetheless, Mawson remained Australia's preeminent Antarctic explorer, and used that position to repeatedly press both the British and Australian governments to claim the massive quadrant of Antarctic territory whose coastline he and his companions had explored in the summer of 1912. Although those governments refused to make a formal claim during the war, Mawson's pressure helped to convince the British government to decide secretly in 1919 to gradually claim all of Antarctica for the British Empire. Britain based its claim to the so-called Australian quadrant on the work of his expedition.[26]

Mawson was enlisted to buttress the claim by voyaging to Antarctica in 1929, and again in 1930, to raise the British flag anew on the coastline he had first sighted in 1912. There would be no sledge journeys this time. Indeed, he would hardly step foot on the continent during the months he spent down south. Some times, Mawson would remain in his launch and just toss a flag and its pole onto a rocky shore. Other times, he would drop a flag from an aircraft flying overhead. And occasionally he would step ashore and raise a flagpole, and read out the proclamation required to make that part of the continent securely British. On January 5, 1931, he stepped ashore at Commonwealth Bay and visited the old hut, with its timbers windblown and its interior filled with ice. Mawson had first raised the flag there in February 1912, and now did so again nearly twenty years later, providing a legal basis for the formal territorial claim that Britain and Australia would subsequently make. The physical presence of the hut, the story of Mawson's journey, and the gradual publication of the expedition's scientific volumes combined to provide symbolic support to the claim and to engender an enduring sense of Australian ownership. One of his great aims had been achieved.

There was much more that Mawson had wanted to achieve from his expedition, which had been grand in its conception, but poorly executed and limited in its immediate results. Apart from the hoped-for geographical discoveries, which were only partly achieved because of the terrible climate, he had wanted to discover a rewarding economic resource in Antarctica that would profit Australia, and himself, and make the whole effort worth doing. But there were no gold mines or valuable mineral resources, and the penguins, seals, and birds were not worth the expense and danger that would be involved in their exploitation. There were only whales, and the technology that would allow their economic exploitation by factory ships was still to be developed. Mawson had trumpeted the expedition as a scientific one, and indeed it was the scientific observations and specimens, of which there were many, which have become more valuable over time as a baseline for present-day observations and specimens. They came at a dreadful cost, with the loss of Ninnis and Mertz. The careful crafting of the expedition story by Mawson, and the non-publication until recently of other expedition members' own diaries and accounts, has allowed Mawson to cast such a big shadow in Antarctica that it has obscured the serious flaws that characterized his ill-fated venture.

Notes

Preface

1 J. W. Madigan, *Madigan's Account: The Mawson Expedition. The Antarctic Diaries of C.T. Madigan 1911–1914*, Wellington Bridge Press, Hobart, 2012.

Chapter One: To the South Magnetic Pole

1 It is often claimed that Xavier Mertz died from an excess of Vitamin A, after eating too many dog livers. It was later suggested that starvation was the more likely cause of his death. Both claims are wrong. See David J. C. Shearman, "Vitamin A and Sir Douglas Mawson," *British Medical Journal*, February 4, 1978; and Denise Carrington-Smith, "Mawson and Mertz: A Re-evaluation of Their Ill-fated Mapping Journey During the 1911–1914 Australasian Antarctic Expedition," *Medical Journal of Australia*, Vol. 183, Number 11/12, December 5–19, 2005.

2 Philip Ayres, *Mawson: A Life*, Melbourne University Press, Carlton, 1999, pp. 11–13; Fred Jacka and Eleanor Jacka (eds.), *Mawson's Antarctic Diaries*, Unwin Hyman, London, 1988, p. xxvii.

3 David Crane, *Scott of the Antarctic*, HarperCollins, London, 2005, Chaps. 11–15; Roland Huntford, *Shackleton*, Hodder and Stoughton, London, 1985, Chaps. 4–12; Roland Huntford, *Scott and Amundsen*, Hodder and Stoughton, London, 1979, pp. 168–76.

4 Huntford, *Shackleton*, Chaps. 13–15.

5 David Branagan, *T.W. Edgeworth David: A Life*, National Library of Australia, Canberra, 2005, pp. 139–44.

6 Mawson diary, November 24, 1908, in Jacka and Jacka (eds.), *Mawson's Antarctic Diaries*; Ayres, *Mawson*, pp. 11–13.

7 Huntford, *Shackleton*, Chaps. 19–26.

8 Branagan, *T.W. Edgeworth David*, pp. 162–75.

9 Huntford, *Shackleton*, pp. 235–36.

10 Mawson diary, November 24, 1908; Branagan, *T.W. Edgeworth David*, pp. 177–78.

11 Granville Allen Mawer, *South by Northwest: The Magnetic Crusade and the Contest for Antarctica*, Wakefield Press, Adelaide, 2006, p. 176; Mawson diary, October 5, 1908; Branagan, *T.W. Edgeworth David*, pp. 179–80; Huntford, *Shackleton*, pp. 195, 233–34.

12 Mawson diary, October 10–29, 1908.

13 Ernest Shackleton, *The Heart of the Antarctic*, William Heinemann, London, 1910, p. 269; Mawson diary, October 4–8, 1908.

14 Mawson diary, October 4–8 and 19–20, 1908.

15 Although called "Dry Valley" by Mawson, there are three adjacent valleys that are free of ice. They are now known as the Dry Valleys.

16 Mawson diary, October 23, 1908; Branagan, *T.W. Edgeworth David*, pp. 182–85; Shackleton, *The Heart of the Antarctic*, p. 270.

17 Mawson diary, October 29, 1908; Branagan, *T.W. Edgeworth David*, p. 186; Shackleton, *The Heart of the Antarctic*, p. 276.

18 Mawson diary, October 30–31, and November 1–3, 22, and 28, 1908; Shackleton, *The Heart of the Antarctic*, pp. 273–76.

19 Mawson diary, November 22, 1908.

20 Mawson diary, November 18 and 23, 1908.

21 Mawson diary, November 28–December 16, 1908; Branagan, *T.W. Edgeworth David*, pp. 189–91.

22 Mawson diary, November 28–December 16, 1908.

23 Mawson diary, December 16–27, 1908; Branagan, *T.W. Edgeworth David*, p. 191.

24 Mawson diary, December 30–31, 1908; Branagan, *T.W. Edgeworth David*, pp. 191–92.

25 Mawson diary, December 31, 1908 and January 1 and 3, 1909.

26 Mawson diary, January 4–5 and 10, 1909.

27 Mawson diary, January 13, 1909; Shackleton, *The Heart of the Antarctic*, pp. 308–09.

28 Mawson diary, January 15–16, 1909; Branagan, *T.W. Edgeworth David*, pp. 192–93.

29 Mawson diary, January 18–February 4, 1909; Branagan, *T.W. Edgeworth David*, pp. 195–98.

30 Mawson diary, February 4, 1909; Branagan, *T.W. Edgeworth David*, pp. 198–201.

31 Ayres, *Mawson*, p. 29.

Chapter Two: A Leader at Last

1 Ayres, *Mawson*, pp. 30–31.

2 Ayres, *Mawson*, pp. 33–35; Jacka and Jacka (eds.), *Mawson's Antarctic Diaries*, p. 53.

3 Ayres, *Mawson*, pp. 34–35; Huntford, *Shackleton*, pp. 324–25.

4 Ayres, *Mawson*, pp. 35–36.

5 Ayres, *Mawson*, pp. 39–40; Huntford, *Shackleton*, pp. 325–28.

6 Ayres, *Mawson*, pp. 44–46; Jacka and Jacka (eds.), *Mawson's Antarctic Diaries*, pp. 51–54.

7 Jacka and Jacka (eds.), *Mawson's Antarctic Diaries*, pp. 55–56; Ayres, *Mawson*, pp. 44–53; Letters, Mawson to Horn, March 28, 1911, and Mawson to Manager, Horlicks Malted Milk Co., March 30, 1911, Folder 13AAE/1, and documents in Folder 13AAE/2, Box 3, MC.

8 Ayres, *Mawson*, p. 51; David Day, *Contraband and Controversy: The Customs History of Australia from 1901*, Australian Government Publishing Service, Canberra, 1996, pp. 108–09.

9 Lady Kennet, *Self-Portrait of an Artist*, John Murray, London, 1949, p. 93; For a biography of Kathleen Scott, see the book by her granddaughter, Louisa Young, *A Great Task of Happiness: The Life of Kathleen Scott*, Macmillan, London, 1995.

10 Letter, [Kathleen Scott] to [Scott] unsigned and undated and loosely enclosed in Folder C/1, Kennet Papers, CUL.

11 Letter, Mawson to Kathleen Scott, April 5, 1911, MS 1453/138, CUL.

12 Kathleen Scott diary, April 8 and 10, 1911, Kennet Papers, CUL; Ayres, *Mawson*, pp. 48–49; For details of Mawson's lecture, see Douglas Mawson, "The Australasian Antarctic Expedition," *Geographical Journal*, Vol. 37, No. 6, June 1911.

13 Letters, Kathleen Scott to Mawson, April 25, 1911, Folder 13AAE/2, Box 3, and April 26, 1920, Folder 51DM/1, Box 59, MC; Ayres, *Mawson*, pp. 48–49; Peter FitzSimons, *Mawson and the Ice Men of the Heroic Age: Scott, Shackleton and Amundsen*, Random House, Sydney, 2011, pp. 237–41, 286–87.

14 Ayres, *Mawson*, pp. 49–50; Letter, Kathleen Scott to Mawson, April 25, 1911, Folder 13AAE/2, Box 3, MC; Kathleen Scott diary, May 5, 1911, Kennet Papers, CUL.

15 Kathleen Scott diary, May 6 and 27, June 19, and July 7, 1911, Kennet Papers, CUL.

16 See docs in Folder 135AAE, Box 14 and Folder 13AAE/3, Box 4, MC.

17 Shackleton, *The Heart of the Antarctic*, p. 9.

18 Shackleton, *The Heart of the Antarctic*, pp. 5–6, 98; Huntford, *Shackleton*, pp. 91, 251.

19 Shackleton, *The Heart of the Antarctic*, pp. 5–6, 98.

20 Letter, Lucas to Mawson, July 8, 1911, Folder 13AAE/3, Box 4, MC.

Chapter Three: Choosing a team

1 Letter, Ninnis to Meade, May 15, 1911, Ninnis Papers, MS 1564/1, SPRI.

2 Letter, Mertz to Mawson, c. May 1911, Folder 13AAE/4, Box 4, MC.

3 Anna Lucas, "Mertz in Hobart: Impressions of One of Mawson's Oen While Preparing for Antarctic Adventure," in *Papers and Proceedings of the Royal Society of Tasmania*, Vol. 146, 2012, pp. 37–38; Letter, Mawson to Mrs. Mertz, March 17, 1914, Box 22, Folder 175AAE, MC.

4 Anna Lucas, "Mertz in Hobart," pp. 37–38.

5 Letter, Lowless & Co to Mawson, August 10, 1911, Box 15, Folder 141AAE/1, MC; Letter, Ninnis to Meade, July 31, 1911, Ninnis Papers, MS 1564/2, SPRI.

6 Kathleen Scott diary, July 15, 1911, Kennet Papers, CUL; Letter, Mawson to Bickerton, June 22, 1911, Box 3, Folder 12/AAE, MC; Stephen Haddelsey, *Born Adventurer: The Life of Frank Bickerton, Antarctic Pioneer*, Sutton Publishing, Stroud, 2005, pp. 14–16.

7 Percival Gray diary, December 5, 1911 and January 3, 1912, "Antarctic Voyages": Diary aboard the *Aurora*, 1911–14, AAD; Angie Butler, *The Quest for Frank Wild*, Jackleberry Press, Warwick, 2011.

8 Jacka and Jacka (eds.), *Mawson's Antarctic Diaries*, pp. 55–56; Letters, Reid to Mawson, July 28, and August 4, 1911, Box 15, Folder 141AAE/1, MC.

9 Haddelsey, *Born Adventurer*, pp. 18–19.

10 Letter, Mawson to Reid, September 22, 1911, Box 15, Folder 141AAE/2, MC.

11 Ayres, *Mawson*, p. 52.

12 A detailed discussion of the expedition camera and film can be found in Quentin Turnour, "'A.K.A. *Home of the Blizzard*': Fact and Artefact in the Film on the Australian Antarctic Expedition, 1911–14," *NFSA Journal*, Vol. 2, No. 4, 2007.

13 *Mercury*, Hobart, December 1, 1911; Hunter diary, June 9, 1912, in Jenny Hunter (ed.), *Rise and Shine: Diary of John George Hunter, Australasian Antarctic Expedition 1911–1913*, Hunter House Publications, Hinton, 2011, p. 96.

14 *Register*, Adelaide, August 30, 1911; Ayres, *Mawson*, p. 69.

15 Madigan diary, August 1, 1913.

16 Details of Hunter's background can be found in Hunter (ed.), *Rise and Shine*, pp. viii–xii.

17 FitzSimons, *Mawson and the Ice Men of the Heroic Age*, pp. 320–22.

18 Ross McMullin, *Farewell, Dear People*, Scribe, Melbourne, 2012, Chap. 6; Hunter diary, July 5, 1912.

19 Bernadette Hince, *Still No Mawson: Frank Stillwell's Antarctic Diaries 1911–13*, Australian Academy of Science, Canberra, 2012, pp. 1–3.

20 Hunter diary, May 31, 1912; J. W. Madigan, *Madigan's Account*, p. 493;

Interview with Eric Norman Webb by Lennard Bickel, 1975, NLA.

21 For a biography of Murphy, see Heather Rossiter, *Lady Spy, Gentleman Explorer: The Life of Herbert Dyce Murphy*, Random House, Sydney, 2001.

22 See David Day, *Antarctica: A Biography*, Random House, Sydney, 2012, pp. 141–42.

23 Madigan diary, November 21, 1911.

24 Newspaper cuttings, c. 1911, Newspaper Cuttings Book, AAD.

25 Madigan diary, November 26, 1911.

26 Diary of Xavier Mertz, October 17–18, November 4–December 2, 1911, translated by Robyn Mundy, MC; Letters, Ninnis to Meade, August 24 and October 19, 1911, Ninnis Papers, MS 1564/3–4, SPRI.

27 Madigan diary, November 21, 1911.

28 Letter, Mawson to Reid, September 22, 1911, Box 15, Folder 141AAE/2, MC; Rossiter, *Lady Spy, Gentleman Explorer*, pp. 131–32, 150.

29 *Mercury*, Hobart, November 27, 1911.

30 Letter, Mawson to Mrs. Mertz, March 17, 1914, Box 22, Folder 175AAE, MC.

31 Madigan diary, November 27–29, 1911; *Mercury*, Hobart, November 28, 1911.

32 Letter, Kathleen Scott to Mawson, September 1912, Box 59, Folder 51DM/1, MC; Madigan diary, December 2, 1911; *Mercury*, Hobart, December 1, 2, and 4, 1911; Anna Lucas, "Mertz in Hobart: Impressions of One of Mawson's Men While Preparing for Antarctic Adventure," in *Papers and Proceedings of the Royal Society of Tasmania*, Vol. 146, 2012, p. 41.

33 Letters, Ninnis to Meade, August 24, October 19, and December 1, 1911, Ninnis Papers, MS 1564/3–5, SPRI.

34 *Mercury*, Hobart, December 4, 1911; Mertz diary, November 10–December 2, 1911.

Chapter Four: Into the Southern Ocean

1 Harrisson diary, December 2, 1911, in Heather Rossiter (ed.), *Mawson's Forgotten Men*, Pier 9, Sydney, 2011, p. 2.

2 Madigan diary, December 2, 1911.

3 Douglas Mawson, "Australasian Antarctic Expedition," *Geographical Journal*, Vol. 44, No. 3, September 1914.

4 Nancy Robinson Flannery, *This Everlasting Silence: The Love Letters of Paquita Delprat and Douglas Mawson, 1911–1914*, Melbourne University Press, Carlton, 2000, p. 22.

5 Madigan diary, November 29 and December 2–3, 1911.

6 Madigan diary, December 3, 1911; Rossiter, *Lady Spy, Gentleman Explorer*, p. 150.

7 Madigan diary, December 2–4, 1911.

8 Madigan diary, December 7–10, 1911.

9 Chris Viney (ed), *Macquarie Island*, Tasmanian Parks and Wildlife Service, Hobart, 2012.

10 Madigan diary, December 11, 1911.

11 Harrisson diary, December 13, 1911; Madigan diary, December 11, 1911.

12 Madigan diary, December 13–14, 1911.

13 Madigan diary, December 14–15, 18–19, 1911.

14 Antarctic diary of Robert Bage, November 1911–January 1912, MS14209, Box 4176/3, SLV; Madigan diary, December 19–20, 1911.

15 Madigan diary, December 21–23, 1911.

16 Madigan diary, December 24, 1911; Bage diary, November 1911–January 1912; Mertz diary, December 24, 1911.

17 Harrisson diary, December 25, 1911.

18 Madigan diary, December 25, 1911; Bage diary, November 1911–January 1912, MS14209, Box 4176/3; Mertz diary, December 25, 1911.

19 Madigan diary, December 26–29, 1911.

20 Madigan diary, December 30, 1911.

21 Bage diary, December 30, 1911.

22 Madigan diary, December 30, 1911.

23 Mertz diary, December 29–31, 1911.

24 Harrisson diary, January 1, 1912; Bage diary, January 1, 1912; Madigan diary, January 1, 1912.

25 Bage diary, January 1, 1912; Madigan diary, January 1–2, 1912.

26 Madigan diary, January 2, 1912.

27 Madigan diary, January 2, 1912; Bage diary, January 4, 1912; Rossiter, *Lady Spy, Gentleman Explorer*, pp. 161–62.

28 Rossiter, *Lady Spy, Gentleman Explorer*, pp. 168–70.

29 Gray diary, January 3, 1912; Bage diary, January 4, 1912; Madigan diary, January 3, 1912; Stillwell diary, January 3, 1912.

30 Letter, Ninnis to Meade, January 6, 1912, Ninnis Papers, MS 1564/6, SPRI; Letter, Mawson to Paquita, January 3, 1912, in Flannery, *This Everlasting Silence*, pp. 25–28.

Chapter Five: The Windiest Place on Earth

1 Letter, Mawson to Paquita, January 3, 1912, in Flannery, *This Everlasting Silence*, pp. 25–28.

2 Madigan diary, January 4 and 5, 1912.

3 Letter from Frank Stillwell, January 6, 1912, in Hince, *Still No Mawson*, p. 233; Madigan diary, January 5, 1912.

4 Madigan diary, January 8, 1912; Bage diary, January 4, 1912; Mertz diary, January 8–9, 1912.

5 Madigan diary, January 9, 10, and 11, 1912.

6 Madigan diary, January 12, 13, 14, and 15, 1912; Mertz diary, January 16, 1912.

7 Madigan diary, January 18 and 19, 1912; Bage diary, January 19, 1912; Mertz diary, January 17 and 19, 1912; Hunter diary, January 19, 1912.

8 Letter by Frank Stillwell, January 6, 1912, in Hince, *Still No Mawson*, p. 240; Madigan diary, January 18, 1912.

9 Madigan diary, January 14 and 17, 1912.

10 I am grateful to Mark Pharaoh of the South Australian Museum for bringing this to my attention.

11 Madigan diary, January 26 and 27 and February 2, 1912.

12 Mertz diary, January 20–29, 1912; Hunter diary, January 30, 1912; Stillwell diary, January 30, 1912.

13 Madigan diary, January 30 and 31 and February 1 and 3, 1912.

14 Hunter diary, February 1, 1912.

15 Madigan diary, February 6–7, 1912; Bage diary, February 1–7, 1912.

16 It was one of 37 sledges bought by Mawson, 20 of them from Norway and 17 from Australia. Ayres, *Mawson*, p. 51.

17 Madigan diary, February 15, 16, and 17, 1912; Bage diary, February 13, 1912.

18 Madigan diary, February 25, 1912; Hunter diary, February 25, 1912.

19 Madigan diary, February 27 and 28, 1912; Bage diary, February 29, 1912.

20 Madigan diary, February 29 and March 1 and 3, 1912; Mawson diary, February 29 and March 1–2, 1912.

21 Madigan diary, May 25, 1912.

22 Mawson diary, March 6, 1912.

23 Madigan diary, March 5, 6, 7, 8, and 11 and April 4, 1912.

24 Mawson diary, March 15, 1912.

25 Jacka and Jacka (eds), *Mawson's Antarctic Diaries*, p. 63; Mawson, *The Home of the Blizzard*, Vol. II, p. 314; Hunter diary, February 21, 1912.

26 Madigan diary, April 24, 1912; Hunter diary, February 28, March 26, and April 13, 1912.

27 Madigan diary, June 11 and 13, 1912; Mertz diary, June 12–19, 1912.

28 Hunter diary, June 13, 1912.

29 Madigan diary, April 30, 1912.

30 Hunter diary, March 11, 1912.

31 Madigan diary, May 17, 18, 20, 21, and 24, 1912.

32 Madigan diary, May 24, 1912.

33 Madigan diary, April 5, 6, and 7 and May 26, 1912.

34 Hunter diary, May 31, 1912.

35 Letter, Smythe to Eitel, April 7, 1912, PRG 523/11/2, Mawson Collection, SLSA.

36 Hunter diary, April 17, 1912.

37 See docs in Box 16, Folder 143AAE, MC.

38 Bage diary, February 14, 1912; Haddelsey, *Born Adventurer*, p. 60.

39 Rossiter, *Lady Spy, Gentleman Explorer*, p. 195.

40 Agreement between Mawson and Harrisson, December 1, 1911, Folder 179AAE–181AAE, Box 23, MC.

41 Hunter diary, June 12, 1912; Madigan diary, August 27 and 30, 1912.

42 Madigan diary, June 20 and 21, 1912; McLean diary, June 21, 1912; Mertz diary, June 21, 1912; Hunter diary, June 21, 1912; Mawson diary, June 21, 1912.

Chapter Six: Preparing for the Unknown

1 Madigan diary, July 10, 1912.

2 Madigan diary, July 10, 1912.

3 Madigan diary, July 17, 1912; Mertz diary, July 16, 1912; Mawson diary, July 16, 1912.

4 Madigan diary, July 27, 1912.

5 Hunter diary, July 9, 1912; Stillwell diary, July 5, 1912.

6 Madigan diary, July 17 and 21, 1912.

7 Madigan diary, July 22, 1912.

8 Hunter diary, June 22 and July 15, 1912; Stillwell diary, July 10 and 15, 1912.

9 Madigan diary, July 31, 1912.

10 Hunter diary, July 31 and August 1, 1912; Mawson diary, July 31, 1912; Mertz diary, July 30, 1912.

11 Madigan diary, July 23 and August 20, 1912.

12 Madigan diary, August 1 and 3, 1912; Hunter diary, August 1, 1912; Mawson diary, August 1, 1912.

13 Mertz diary, August 1, 1912.

14 Madigan diary, August 2 and 3, 1912; Stillwell diary, July 23, 1912.

15 Madigan diary, August 5–8, 1912.

16 Stillwell diary, August 9, 1912.

17 Mawson diary, August 9, 1912.

18 Madigan diary, August 9–13, 1912; Mawson diary, August 10–12, 1912.

19 Madigan diary, August 13, 1912; Mawson diary, August 13, 1912.

20 Madigan diary, August 13, 1912; Mawson diary, August 13, 1912.

21 Madigan diary, August 14, 1912; Mawson diary, August 14, 1912.

22 Stillwell notes how "Madigan and Ninnis were rather tired of [Mawson] in a 3-man sleeping bag." Stillwell diary, August 15, 1912.

23 Madigan diary, August 15, 1912; Mawson diary, August 14, 1912.

24 Madigan diary, August 15, 1912; Mawson diary, August 15 ,1912; Stillwell diary, August 15, 1912; Hunter diary, August 15, 1912.

25 Mertz diary, August 16, 1912.

26 Madigan diary, August 20–25, 1912; Mertz diary, August 17–25, 1912; Mawson diary, August 16–25, 1912.

Chapter Seven: Madigan Proves Himself

1 Madigan diary, August 23, 1912.

2 Madigan diary, September 1 and 3, 1912; Mertz diary, September 1, 1912.

3 Madigan diary, August 23, 1912.

4 Madigan diary, August 22, 1912.

5 Madigan diary, August 26, 1912.

6 Madigan diary, September 7, 1912.

7 Madigan diary, August 27 and 30, 1912; Hunter diary, August 27, 1912.

8 Madigan diary, September 4 and 7, 1912; Mawson diary, March 20, June 18 and July 20, 1912; Hunter diary, June 14, 1912; Rossiter, *Lady Spy, Gentleman Explorer*, pp. 224–27; "Routine Duties," notice by Mawson, March 19, 1912, Box 10, Folder 42AAE–43AAE, MC.

9 Stillwell diary, September 4, 1912.

10 Madigan diary, October 1, 1912; Hunter diary, September 12, 1912.

11 Madigan diary, August 27, 1912.

12 Mertz diary, September 11–17, 1912; Stillwell diary, September 7–16, 1912; Hunter diary, September 16–17 and 26, 1912; Mawson diary, September 16–17 and 26, 1912.

13 Mawson diary, September 18, 23, and 24, 1912; Hunter diary, September 22, 1912; Madigan diary, October 1, 1912.

14 Madigan diary, October 1, 1912.

15 ibid.

16 ibid.

17 Madigan diary, October 5, 1912; Hunter diary, September 26, 1912.

18 Madigan diary, October 1, 1912; Mawson diary, September 18 and 24, 1912; Hunter diary, September 26, 1912.

19 Madigan diary, October 3, 1912; Stillwell diary, October 3, 1912; Mawson diary, May 18, September 25, and October 3, 1912; Hunter diary, June 4 and October 3, 1912; Haddelsey, *Born Adventurer*, p. 69; Rossiter, *Lady Spy, Gentleman Explorer*, pp. 258–60.

20 Madigan diary, October 6, 1912; Stillwell diary, October 12, 1912.

21 Madigan diary, October 6 and 12, 1912; Hunter diary, October 12, 1912.

22 Madigan diary, October 8, 1912; Hunter diary, June 25, 1912; Mawson, *The Home of the Blizzard*, Vol. II, pp. 6–8.

23 Madigan diary, October 13, 1912.

24 Mertz diary, October 12, 1912.

25 Madigan diary, October 21, 1912; Mertz diary, October 15 and 20–22, 1912.

26 Mawson diary, October 5, 10, 12, and 19–20, 1912; Madigan diary, October 14 and 16, 1912.

27 Stillwell diary, October 19, 1912.

28 Bage diary, October 20, 1912; McMullin, *Farewell, Dear People*, pp. 349–50.

29 Madigan diary, October 5, 11, and 21, 1912.

30 Madigan diary, October 22, 1912; Stillwell diary, October 26, 1912.

31 Madigan diary, October 23, 1912.

32 Madigan diary, October 25, 1912.

33 Stillwell diary, October 27–28, 1912; Mawson diary, October 21, 1912.

34 Madigan diary, October 25 and 27, 1912; Haddelsey, *Born Adventurer*, p. 72.

35 Narrative of Southern Sledging Journey, Bage diary, SLV; Stillwell diary, November 8, 1912.

36 Madigan diary, November 8–10, 1912; Bage diary, November 7, 1912.

Chapter Eight: Into the White Wilderness

1 Madigan diary, November 8, 1912, p. 297; Stillwell diary, November 8, 1912; Mertz diary, November 8, 1912.

2 "General Instructions During My Absence," by Mawson, November 9, 1913, and "Instructions to Hut Party to Arrival of Murphy," by Mawson, Box 10, Folders 42AAE and 43AAE, MC.

3 Jacka and Jacka (eds), *Mawson's Antarctic Diaries*, pp. 127–28; Emma McEwin, *An Antarctic Affair*, East Street Publications, Bowden, 2008, p. 69; Mertz diary, November 9–10, 1912.

4 Mawson, "Australasian Antarctic Expedition, 1911–1914," *Geographical Journal*, Vol. 44, No. 3, September 1914.

5 Mawer, *South by Northwest*, pp. 194–95.

6 Bage diary, November 7, 1912; Haddelsey, *Born Adventurer*, pp. 70–72.

7 Jacka and Jacka (eds), *Mawson's Antarctic Diaries*, p. 128.

8 Hunter diary, September 28, 1912.

9 Mawson diary, November 2, 1912; Mawson, *The Home of the Blizzard*, Vol. 1, p. 220.

10 Mawson diary, November 10, 1912.

11 Mertz diary, November 10, 1912.

12 Madigan diary, November 8–10, 1912; Stillwell diary, November 9, 1912.

13 Madigan diary, November 10, 1912; Stillwell diary, November 10, 1912.

14 Madigan diary, November 10, 1912.

15 Stillwell diary, November 11, 1912.

16 Mawson diary, November 10, 1912; Bage diary, November 7, 1912.

17 Mawson diary, November 10, 1912.

18 Mawson, *The Home of the Blizzard*, Vol. II, Chap. XVII.

19 Mawson diary, November 11, 1912; Mertz diary, November 11, 1912.

20 Mawson diary, November 11–15, 1912; Mertz diary, November 11–15, 1912; Madigan diary, November 16, 1912.

21 Madigan diary, November 14, 1912; Mertz diary, November 16, 1912; Stillwell diary, November 15, 1912.

22 Stillwell diary, November 17, 1912; Mertz diary, November 17, 1912.

23 Mawson diary, November 16–17, 1912; Madigan diary, November 17, 1912.

24 Madigan diary, November 11, 1912; Mawson, *Home of the Blizzard*, Vol. 1, p. 313.

25 Although Mawson mentions the Mertz glacier, it was not named that until after Mertz's death. Mawson, *Home of the Blizzard*, Vol. 1, pp. 316–17.

26 Madigan diary, November 16–17, 1912.

27 Madigan diary, November 17, 1912; Mertz diary, November 17, 1912; Mawson diary, November 17, 1912.

28 Madigan diary, November 18–19, 1912; Stillwell diary, November 18, 1912.

29 Stillwell diary, November 17–27, 1912.

Chapter Nine: Making Their Mark

1 Bage diary, November 7, 1912; Narrative of Southern Sledging Journey November 1911–January 1912, Bage Papers, MS 14209, Box 4176/3, SLV.

2 Narrative of Southern Sledging Journey November 1911–January 1912, Bage Papers, MS 14209, Box 4176/3, SLV; Hurley diary, November 10, 1912, in Robert Dixon and Christopher Lee (eds.), *The Diaries of Frank Hurley, 1912–1941*, Anthem Press, London, 2011, p. 1; Rossiter, *Lady Spy, Gentleman Explorer*, pp. 268–69.

3 Narrative of Southern Sledging Journey November 1911–January 1912, Bage Papers, MS 14209, Box 4176/3, SLV; Mawson, *The Home of the Blizzard*, Vol. 1, pp. 274–75.

4 Narrative of Southern Sledging Journey November 1911–January 1912, Bage Papers, MS 14209, Box 4176/3, SLV; Mawson, *The Home of the Blizzard*, Vol. 1, p. 288.

5 Narrative of Southern Sledging Journey November 1911–January 1912, Bage Papers, MS 14209, Box 4176/3, SLV.

6 Narrative of Southern Sledging Journey November 1911–January 1912, Bage Papers, MS 14209, Box 4176/3, SLV.

7 Hurley diary, November 12–14, 1912.

8 Hurley diary, November 19, 1912; Hunter diary, November 18–20, 1912; Mawson, *The Home of the Blizzard*, Vol. 1, pp. 278–81.

9 Hunter diary, November 22, 1912; Hurley diary, November 24–December 3, 1912.

10 Hurley diary, December 6, 1912.

11 Mawson, *The Home of the Blizzard*, Vol. 1, pp. 293–94; Hurley diary, December 13, 1912.

12 Mawson, *The Home of the Blizzard*, Vol. 1, pp. 294–97; Hurley diary, December 19–22, 1912.

13 Madigan diary, November 20–21, 1912.

14 Madigan diary, November 22, 1912.
15 Madigan diary, November 11, 1912.
16 Madigan diary, November 23, 1912.
17 Madigan diary, November 24–26, 1912.
18 Madigan diary, November 28, 1912.
19 Madigan diary, December 3–8, 1912.
20 Madigan diary, December 6–10, 1912.
21 Madigan diary, December 11–18, 1912; Mawson, *The Home of the Blizzard*, pp. 319, 333.
22 Madigan diary, December 12–18, 1912.
23 Mawson, *The Home of the Blizzard*, p. 330; Madigan diary, December 14, 1912.
24 Madigan diary, December 16 and 18, 1912.

Chapter Ten: Crossing the Great Divide

1 Mawson diary, November 18, 1912.
2 Mawson diary, November 18, 1912; Mertz diary, November 18, 1912.
3 Mertz diary, November 18, 1912; Mawson diary, November 18–21, 1912.
4 Mawson diary, November 19–20, 1912; Mertz diary, November 19–20, 1912.
5 Mawson diary, November 20–22, 1912.
6 Mawson diary, November 18–December 1, 1912; Mertz diary, November 23 and 26–28, 1912.
7 Mawson diary, November 29–December 1, 1912; Mertz diary, November 24 and 29, 1912.
8 Mawson diary, December 1–10, 1912; Mertz diary, November 27, 1912.
9 Mertz diary, November 30, 1912.
10 Mawson diary, November 27 and 29 and December 1, 1912; Mertz diary, November 30, 1912.
11 Mawson diary, December 7 and 9, 1912; Mertz diary, December 6, 9, and 10, 1912.
12 Mawson diary, December 8–12, 1912; Mertz diary, December 10 and 12, 1912.
13 Mawson diary, December 13, 1912; Mertz diary, December 13, 1912; Lucas and Leane, "Two Pages of Xavier Mertz's Pissing Antarctic Diary," p. 5.
14 Mawson diary, December 13, 1912; Mawson, "Australasian Antarctic Expedition, 1911–1914," *Geographical Journal*, Vol. 44, No. 3, September 1914, p. 272.
15 Shackleton, *The Heart of the Antarctic*, p. 265.
16 Mawson diary, December 13–14, 1912.
17 Mertz diary, December 13, 1912.
18 Mertz diary, December 16, 1912; Mawson diary, December 14, 1912; Mawson, "Australasian Antarctic Expedition, 1911–1914," *Geographical Journal*, Vol. 44, No. 3, September 1914, p. 270.

19 Mawson diary, December 13, 1912.

20 Mertz diary, December 14, 1912; Lucas and Leane, "Two Pages of Xavier Mertz's Missing Antarctic Diary," p. 5.

21 Mawson diary, December 14, 1912; Mawson, *The Home of the Blizzard*, Vol. 1, pp. 237–38; Lucas and Leane, "Two Pages of Xavier Mertz's Missing Antarctic Diary," p. 5.

22 Mawson diary, December 14, 1912; Mawson, *The Home of the Blizzard*, Vol. 1, pp. 238–40; Lucas and Leane, "Two Pages of Xavier Mertz's Missing Antarctic Diary," p. 5.

23 Mawson diary, December 14, 1912; Mawson, *The Home of the Blizzard*, Vol. 1, pp. 238–40; Mertz diary, December 14–16, 1912; Interview with Eric Norman Webb by Leonard Bickel, 1975, NLA.

Chapter Eleven: A Cascade of Calamities

1 Mawson diary, December 14, 1912; Mawson, *The Home of the Blizzard*, Vol. 1, pp. 239–40; Mertz diary, December 14, 1912; Lucas and Leane, "Two Pages of Xavier Mertz's Missing Antarctic Diary."

2 Mawson, "Australasian Antarctic Expedition, 1911–1914," p. 272.

3 Mawson diary, December 14, 1912; Mawson, *The Home of the Blizzard*, Vol. 1, pp. 239–40; Mertz diary, December 14, 1912; Lucas and Leane, "Two Pages of Xavier Mertz's Missing Antarctic Diary."

4 Mawson diary, December 14, 1912; Lucas and Leane, "Two Pages of Xavier Mertz's Missing Antarctic Diary"; Mawson, *The Home of the Blizzard*, Vol. 1, p. 241.

5 Mawson diary, December 14, 1912; Lucas and Leane, "Two Pages of Xavier Mertz's Missing Antarctic Diary"; Mawson, *The Home of the Blizzard*, Vol. 1, p. 241.

6 Mawson, *The Home of the Blizzard*, Vol. 1, p. 241.

7 Mawson, "Australasian Antarctic Expedition, 1911–1914."

8 Mawson diary, December 14, 1912; Mawson, "Australasian Antarctic Expedition, 1911–1914," p. 272; Lucas and Leane, "Two Pages of Xavier Mertz's Missing Antarctic Diary."

9 Mawson diary, December 14–15, 1912; Mawson, *The Home of the Blizzard*, Vol. 1, p. 245; Mertz diary, December 16, 1912.

10 Mawson diary, December 16, 1912; Mertz diary, December 17, 1912.

11 Mawson diary, December 17–18, 1912; Mertz diary, December 17–18, 1912.

12 Mawson diary, December 19–21, 1912.

13 Mertz diary, December 21, 1912; Mawson diary, December 27 and 29, 1912.

14 For the argument proposing vitamin A as the cause of Mertz's death, see David J. C. Shearman, "Vitamin A and Sir Douglas Mawson," *British Medical Journal*, February 4, 1978; For the details of the food they consumed until

the death of Mertz, see Mertz diary, December 14, 1912–January 1, 1913; Mawson diary, December 14, 1912–January 7, 1913.

15 Vilhjalmur Stefansson, *My Life with the Eskimo*, Macmillan, New York, 1913, pp. 27–28, 140–41.

16 Mawson diary, December 21–22, 1912.

17 Mawson diary, December 23–24, 1912; Mertz diary, December 23–24, 1912; FitzSimons, *Mawson and the Ice Men of the Heroic Age*, p. 305.

18 Mawson diary, December 23–25, 1912.

19 Mertz diary, December 23–24, 1912.

20 Note by Mawson, December 25, 1912, Folder 49AAE, MC.

21 Mawson diary, December 26, 1912.

22 Mawson diary, December 27–28, 1912; Mertz diary, December 27–28, 1912.

23 Mawson diary, December 27–30, 1912; Mertz diary, December 29–30, 1912.

24 Mawson diary, December 31, 1912.

25 Mertz diary, January 1, 1913.

26 Mawson diary, January 1–3, 1913.

27 Mawson diary, January 5, 1913.

28 Mawson diary, January 6, 1913.

Chapter Twelve: Racing Home

1 Transcript of Hurley diary, December 21, 1912, ML MSS 389, ML.

2 Mawson, *The Home of the Blizzard*, Vol. 1, p. 298; Hurley diary, December 21–22 ,1912.

3 Hurley diary, December 25–27, 1912.

4 Hurley diary, December 27–30, 1912; Mawson, *The Home of the Blizzard*, Vol. 1, pp. 299–301.

5 Mawson, *The Home of the Blizzard*, Vol. 1, pp. 297–98; Hurley diary, December 24 and 30, 1912 and January 1, 1913.

6 Hurley diary, January 1–5, 1913; Mawer, *South by Northwest*, p. 200.

7 Hurley diary, January 6–7. 1913; Mawson, *The Home of the Blizzard*, Vol. 1, pp. 303–05.

8 Hurley diary, January 8, 1913; Mawson, *The Home of the Blizzard*, Vol. 1, pp. 305–06.

9 Hurley diary, January 8–9, 1913; Interview with Eric Norman Webb by Lennard Bickel, 1975, NLA; Mawer, *South by Northwest*, p. 201.

10 Mawer, *South by Northwest*, p. 201; Hunter (ed.), *Rise and Shine*, p. 189; Hince (ed.), *Still No Mawson*, p. 213.

11 Hurley diary, January 10, 1913.

12 Stillwell diary, January 13, 1913.

13 Hunter diary, January 13, 1913.

14 Hunter diary, January 16, 1913.

15 McLean diary, December 15 and 18, 1912; Madigan diary, December 15 and 19, 1912.

16 McLean diary, December 20, 1912; Madigan diary, December 20, 1912.

17 Madigan diary and Sledging Notebook, December 20–21 and 24, 1912; McLean diary, December 20–21, 1912.

18 Madigan diary, December 22 and 25, 1912; McLean diary, December 22 and 25, 1912.

19 Madigan diary, December 26–31, 1912 and January 1–2, 1913; McLean diary, December 26–31, 1912 and January 1–2, 1913.

20 Madigan diary, January 2–4, 1913; McLean diary, January 2–4, 1913.

21 Madigan diary, January 5–7, 1913; McLean diary, January 5–7, 1913.

22 Madigan diary, January 8–10, 1913; McLean diary, January 8–10, 1913.

23 Madigan diary, January 10–12, 1913; McLean diary, January 10–12, 1913.

24 Madigan diary, January 12–16, 1913; McLean diary, January 12–16, 1913.

25 Madigan diary, January 16, 1913; McLean diary, January 16, 1913.

26 Hunter diary, January 16, 1913.

27 Hunter diary, January 17–18, 1913.

28 Mawson, *The Home of the Blizzard*, Vol. 2, pp. 6–18; Haddelsey, *Born Adventurer*, pp. 77–79.

29 Mawson, *The Home of the Blizzard*, Vol. 2, pp. 6–18; Haddelsey, *Born Adventurer*, pp. 92–103.

30 Hunter diary, January 16, 1913.

31 McLean diary, January 20–21, 1913; Stillwell diary, January 20–21, 1913.

32 Hunter diary January 24–February 7, 1913.

33 Stillwell diary, January 24, 1913.

34 McLean diary, January 25–29, 1913; Hunter diary January 24–February 7, 1913; Stillwell diary, January 29, 1913.

35 Mawson, *The Home of the Blizzard*, Vol. II, p. 36; McLean diary, December 22–25, 1912; McMullin, *Farewell, Dear People*, p. 364; Madigan diary, February 13, 1913; Haddelsey, *Born Adventurer*, p. 106; Rossiter, *Lady Spy, Gentleman Explorer*, pp. 305–11.

36 Stillwell diary, January 27, 1913.

37 Mawson, *The Home of the Blizzard*, Vol. II, pp. 41–42.

38 Mawson, *The Home of the Blizzard*, Vol. II, p. 42; Stillwell diary, January 31, 1913.

Chapter Thirteen: Stumbling into History

1 Mawson diary, January 7, 1913.

2 These issues are discussed in David J. C. Shearman, "Vitamin A and Sir Douglas Mawson," *British Medical Journal*, February 4, 1978; and Denise Carrington–Smith, "Mawson and Mertz: A Re-evaluation of Their Ill-fated

Mapping Journey During the 1911–1914 Australasian Antarctic Expedition," *Medical Journal of Australia*, Vol. 183, Number 11/12, December 5–19, 2005.

3 Mawson diary, January 6 and 8, 1913.

4 Mawson diary, January 8–9, 1913.

5 Mawson diary, December 28, 1912–January 10, 1913.

6 Beau Riffenburgh, *Aurora: Douglas Mawson and the Australasian Antarctic Expedition 1911–14*, Erskine Press, Norwich, 2011, pp. 319–21.

7 Ayres, *Mawson*, pp. 78–79.

8 Mawson diary, January 9–11, 1913.

9 Mawson diary, January 11–12, 1913.

10 Note by Mawson, January 12, 1913, Folder 49AAE, MC.

11 Mawson diary, January 13–16, 1913.

12 Mawson diary, January 16–17, 1913.

13 Mawson diary, January 17, 1913; Mawson, *The Home of the Blizzard*, Vol. 1, pp. 264–65.

14 Newspaper cuttings, c. 1914, Newspaper Cuttings Book, AAD; Narrative of the Eastern Coastal Party A.A.E 1911–14, in Madigan, *Madigan's Account*; Bage diary, February 13, 1912; Mawson diary, January 17, 1913; *Weekend Australian*, Sydney, December 1–2, 2012.

15 Mawson diary, January 17, 1913; Mawson, *The Home of the Blizzard*, Vol. 1, pp. 264–65.

16 Mawson diary, January 17–18, 1913.

17 Mawson diary, January 18–20, 1913.

18 Mawson diary, January 19–22, 1913.

19 Mawson diary, January 22–23, 1913.

20 Mawson diary, January 23–24, 1913.

21 Mawson diary, January 25, 1913.

22 Mawson diary, January 26, 1913.

23 Mawson diary, January 27–28, 1913.

Chapter Fourteen: Home at Last

1 Mawson diary, January 29–30, 1913 and Note by McLean, January 29, 1913.

2 Mawson diary, January 29–30, 1913.

3 Mawson diary, January 29–February 1, 1913.

4 Mawson diary, January 29–February 1, 1913.

5 Mawson diary, February 2–3, 1913; Branagan, *T.W. Edgeworth David*, p. 173.

6 Mawson diary, February 4–7, 1913.

7 Mawson diary, February 8, 1913; Madigan diary, August 11–15, 1912.

8 Mawson diary, February 8, 1913; Douglas Mawson, "Australasian Antarctic Expedition, 1911–1914," p. 274; Mawson, *The Home of the Blizzard*, Vol. 1, p. 271.

9 Mawson diary, February 1–8, 1913; Mawson, *The Home of the Blizzard*, Vol. 1, p. 271 and Vol. II, p. 43.

10 Mawson diary, February 8, 1913; Mawson, "Australasian Antarctic Expedition, 1911–1914," p. 274; Mawson, *The Home of the Blizzard*, Vol. 1, p. 271.

11 Mawson, *The Home of the Blizzard*, Vol. II, pp. 42–43; Hunter diary, January 24–February 7, 1913.

12 Hunter diary, January 24–February 7, 1913.

13 Stillwell diary, February 6 and 8, 1913; Hunter diary, January 24–February 7, 1913.

14 Stillwell diary, February 8, 1913; Hunter diary, February 8, 1913; Taylor diary, February 8, 1913, in Stanley Gordon Roberts Taylor, *Antarctic Diary*, Irene Gale, Kensington Park, 2011, pp. 155–56.

15 Taylor diary, February 8, 1913.

16 Madigan diary, February 13, 1913; McLean diary, February 8, 1913.

17 Madigan diary, February 13, 1913; McLean diary, February 8, 1913.

18 Mawson diary, February 8, 1913.

19 Madigan diary, February 13, 1913; McLean diary, February 8, 1913; Hunter diary, February 8. 1913.

20 Madigan diary, February 13, 1913; Hunter diary, February 9, 1913; Stillwell diary, February 9, 1913.

21 Mawson diary, February 9, 1913; Hunter diary, February 9, 1913; McLean diary, January 13, 1913; Mawson diary, February 9, 1913.

Chapter Fifteen: The Final Year

1 Letter, Davis to Mawson, February 1, 1913, Box 10, Folder 44AAE, MC.

2 Madigan diary, February 16, 1913.

3 Mawson diary, February 8, 11, and 12 and March 23, 1913.

4 Wireless messages, Mawson to Davis, February 10, 1913, Box 9, Folder 28AAE, MC.

5 ibid.

6 Wireless message, Mawson to Eitel, c. March 1913, Box 9, Folder 28AAE, MC.

7 Wireless message, Mawson to David, c. February 1913, Box 9, Folder 28AAE, MC.

8 Wireless message, David to Mawson, c. February 1913, Box 9, Folder 28AAE, MC.

9 Wireless messages, Mawson to Davis, February 10, 1913, and Mawson to Eitel, cMarch 1913, Box 9, Folder 28AAE, MC.

10 Wireless message, Mawson to David, c. March 1913, Box 9, Folder 28AAE, MC.

11 Wireless messages, David to Mawson, c. April 1913, Mawson to David,

April 4, 1913, Mawson to Davis, c. April 1913, Eitel to Mawson, August 5, 1913, and Mawson to Eitel, August 6, 1913, Box 9, Folder 28AAE, and Letter, Wild to Mawson, September 29, 1913, Box 22, Folder 175AAE, MC.

12 Letter, Wild to Mawson, September 29, 1913, Box 22, Folder 175AAE, MC; *Mercury*, Hobart, May 1, 1913; *New York Times*, June 2, 1913.

13 McLean diary, February 13, 1913.

14 Madigan diary, February 13, 1913.

15 McLean diary, January 13, February 28, and March 2, 1913; Madigan diary, February 16, 1913.

16 Madigan diary, February 13 and 16, 1913.

17 Madigan diary, February 14–16, 25, and 28, 1913.

18 Madigan diary, February 13 and 20 and March 3–4, 1913; McLean diary, March 6 and 11, 1913.

19 McLean diary, March 3, 1913.

20 Madigan diary, March 4, 1913; McLean diary, March 3 and 12, 1913.

21 Jacka and Jacka (eds), *Mawson's Antarctic Diaries*, p. 186; Rossiter, *Lady Spy, Gentleman Explorer*, pp. 256–57.

22 Wireless messages, Mawson to Eitel, c. March 1913, and Mawson to Denman, April 1, 1913, Box 9, Folder 28AAE, MC.

23 Kathleen Scott diary, February 19, 20, and 27, 1913, Kennet Papers, CUL; Young, *A Great Task of Happiness*, pp. 153–56.

24 Wireless messages, Lady Scott to Mawson, c. March 1913, Box 9, Folder 28AAE, and Mawson to Lady Scott, c. March 1913, Box 10, Folder 44AAE, MC.

25 Flannery, *This Everlasting Silence*, p. 53.

26 Madigan diary, March 6–20 and April 21, 1913; McLean diary, February 21 and 28, 1913; Mawson diary, February 21–March 8, 1913.

27 McLean diary, March 9 and 18, 1913.

28 McLean diary, February 23, 1913; Mawson diary, February 22, 1913.

29 Letters, Heinemann to Eitel, October 11 and 25, 1912, Box 16, Folder 143AAE, MC.

30 Madigan diary, March 9, 1913.

31 Madigan diary, March 9, 1913.

32 Mawson diary, January 9, 1913.

33 Madigan diary, March 10–14, 1913; McLean diary, March 12 and 17, 1913.

34 Madigan diary, March 18, 1913.

35 Mawson diary, March 22–23, 1913.

Chapter Sixteen: The End of Exile

1 Madigan diary, March 27, 1913; McLean diary, March 27, 1913.

2 Madigan diary, April 1 and 9, 1913.

3 McLean diary, June 4, 1913.

4 Madigan diary, April 16, 1913; Mawson's diary has a composite entry for the dates, April 12–16, which notes simply "Bad wireless, good aurora." Mawson diary, April 12–16, 1913.

5 Madigan diary, April 16 and 19, 1913.

6 Madigan diary, April 16 and 19, 1913.

7 McLean diary, May 5, 1913; Mawson diary, May 5, 1913.

8 Madigan diary, May 22, 1913.

9 Madigan diary, May 29, 1913.

10 Madigan diary, May 22, 1913.

11 Madigan diary, May 28 and 30 and June 10 and 20, 1913.

12 Mawson diary, April 1–6, 17, and 29 and May 15–22, 1913.

13 Mawson diary, June 8, 1913.

14 Mawson diary, May 25 and June 13–15, 1913; McLean diary July 25, 1913.

15 Madigan diary, May 22 and 29 and August 31, 1913.

16 McLean diary, April 20 and 25 and May 29, 1913.

17 McLean diary, May 13, 1913.

18 McLean diary, April 29 and 30, 1913; Madigan diary, June 2, 1913.

19 Madigan diary, June 4, 1913.

20 Madigan diary, April 23 and May 10, 1913; Mawson diary, April 23–25, 1913.

21 Madigan diary, June 20 and 26, 1913.

22 McLean diary, June 22, 1913; Madigan diary, June 22, 1913.

23 McLean diary, July 12, 1913; Madigan diary, July 7–12, 1913; Mawson diary, July 7–12, 1913.

24 Madigan diary, July 17, 1913; Mawson diary, July 21, 1913.

25 McLean diary, August 10, 1913.

26 Madigan diary, September 25, 1913.

27 Mawson diary, July 30 and August 1–September 21, 1913.

28 Mawson diary, November 1–2, 1913; Madigan diary, November 3, 1913; McLean diary, November 3, 1913.

29 Letters, Mawson to Davis, and Mawson to David, November 19, 1913, Box 10, Folder 44AAE, MC.

30 McLean diary, November 24, 1913; Mawson diary, November 24, 1913.

31 Madigan diary, November 24–December 10, 1913; Mawson diary, November 24–December 12, 1913.

32 Mawson diary, December 11, 1913; Madigan diary, December 22, 1913.

33 Mawson diary, December 12, 1913; Madigan diary, December 22, 1913; Haddelsey, *Born Adventurer*, p. 122.

34 McLean diary, December 12, 1913; Mawson diary, December 12, 1913; Madigan diary, December 22, 1913; Haddelsey, *Born Adventurer*, p. 122.

Chapter Seventeen: Creating a Hero

1 Haddelsey, *Born Adventurer*, pp. 122–23; Madigan diary, December 22–23, 1913; Mawson diary, December 18–23, 1913; McLean diary, December 13–18, 1913.

2 Madigan diary, December 23, 1913.

3 McLean diary, December 22, 1913.

4 Mawson diary, December 23–25, 1913; Madigan diary, December 23–25, 1913; McLean diary, December 24–25, 1913.

5 Madigan diary, December 26, 1913–February 24, 1914; Mawson diary, December 26, 1913–February 16, 1914; Gray diary, January 11 and February 6 and 24, 1914; McLean diary, February 24, 1914.

6 *New York Times*, February 27, 1914.

7 Ayres, *Mawson*, pp. 99–100.

8 See docs in Box 15, Folder 141AAE/1, MC.

9 Ayres, *Mawson*, pp. 103–04.

10 Letter, Mawson to Mrs. Mertz, March 17, 1914, Box 22, Folder 175AAE, MC.

11 ibid.

12 Letters, Mawson to Mr. Mertz, May 16, 1914, and Mertz to Mawson, May 19, 1914, and Mawson to Mertz, July 8, 1914, Box 22, Folder 175AAE, MC; *New York Times*, February 27, 1914.

13 Letter, McLean to Mawson, July 13, 1914, Box 23, Folder 178AAE, MC; Ayres, *Mawson*, pp. 100–101.

14 Mawson, "Australasian Antarctic Expedition, 1911–1914," *Geographical Journal*, Vol. 44, No. 3, September 1914, p. 257.

15 Ayres, *Mawson*, pp. 102–04.

16 Letter, Webb to Mawson, October 22, 1914, Box 22, Folder 175AAE, Mawson Papers, MC.

17 Ayres, *Mawson*, pp. 105–09; Letter, Mackellar to Mawson, March 16, 1915, Box 59, Folder 51DM/1, MC.

18 McMullin, *Farewell, Dear People*, pp. 384–87.

19 Letter, Mawson to Webb, August 16, 1915, Box 22, Folder 175AAE, MC.

20 Letters, Madigan to Mawson, September 4, 1914, January 3 and December 18, 1915, Box 22, Folder 175, AAE, MC; Branagan, *T.W. Edgeworth David*, pp. 257–59, 288.

21 Letter, Mawson to Ninnis, January 1, 1915, Box 22, Folder 175AAE, MC.

22 Ayres, *Mawson*, pp. 111–12.

23 See docs in Box 47, Folder 10DM/1&2, MC.

Chapter Eighteen: Mawson's War

1 Ayres, *Mawson*, pp. 112–13; Kathleen Scott diary, May 16 and 20, 1916, Kennet Papers, CUL; Roland Huntford, *Shackleton*; Paquita Mawson, *Mawson of the Antarctic*, Longmans, London, 1964, pp. 127–31.

2 Letter, Mawson to Scott, undated c. 1916, PRG 523/6/4/4, SLSA.

3 Letter, Mawson to his wife, June 2, 1916, PRG 523/3/1/7, SLSA.

4 See docs in Box 47, Folder 10DM/1&2, MC; Ayres, *Mawson*, pp. 114–16.

5 Letter, Mawson to Scott, May 20, 1916, PRG 523/6/4/4, SLSA.

6 Kathleen Scott diary, May 16 and 25, 1916, Kennet Papers, CUL; Young, *A Great Task of Happiness*, pp. 166–70.

7 Kathleen Scott diary, June 10–12, 1916, Kennet Papers, CUL; Letter, Kathleen Scott to Mawson, April 26, 1920, Folder 51DM/1, Box 59, MC.

8 Kathleen Scott diary, June 15–24, 1916, Kennet Papers, CUL.

9 Letter, Mawson to Scott, June 27, [?1916], PRG 523/6/4/4, SLSA; See docs in Box 47, Folder 10DM/1&2, MC; Ayres, *Mawson*, pp. 114–16.

10 Kathleen Scott diary, July 1–16, 1916, Kennet Papers, CUL.

11 See docs in Box 47, Folder 10DM/1&2, MC; Ayres, *Mawson*, pp. 117; Letter, Smith to Mawson, July 27, 1916, PRG 523/6/1/4, SLSA.

12 Ayres, *Mawson*, p. 117.

13 Kathleen Scott diary, July 30, 1916, Kennet Papers, CUL.

14 Letter, Mawson to Scott, September 4, 1916, PRG 523/6/4/4, SLSA; Ayres, *Mawson*, p. 118.

15 Letter, Mawson to Vickers, November 18, 1916, Box, 15, Folder 141AAE/1, MC.

16 Letter, Mawson to Hughes, October 19, 1916, Box 23, Folder 183AAE, MC.

17 Letter, McLean to Mawson, July 4, 1916, Box 23, Folder 178AAE, MC.

18 Ayres, *Mawson*, p. 119; Paquita Mawson, *Mawson of the Antarctic*, pp. 134–35; Documents in Box 47, Folder 10DM/1&2, MC.

19 See docs in Box 47, Folder 10DM/1&2, MC.

20 Ayres, *Mawson*, pp. 120–22.

21 Letters, Mawson to Masson, October 3, 1917, and Lightfoot to Mawson, 5 March 1918, PRG 523/6/1/4, SLSA.

22 Ayres, *Mawson*, p. 122; Letter, Mawson to Smith, March 20, 1918, PRG 523/6/1/4, SLSA.

23 Lady Kennet, *Self-Portrait of an Artist*, p. 172.

24 Letter, Scott to Mawson, April 26, 1920, Box 59, Folder 51DM/1, MC.

25 Letter, Scott to Mawson, November 11, 1926, PRG 523/6/4/4, SLSA.

26 For details of the secret British plan and its ultimately failed implementation, see Day, *Antarctica: A Biography*, Chaps. 9–13.

Select Bibliography

Manuscript Sources

Abbreviations
AAD   Australian Antarctic Division Library, Hobart
CUL   Cambridge University Library
MC   Mawson Collection, South Australian Museum
ML   Mitchell Library, Sydney
NAA   National Archives of Australia
NLA   National Library of Australia, Canberra
SLSA   State Library of South Australia, Adelaide
SLV   State Library of Victoria, Melbourne
SPRI   Scott Polar Research Institute, Cambridge

Primary Sources

Private Papers
Australasian Antarctic Expedition papers, ML
Robert Bage, Antarctic diary, SLV
Frank Bickerton papers, SPRI
Percival Gray, "Antarctic Voyages": Diary aboard the *Aurora*, 1911–14,
    AAD
Walter Hannam diary, ML
Frank Hurley papers, ML
Sidney Jeffryes correspondence, ML
Charles Laseron diary, ML

Archibald McLean papers, ML
Douglas Mawson papers, ML
Douglas Mawson papers, SLSA
Douglas Mawson papers, SPRI
Mawson papers, MC
Belgrave Ninnis papers, SPRI
Lady Kathleen Scott diaries and letters, CUL

Books

Roald Amundsen, *My Life as an Explorer*, William Heinemann, London, 1927
Roald Amundsen, *The South Pole: An Account of the Norwegian Antarctic Expedition in the "Fram," 1910–1912*, [first published, 1912] C. Hurst, London, 1976
J. K. Davis, *High Latitude*, Melbourne University Press, Melbourne, 1962
John K. Davis, *With the "Aurora" in the Antarctic 1911–1914*, Andrew Melrose, London, 1919
Robert Dixon and Christopher Lee (eds.), *The Diaries of Frank Hurley, 1912–1941*, Anthem Press, London, 2011
Wilhelm Filchner, *To the Sixth Continent: The Second German South Polar Expedition*, Bluntisham Books, Bluntisham, 1994
Nancy Robinson Flannery, *This Everlasting Silence: The Love Letters of Paquita Delprat and Douglas Mawson, 1911–1914*, Melbourne University Press, Melbourne, 2000
Bernadette Hince, *Still No Mawson: Frank Stillwell's Antarctic Diaries 1911–13*, Australian Academy of Science, Canberra, 2012
Jenny Hunter (ed.), *Rise and Shine: Diary of John George Hunter, Australasian Antarctic Expedition 1911–1913*, Hunter House Publications, Hinton, 2011
Frank Hurley, *Argonauts of the South: Being a Narrative of Voyagings and Polar Seas and Adventures in the Antarctic with Sir Douglas Mawson and Sir Ernest Shackleton*, G.P. Putnam's Sons, New York, 1925
Fred Jacka and Eleanor Jacka (eds.), *Mawson's Antarctic Diaries*, Unwin Hyman, London, 1988
Lady Kennet, *Self-Portrait of an Artist*, John Murray, London, 1949
Charles Laseron, *South with Mawson: Reminiscences of the Australasian Antarctic Expedition, 1911–1914*, Australasian Publishing, Sydney, 1947

C. T. Madigan, *Central Australia*, Oxford University Press, Melbourne, 1944

C. T. Madigan, *Crossing the Dead Heart*, Rigby, Adelaide, 1974

J. W. Madigan, *Madigan's Account: The Mawson Expedition. The Antarctic Diaries of C.T. Madigan 1911–1914*, Wellington Bridge Press, Hobart, 2012

Douglas Mawson, *The Home of the Blizzard*, 2 vols., William Heinemann, London, 1915

Paquita Mawson, *Mawson of the Antarctic*, Longmans, London, 1964

Heather Rossiter (ed.), *Mawson's Forgotten Men: The 1911–1913 Antarctic Diary of Charles Turnbull Harrisson*, Pier 9, Sydney, 2011

Robert F. Scott, *The Voyage of the "Discovery,"* 2 vols., Macmillan, London, 1905

Ernest Shackleton, *The Heart of the Antarctic*, William Heinemann, London, 1910

Shirase Expedition Supporters Association, *The Japanese South Polar Expedition 1910–12, A Record of Antarctica*, [Originally published in Japanese, 1913, translated by Lara Dagnell and Hilary Shibata] Erskine Press and Bluntisham Books, Norwich and Bluntisham, 2012

Vilhjalmur Stefansson, *My Life with the Eskimo*, Macmillan, New York, 1913

Stanley Gordon Roberts Taylor, *Antarctic Diary*, Irene Gale, Kensington Park, 2011

Edward Wilson, *Diary of the Terra Nova Expedition to the Antarctic 1910–1912*, Blandford Press, London, 1972

Secondary Sources

Books

Philip Ayres, *Mawson: A Life*, Melbourne University Press, Melbourne, 1999

David Branagan, *T.W. Edgeworth David: A Life*, National Library of Australia, Canberra, 2005

Angie Butler, *The Quest for Frank Wild*, Jackleberry Press, Warwick, 2011

David Crane, *Scott of the Antarctic*, HarperCollins, London, 2005

David Day, *Antarctica: A Biography*, Random House, Sydney, 2012

Margery and James Fisher, *Shackleton*, Barrie, London, 1957

Peter FitzSimons, *Mawson and the Ice Men of the Heroic Age: Scott, Shackleton and Amundsen*, William Heinemann, Sydney, 2011

Tom Griffiths, *Slicing the Silence: Voyaging to Antarctica*, Harvard University Press, Cambridge, 2007

Alan Gurney, *The Race to the White Continent*, Norton, New York, 2000

Stephen Haddelsey, *Born Adventurer: The Life of Frank Bickerton, Antarctic Pioneer*, Sutton Publishing, Stroud, 2005

Brigid Hains, *The Ice and the Inland: Mawson, Flynn, and the Myth of the Frontier*, Melbourne University Press, Melbourne, 2002

Trevor Hatherton (ed), *Antarctica: the Ross Sea Region*, DSIR Publishing, Wellington, 1990

William Hunt, *Stef: A Biography of Vilhjalmur Stefansson*, University of British Columbia Press, Vancouver, 1986

Roland Huntford, *Scott and Amundsen*, Hodder and Stoughton, London, 1979

Roland Huntford, *Shackleton*, Hodder and Stoughton, London, 1985

Tim Jarvis, *Mawson: Life and Death in Antarctica*, Miegunyah Press, Carlton, 2008

Max Jones, *The Last Great Quest: Captain Scott's Antarctic Sacrifice*, Oxford University Press, Oxford, 2003

Emma McEwin, *An Antarctic Affair*, East Street Publications, Bowden, 2008

David McGonigal (ed.), *Antarctica: Secrets of the Southern Continent*, Simon and Schuster, Sydney, 2001

Ross McMullin, *Farewell, Dear People: Biographies of Australia's Lost Generation*, Scribe, Melbourne, 2012

Granville Allen Mawer, *South by Northwest: The Magnetic Crusade and the Contest for Antarctica*, Wakefield Press, Adelaide, 2006

Hugh Robert Mill, *The Life of Sir Ernest Shackleton*, William Heinemann, London, 1923

Beau Riffenburgh, *Aurora: Douglas Mawson and the Australasian Antarctic Expedition 1911–14*, Erskine Press, Norwich, 2011

Beau Riffenburgh, *Racing with Death: Douglas Mawson — Antarctic Explorer*, Bloomsbury, London, 2008

David Roberts, *Alone on the Ice: The Greatest Survival Story in the History of Exploration*, Norton, New York, 2013

Heather Rossiter, *Lady Spy, Gentleman Explorer: The Life of Herbert Dyce Murphy*, Random House, Sydney, 2001

Chris Turney, *1912: The Year the World Discovered Antarctica*, Text, Melbourne, 2012

Louisa Young, *A Great Task of Happiness: The Life of Kathleen Scott*, Macmillan, London, 1995

Booklets

Chris Viney (ed), *Macquarie Island*, Tasmanian Parks and Wildlife Service, Hobart, 2012

Theses

Noel Barrett, "Was Australian Antarctic Won Fairly?," Honors Thesis, Bachelor of Antarctic Studies, University of Tasmania, November 2007

Christy Collis, "The Edge Men: Narrating Late Twentieth Century Exploration on Australia's Desert and Antarctic Frontiers," PhD, La Trobe University, 2000

Journal and Magazine Articles

"The Australasian Antarctic Expedition, 1911–1914," *Bulletin of the American Geographical Society*, Vol. 47, No. 1, 1915

Denise Carrington-Smith, "Mawson and Mertz: A Re-evaluation of Their Ill-fated Mapping Journey During the 1911–1914 Australasian Antarctic Expedition," *Medical Journal of Australia*, Vol. 183, Number 11/12, December 5–19, 2005

Anna Lucas, "Mertz in Hobart: Ompressions of One of Mawson's Men While Preparing for Antarctic Adventure," in *Papers and Proceedings of the Royal Society of Tasmania*, Vol. 146, 2012

Anna Lucas and Elizabeth Leane, "Two Pages of Xavier Mertz's Missing Antarctic Diary: A Contextualization and Reconstruction," in *Polar Record*, [details] 2012

Douglas Mawson, "Australasian Antarctic Expedition, 1911–1914," *Geographical Journal*, Vol. 44, No. 3, September 1914

Douglas Mawson, "The Australasian Antarctic Expedition," *Geographical Journal*, Vol. 37, No. 6, June 1911

"Scott and Amundsen: An Exchange Between Roland Huntford and Wayland Young," *Encounter*, November 1980

David J. C. Shearman, "Vitamin A and Sir Douglas Mawson," *British Medical Journal*, February 4, 1978

"Sir Douglas Mawson in New York," *Bulletin of the American Geographical Society*, Vol. 47, No. 2, 1915

Quentin Turnour, "'A.K.A. *Home of the Blizzard*': Fact and Artefact in the Film on the Australian Antarctic Expedition, 1911–14," *NFSA Journal*, Vol. 2, No. 4, 2007

Wayland Young, "On the Debunking of Captain Scott: A Critique Against Myths, Errors and Distortions," *Encounter*, May 1980

Index